Institutional Diversity and Political Economy

Institutional Diversity and Political Economy

The Ostroms and Beyond

PAUL DRAGOS ALIGICA

OXFORD
UNIVERSITY PRESS

OXFORD
UNIVERSITY PRESS

Oxford University Press is a department of the University of Oxford.
It furthers the University's objective of excellence in research, scholarship,
and education by publishing worldwide.

Oxford   New York
Auckland   Cape Town   Dar es Salaam   Hong Kong   Karachi
Kuala Lumpur   Madrid   Melbourne   Mexico City   Nairobi
New Delhi   Shanghai   Taipei   Toronto

With offices in
Argentina   Austria   Brazil   Chile   Czech Republic   France   Greece
Guatemala   Hungary   Italy   Japan   Poland   Portugal   Singapore
South Korea   Switzerland   Thailand   Turkey   Ukraine   Vietnam

Oxford is a registered trademark of Oxford University Press
in the UK and certain other countries.

Published in the United States of America by
Oxford University Press
198 Madison Avenue, New York, NY 10016

Library of Congress Cataloging-in-Publication Data
Aligica, Paul Dragos
Institutional diversity and political economy : the Ostroms and beyond / Paul Dragos Aligica.
pages cm
Includes bibliographical references and index.
ISBN 978–0–19–984390–9 (alk. paper)
1. Institutional economics.   2. Social institutions.   3. Public institutions.   4. Ostrom,
Elinor.   I. Title.
HB99.5.A47 2013
306.3—dc23
2013011721

3 5 7 9 8 6 4
Printed in the United States of America
on acid-free paper

Contents

Acknowledgments

THIS PROJECT OWES immensely to the advice and encouragement I have received over the years from my professors at Indiana University Bloomington and from my colleagues at George Mason University. Needless to say, Vincent and Elinor Ostrom top this list. I am deeply indebted to Brian Hooks, Claire Morgan, Pete Boettke, and Tyler Cowen and their efforts in creating a hospitable and productive setting at the Mercatus Center at George Mason University for an entire research program, to which this book is just a small contribution. Pete Boettke, the Director of the F. A. Hayek Program for Advanced Study in Philosophy, Politics and Economics at the Mercatus Center, has inspired and incessantly fuels this research program with new ideas. I acknowledge with gratitude his multifaceted influence. Special thanks to Claire Morgan for her belief in this project, which in fact started as a result of a conversation with her.

The book project had the privilege of being the beneficiary of a book manuscript review conference in August 2012, at George Mason University, organized and sponsored by the Mercatus Center. I am profoundly grateful to the participants: Jack Goldstone, Barbara Allen, William Blomquist, Peter Boettke, Roberta Herzberg, Marco Janssen, James Johnson, Jack Knight, Mike McGinnis, Margaret Polski, Hilton Root, Filippo Sabetti, Amy Stabler, and Richard Wagner. My gratitude also goes to Claire Morgan and Erica Christensen for coordination and organizing the event. Individual chapters of the book or ideas and arguments expressed in sections and fragments of various chapters were read and most helpfully commented on by Nicholas Rescher, Xavier Basurto, Bill Blomquist, Peter DeLeon, Mike McGinnis, Ron Oakerson, Roger B. Parks, Edella Schlager, Karol Soltan, Bruno Grancelli, Janos Matyas Kovacs, Eileen Norcross, Christopher Weible, and Bruno Dallago. Their feedback and help is gratefully acknowledged.

An initial version of chapter 1 was discussed at the 2011 American Political Science Association Annual Meeting, Seattle, and at the 2011 Southern Economic Association Annual Meeting, Washington, DC. The comments received on these occasions from Jessica Green, David Victor, Liliana Andonova, Robert Keohane, Emily Chamlee-Whright, Jayme Lemke, Peter Calcagno, and Virgil Storr are hereby acknowledged with gratitude. Chapter 2 includes material published in "Polycentricity: From Polanyi to Ostrom and Beyond," coauthored with Vlad Tarko for *Governance: An International Journal of Policy, Administration, and Institutions*, vol. 25, March 2012. I thank John Wiley & Sons for permission to reprint this material. Two sections of chapter 3 were part of "Institutional and Stakeholder Mapping: Frameworks for Policy Analysis and Institutional Change," *Public Organization Review*, vol. 6, June 2006. I thank Springer for permission to reprint this material.

The help of my research assistants, Vlad Tarko (assisting the work in chapter 4) and Sathya Mathavan (editing the bibliography) is gratefully acknowledged. A different sort of debt is owed to Terry Vaughn, Cathryn Vaulman and Bharathy Surya Prakash. They supported the project with professionalism, easing the progress of the book from submission to the final stage. I remain responsible for any errors or omissions. Last but not least, I would like to express my deepest gratitude to Lin Ostrom. In the difficult month of May 2012, she found the resources to read the manuscript with astonishing care, offering invaluable feedback with a level of attention and intensity that reached the point of fixing minor typos. As an alumnus and affiliate of the Ostroms' Workshop in Political Theory and Policy Analysis at Indiana University in Bloomington, I was familiar with the amazing dedication Lin and Vincent always had for their students and collaborators. Yet I was totally unprepared for this last gift, received in such tragic moments.

I dedicate this book to the memory of Elinor and Vincent Ostrom.

Introduction

ONE OF THE most profound but not always fully understood challenges to modern political economy and institutional theory is the diversity of institutional forms that give substance and structure to political and economic life. Diversity shouldn't be a surprise. Institutional arrangements are intricate clusters of rules and human interactions, shaped in large measure by the variety of situations of social life. The mere diversity of situations is enough to create a wide variety of possible arrangements. If we add to all that the variety of individuals' possible preferences, beliefs, interpretations, and strategies, all leading to possible new rules and situations, we start to grasp the huge range of potential combinations in their evolving dynamism. All of the above suggest the measure in which institutional diversity is indeed messy and complex. It doesn't lend itself easily to analysis. When it comes to institutions, "carving nature at its joints" and arranging it in classes is not a simple and straightforward process. And yet, more often than not, in our institutional theories and in our designs we tend to brush off this profound challenge. More often than not, homogeneity is assumed or expected, while heterogeneity is considered as marginal, unessential, of limited relevance. The limits of this strategy may not be so obvious as long as one is operating mainly as a social scientist, following the notion that social scientists produce generalizations and test them, while the burden of applying the insights thus gained to practical problems and social dilemmas is the business of "practitioners."

But what happens if, instead of the typical approach, which gives a position of preeminence to theoretical generalizations and considers the applied level an extension of peripheral interest, we start by focusing on tangible, applied problems and puzzles, and we consider institutional theory in the light of its instrumental value to contextualized analysis and institutional design? Elinor and Vincent Ostrom's lifework is a case study giving many clues and some possible answers to this question. Their approach is well known for aiming not for grand generalizations but for understanding the nature and possible solutions to specific problems of collective action, governance, and social dilemmas in various settings and circumstances. Making governance dilemmas and the applied dimension the starting point, as well as the filter of our interest, reveals a different configuration of concepts and themes marking and linking the practice-to-theory continuum. And it is noteworthy that at the core of this configuration the problem of diversity and heterogeneity emerges as salient and pivotal.

"The presence of order in the world," writes E. Ostrom (1998), "is largely dependent upon the theories used to understand the world. We should not be limited, however, to only the conceptions of order derived from the work of Smith and Hobbes." That is to say, we should not limit our approaches to theoretical frameworks of the State and to theoretical frameworks of the Market. We need theories that match the extensive variety of institutional arrangements existent in the world. In response to that need, the Ostroms have charted and explored a novel domain of the complex institutional reality of social life: the rich institutional arrangements that are neither states nor markets. Small and large, multipurpose or just focused on one good or service, they display a daunting variety of functions and structures: suburban municipalities, neighborhood organizations, churches, voluntary associations, and informal entities like those solving the common-pool resources dilemmas the Ostroms studied and documented around the world. In their work they identified the functional principles behind them, tried to find out whether their very diverse forms could be understood as parts of broader patterns, and charted the logic of the institutional process involved. In many cases they found that such institutional arrangements may be related to, and yet different from, both "the state" and "the market." They also found that, irrespective of what one may call these arrangements, in order to analyze them one needs theoretical lenses that do not well fit the classical dichotomy, defined by two and only two major institutional models. This is the reason why the Ostroms' perspective is so difficult to categorize. Rooted in economics, public policy, and political science, recognized by the most prestigious awards in political science and public administration as well as a Nobel Prize in economics, their work develops new approaches to both familiar and unfamiliar social phenomena, while transcending the constraints and simplifications imposed by existing disciplinary boundaries.

And thus, the Bloomington scholars' work, by drawing our attention to the phenomenon of institutional diversity and its implications for governance and public policy, reminds us at the same time that our theoretical lenses are simplifying devices that allow us to see some things in profound ways but, at the same time, obscure others. We are reminded why in political economy, as in any other social science, the methodological tension between generalization and specification is so intense and consequential and cannot be simply assumed away. In addition to that, we learn that, lured by the beauty and parsimony of our theories and models, we may be missing the remarkable facts of institutional diversity. The Ostroms' studies warn us that a predisposition toward homogenization is profoundly rooted in our models of man, action, and institutional order. The homogenization, super-simplification, and formulaic conceptualization in our theories of institutions is in many respects a function of a parallel homogenization of human agents that we practice at the micro level.

For instance, in her studies on collective action, Elinor Ostrom has repeatedly drawn attention to the problem of actor and social heterogeneity and its implications for institutional order and institutional theory. One of her major concerns has been that in the relevant literature, although "the assumption of homogeneity was made for theoretical reasons," it has been too often used as a close approximation of reality, despite the fact that "heterogeneity is a preeminent aspect." Even more important, although "heterogeneity has been obvious to empirical research," too little work has focused on it and its consequences" (Ostrom and Keohane 1995; Poteete, Jansen, and Ostrom 2010). Her take in this respect is both eye-opening and challenging.

What would happen if we started to look at social order through the twin lenses of heterogeneity and institutional diversity? In a sense, this book is an attempt to chart and explore several avenues entailed by this challenge. Its premise is that whether one likes it or not, the related problems of heterogeneity, institutional diversity, and pluralism are a major (and more often than not, unacknowledged) issue in the literature dedicated to institutionalism, governance, and institutional design. Revisiting this challenge opens up a window into the core of the institutionalist contemporary research agenda and implies an assessment of the state and promise of institutionalism, broadly defined as a family of research programs in which institutional emergence, structure, and change are programmatically used as key dependent and independent variables in the conceptual reconstruction of a discipline, field, or thematic area. The re-examination in this light of some of the key themes and concepts of the Ostroms' contribution becomes thus a vehicle for a discussion not only of their research agenda but also of the future of institutionalism, political economy, and, for that matter, any research program in which the problem of governance and the theory of collective action are central.

The Ostroms' distinctive approach was considered from the very beginning an evolving part of the "public choice revolution" exploding in the 1960s. As William C. Mitchell framed it in his 1988 *Public Choice* article, "Virginia,

Rochester, and Bloomington: Twenty-Five Years of Public Choice and Political Science," the Ostroms' school has established itself rapidly as one of the preeminent centers of the movement. Three distinct schools of thought have appeared, he wrote, changing the ways we understand the economic and political reality. These schools could be labeled based on their geographical locations: Virginia, Rochester, and Bloomington. "At each of these institutions one or two dominant figures led...the effort to construct theories of collective choice: Riker at Rochester, Buchanan and Tullock at various Virginia universities, and the Ostroms at Indiana." In the years after Mitchell's article was published, Bloomington has not only consolidated its position as one of the preeminent centers of the public choice but also transformed its blend of public choice into a unique form of institutional theory. In the process, it created a unique research agenda, becoming one of the most dynamic and productive centers of scholarly work in social sciences in general. The fact that Elinor Ostrom was a recipient of the 2009 Nobel Prize in Economics was a telling recognition of Bloomington school's important contributions to the study of institutions and economic governance.

Yet, in the celebratory and retrospective mood created by such honors and public recognition, the Bloomington agenda is far from making its closing arguments. This book argues that if followed consistently, the logic intrinsic to the agenda developed in the last four decades by Elinor and Vincent Ostrom is leading to a unique brand of institutionalism, a research program taking seriously and dealing systematically with the theoretical, empirical, and normative problems of heterogeneity and its consequence and condition, institutional diversity.

The Ostroms started in the 1960s with a theory of collective action based on a theory of goods, theories that were emerging at that time from the mantle of neoclassical economics as major building blocks of the new, modern political economy. In time, their work on governance created one of the main channels of the transition from public choice to the new institutionalism. Today, looking back to the broad field covered (and in many cases created) by them and revisiting the insights growing from the theoretical and empirical studies of collective action and governance done by a large number of scholars in several disciplines, the main conclusion is that the results are in many respects not quite what one may have desired or expected initially, in the light of the theories and conjectures advanced by authors such as Mancur Olson, Garret Hardin, or even Gordon Tullock. Generalizing proved to be very difficult. A key variable like heterogeneity (of preferences, beliefs, or endowments) may both facilitate and impede collective action, as a function of circumstances and situational logic. What goes for heterogeneity goes for other comparable variables. That may well explain why no general theory of collective action has been offered and may not even be possible: The situational logic circumstances require an approach that goes beyond the simple and global and deals with complex, interactive, and conditional "theoretical scenarios." These results—one may like them or not—have momentous implications. They invite a rethinking of institutional theory and, more generally, any form of political economy or social theory in which collective action is central. We have a situation in which one of the most intense and carefully studied domains in political economy and social sciences leads us to the conclusion that there is an increasing mismatch between, on the one hand, the theoretical-epistemological frameworks used and the expectations based on them, and the phenomena in question, on the other. The process of the growth of knowledge requires a midcourse adjustment.

And thus, exploring the pluralist lines opened by the Ostroms becomes an alternative by necessity. Their thrust is leading to a substantial departure from the conventional wisdom built around theories assuming or expecting homogeneity, "normalization," and "consensus." Indeed, one of the major lessons of the Ostroms' work has been that it is both necessary and possible to deal constructively with the numerous situations in which homogeneity is not assumed, existent, or anticipated. That is to say, it demonstrates the institutional complexity and diversity of possible answers to the problems of governance in conditions of heterogeneity.

In all this, the Ostroms' views converge with a new and innovative agenda advanced in political economy, social philosophy, and political theory: the study of the problem of governance and social order in circumstances of deep heterogeneity, which lack consensus or correspondence of preferences, beliefs, or information. The fact that most authors involved in these efforts happen to be at the same time in search of an alternative to the epistemological credo embraced by the mainstream makes things even more interesting. This book is, in a sense, precisely about this path toward convergence, as seen from the Ostromian side. As such, it shows how, exploring the themes of the Bloomington school, we could both contribute to the contours of the emerging perspective and identify the measure in which the Ostroms provide a core analytical and empirical dimension to this increasingly vibrant agenda.

Needless to say, an approach that makes out of the reality of heterogeneity a key point is more relevant today than ever. Diverse values, identities, principles, and cultures clash in the global arena. Emigration, increasing diverse populations within the boundaries of nation-states, demography and culture, increasing technology-driven social segmentation and cultural heterogeneity—all challenge governance systems not only at the global and national levels but also, increasingly, at the local level. All these phenomena revive the theme of pluralism, diversity, and collective action with an unprecedented intensity. The increasing preoccupation with it in current political and economic theory is unavoidable once heterogeneity is recognized as a key feature of social reality and as a genuine political and economic practical challenge. In what measure is it possible to have an institutional order defined by freedom, justice, prosperity, and peace in an increasingly interdependent world of diverse and conflicting views, beliefs, preferences, values, and objectives? This is a discussion about the fundamental nature of governance (both domestic and international) in the new era. With it, we are at the core of the major political and economic challenges of our age. And at the same time, we are at the cutting edge of contemporary social science and political philosophy. The empirically grounded, applied institutional analysis of the possibility of social order, governance, and economic performance in extreme conditions that lack consensus or convergence of beliefs, preferences, and values seems to be indeed the new frontier.

This project started as an attempt to look at a set of promising concepts and themes that have emerged within the framework of the Ostromian research program and that had a double characteristic. First, they had a central position in the deeper architecture of the Ostromian system. Second, they were still a work in progress, inviting further discussion and elaboration. The plan was to introduce and further elaborate them, while exploring their analytical and operational implications, and thus to offer the reader an introduction to both the existing state and the potential of this important school of institutional theory. An additional thought was at work in this plan: Bloomington institutionalism is better known today mainly for the empirical work on governance and collective action, with specific applications to public economies in metropolitan areas as well as to the management of diverse common-pool resources. However, that is only part of the story. Those lines of research are rooted and embedded in a complex research program, a multifaceted system of ideas that span from social philosophy to applied political economy. Hence the intention was to go beyond the more salient and publicly visible pieces of the research produced by the Bloomington scholars and to identify several concepts that, at a more foundational level, reflect that less-known facet. The assumption has been indeed that those concepts continue to be the bearers of a significant potential for the renewal and advancement of the agenda.

However, as the book project grew, a larger pattern started to take form, a pattern that went beyond the initial objectives, adding a new dimension to the book. The initial plan remained embedded in the project (and the chapters could still be read as separated concept-based vignettes of a broader intellectual landscape). Yet the underlying logic uniting these concepts and their interpretation become more and more salient in the economy of the manuscript, and the emphasis shifted slowly toward it. The broader vision and the logic that gives these key concepts their most profound meaning became, in the end, the tacit theme. Out of it came the implicit conjecture that the emerging perspective toward which the Ostroms' work leads may be one of the boldest and most profound propositions advanced in current social sciences. That is to say, it is a sustained theoretical and analytical effort that (*a*) captures and addresses the structural and functional variety of social institutions, seen as a function of heterogeneity, and (*b*) follows up to the logical conclusion the normative implications of that variety, in a pluralist philosophy of governance.

The two themes, heterogeneity and institutional diversity, are, accordingly, two facets of the same problem, while the Ostrom type of institutionalism is a foundational pillar of the research program that unites these two facets, under a pluralist cupola. This is a pluralist perspective that goes beyond the state-centered views, beyond the markets-versus-states dichotomy, and indeed, beyond the policy models and solutions that assume the presence of large areas of consensus and centralization. Notions such as "polycentricity" or instruments such as the Institutional Analysis and Development (IAD) framework, developed and advanced by Elinor and Vincent Ostrom, are thus to be seen as ways by which this type of institutionalist political economy tries to chart and analyze the complexity and diversity of human institutional arrangements emerging from social and individual heterogeneity.

The book starts with a fresh and perhaps surprising interpretation of the place and significance of the Ostromian perspective in the context of the relevant intellectual developments in the political economy and social philosophy of the second half of the 20th century. Then chapter 1 moves to overview the research agenda focused on heterogeneity and its impact on collective action. The findings growing out of this research line are interpreted and used as an indicator for the current state of institutionalism and, by extension, of a large part of contemporary political economy. The idea is that the evolution of that agenda has reached a point where cumulated theoretical, normative, and epistemological challenges are opening up the way for a novel stage in thinking and theorizing about collective action, governance, and institutional arrangements. The rest of the chapters may be read in a double key: (*a*) as a look at how the Ostromian perspective responds to these theoretical, normative, and epistemological challenges and (*b*) as a presentation, interpretation, and elaboration of several major underlying themes defining this perspective, while placing these themes in the broader context of the relevant literature.

Chapter 2 focuses on one of the ways the Ostroms have tried to conceptualize the complex problem of governance in conditions of heterogeneity and diversity: the notion of polycentricity. Chapter 3 looks at how they have tried to respond to the methodological and epistemological challenge of heterogeneity and institutional diversity via the development of an original instrument: the Institutional Analysis and Development (IAD) framework. Chapter 4 makes a step further and introduces the issue of resilience as a nexus of institutional processes that offers a unique window from the macro level into the inner functioning of complex socioecological systems. The chapter illuminates how institutional diversity and polycentricity serve systemic resilience and reveals how in dealing with this issue, the Bloomington perspective is bringing together the domains of environmental science, economics, and institutionalism. Chapter 5 replicates the approach of the previous chapter, this time from the micro level, and uses as an inside window the problem of institutional design and its agents, a tacit but constant presence in the previous chapters. The chapter looks at this problem through theoretical lenses highlighting the role of ideas, expectations and predictability in social cooperation, notes the crucial position predictability has in the emergence and the study of institutional order, and then explores its implications for the ways we understand the relationship between institutional theory (ideas), institutional theorists, and social reality. Chapter 6 concludes by noting that the overview of Ostroms' work in the light of some of its pivotal concepts (such as polycentricity, institutional diversity, the IAD framework, institutional resilience, institutional design) reveals two things. The first is that this work sets up the stage for a reconstruction of our very approach to institutional theory by challenging us to rethink assumptions, methods, and entire theoretical perspectives. The second is that a certain philosophical profile, unmistakably associable to the pragmatist intellectual tradition, seems to be latent in it, both as an assumption and an implication. The chapter is a first attempt so far to probe and elaborate the link between a foundational pragmatist perspective and Ostromian institutionalism.

The book closes refocusing on the major underlying theme uniting all the chapters: the idea that Ostroms' work has, _in nuce,_ all the attributes needed to inspire and contribute to a powerful agenda, both innovative and consistent with distinguished traditions of theorizing in modern political economy and social philosophy. It is an approach whose defining feature is that it follows steadily the logic of heterogeneity, institutional diversity, and value pluralism up to its epistemic implications and that accepts the normative challenge posed by it. In this respect, it is a natural extension to the next level or the next stage of the current cycle of research on institutions, governance, and collective action. Read in this light, the volume is a contribution to the efforts to further outline the contours of this next stage of debates and intellectual investigations.

Before concluding these introductory comments, I must note that this book tries to capture something of the spirit, not just the letter, of the Ostromian perspective. The Bloomington research agenda has always had a trace of the unconventional, the unorthodox. It has always managed to maintain a certain detachment from the mainstream, sufficiently large to be intriguing, but not large enough to place itself in the domain of the marginal. Now that institutionalism is mainstream and that the specific type of institutional theory the Ostroms have advanced is increasingly accepted and embraced in economics, political science, and social science, it is natural to ask in what measure this spirit of unconventionalism, such a subtle but pregnant feature of the school, may be preserved. This book may be seen as an attempt to articulate one of the possible answers. The major themes discussed in it all point toward some less-traveled paths. They reflect parts of the Ostromian universe that continue to operate at the boundaries of the mainstream. While many ideas advanced by the Ostroms have made it to the current mainstream, none of the themes addressed in this book (from polycentricity and institutional resilience to institutional mapping and the reassessment on pragmatist grounds of the philosophical basis of institutional theory) has reached that level yet. They all imply rich, intriguing, and potentially controversial research agendas that, in some cases, in their further elaborations may even move away from the letter of the original Ostromian line. However, in all cases they retain the bold spirit defining Vincent and Elinor Ostrom's attitude toward science, scholarship, and the life of the mind.

I

Institutional Diversity, Heterogeneity, and Institutional Theory

ELINOR AND VINCENT Ostrom's affinity for the themes of institutional diversity, pluralism, and heterogeneity comes from two major sources. The first is foundational. The Ostroms operate from the perspective of what in social philosophy has been called a pluralistic worldview or paradigm. For them, diversity, pluralism, heterogeneity are "social facts," an inescapable condition of the social world. Similarly, for them the institutional arrangements people generate in response to this inexorable and irreducible feature of the world are and need to be pluralist. In other words, when it comes to organizing human coordination and interdependence in diverse circumstances, with diverse preferences, endowments, and beliefs, institutional pluralism is a fact, a challenge, and a *prima facie* normative answer. If that is the case, then the pluralism of criteria and values should as well define the way institutions and their performance are assessed. Last but not least, all of the above encourage a pluralist approach to the methods and theories used to analyze and explain the nature and functioning of institutions and social order. All in all, Ostromian institutionalism seems to have a strong pluralist bent.

When situated in the context of modern social philosophy, the Ostroms stand indeed in the category of thinkers who subscribe to the view that social heterogeneity and the divergence of values, beliefs, and preferences are the crucial elements of an adequate understanding of the central problem of social, politic, and economic order. Even more interesting, if we follow authors such as Lukes (2003), Tallise (2012), Gaus (2003), and Lassman (2011) we may even distinguish between two different branches or views of pluralism, among the broad range of pluralist scholars.

On the one hand, toward one end of the spectrum, are the "moderates," authors who while acknowledging the profound challenge of diversity and pluralism, still try to build their approach on a common grounding principle, a counterweight to heterogeneity, able to anchor in the last resort both social agents and the theory of social order. John Rawls, James Buchanan, and Jürgen Habermas are among the best-known examples. Yes, the argument says, heterogeneity is a problem, but, fortunately, hidden within diversity is a really deeper focal point or functional principle—diversity may be in the end neutralized via one form or another of homogeneity. A shared "point of view," a shared conception of the fundamental goals, some form of agreement or consensus is somehow possible by definition. We should base our approach on that focal point and consequently progressively shift our main focus away from the issue of diversity. That is to say, general solutions transcending the differences of a heterogeneous social landscape are possible because diversity, at its most basic level, can be circumvented, neutralized, normalized. Ultimately, the approach is based on the supposition that "*if* we could only achieve 'normalization,' if only the problem of social evaluation could be reduced to the reasoning based on a single perspective, then we would have solved the problem of uncovering the social rules (laws, basic structure, or whatever) that would promote the common good" (Gaus 2011, 2).

On the other hand, toward the other end of the spectrum, are the more radical pluralists, scholars who question the faith in universal theoretical or institutional strategies able to offer a general solution via reducing heterogeneity and divergence to some second-best form of convergence and homogeneity. They challenge the assumption that agreement, consensus, and homogeneity should be treated as the natural and default position. Diversity, divergence, disagreement are unavoidable characteristics of our social conditions. In a realistic vein, they claim that we should treat this condition as a state of fact, not as a malfunction, an accidental defect, a transitory deviation from the natural equilibrium point (to be discerned through a combination of analytical reason and intuition by the philosopher-king or the economist-king). At minimum we should be ready to accept that both homogeneity and heterogeneity have a foundational role to play. Consequently, we should be prepared to think in contextual and situational terms, about a variety of solutions to the variety of problems, identified by a variety of people in a variety of circumstances, sometimes involving profound trade-offs and irreconcilable tensions and sacrifices. This is the tradition defined by the work of an entire range of authors starting with Isaiah Berlin's classical take on pluralism and leading to the current exploration of the nature and implications of diversity and heterogeneity advanced by Gerald Gaus (2011) and Scott Page (2007). This is the tradition that looks at the interplay between homogeneity and heterogeneity, never forgetting the importance of the former but focusing mainly on the latter. And this, claims this book, is the tradition toward which leads the logic of the Ostromian project. This book will illuminate how and in what measure the work of the Bloomington scholars is or could be a contribution to the consolidation, renewal, and reconfiguration of this tradition, in the context of the increasingly converging efforts of a group of scholars that sometimes in coordination, sometimes independently, seem to be on the verge of transforming it into a major alternative in contemporary social sciences and social philosophy. However, for now, we need to return to the sources of the Bloomington school institutionalism's affinity for the problems of heterogeneity and pluralism.

If the first source was related to the very foundational assumptions and attitudes, the second is related to the evolution of the research program set into motion on the bases of the initial, original principles and ideas. Indeed it may be debatable in what measures the Ostroms were from the very beginning fully aware of the profound pluralism embedded in their approach. It seems more likely that the all-the-way-down pluralism (sociological, institutional, epistemological, methodological, etc.) grew in time, and was revealed more or less indirectly as the Bloomington research agenda progressed. For instance, the empirical work done in various settings on themes related to governance seems to have been an ongoing source of insights reinforcing a particular trend in the evolution of the Ostroms' thought. In other words, Ostromian pluralism, the focus on heterogeneity and institutional diversity, was not the result of purely axiomatic thinking, the deduction of propositions, conclusions, and corollaries from a particular set of assumptions about social order and its optimal institutional arrangements. Instead, it was a process that was checked, calibrated, and validated step by step, over the years, by the ongoing rethinking and confrontation with the empirical reality—in brief, a long and tenuous process of discovery, growth of knowledge, and self-clarification. This is the reason one presents and discusses it in terms of a trend, a direction toward which leads the logic of the Ostromian approach. And this is the reason why the Bloomington school's contribution to the emerging new paradigm is best seen not in doctrinaire terms but as driven by a series of separated yet related research endeavors, each incrementally bringing to light new elements (or validating already existing ones) as an outcome of an ongoing dialogue between theory and empirical reality.

If that is the case, then, in all probability, the best way to start our discussion of the Ostroms' institutionalism is to use as a vehicle the developments taking place on one of the main research fronts in one of the major areas in which they invested their efforts. Looking at concrete attempts to disentangle the complex factors and forces determining governance and collective action will illustrate the intrinsic logic of their approach and the direction in which it presses on. It is important to note the large measure in which the empirical front is a chief driver of its pluralist orientation. The growth of knowledge taking place on it (as well as the dead ends) invites conceptual, methodological, and epistemological responses, and these responses seem to be more often than not on pluralist lines. Later in the argument the broader and bolder conceptual, methodological, and philosophical facets will be addressed at length. However, for now it is important to show in a concrete way how a specific cycle of research, on a specific key theme, both echos and (possibly) shapes the general direction of the Ostromian perspective.

Given the fact that the Bloomington school is so famous for its work on collective action, the choice of the investigations on these topics as our working example should not come as a surprise. We'll hence take as a starting point the challenge entailed in Elinor Ostrom's remark that although in the relevant literature "the assumption of homogeneity was made for theoretical reasons," it had been too often used as a close approximation of reality, despite the fact that "heterogeneity is a preeminent aspect" (Ostrom and Keohane 1995, 7–11; Ostrom 2005). More precisely, we'll start our incursion into the domain of the institutionalism of diversity and pluralism with a closer look at the research program investigating the impact of heterogeneity on collective action. The choice is reinforced by the conjecture that heterogeneity (understood as operating under conditions of interdependence and imperfect information) is the most profoundly defining element of institutionalism, or at least of the variety of institutionalism advanced by the Ostroms. In brief, this chapter will use the theme of heterogeneity and the conclusions based on research on it as a vehicle. The objective is to show that, if seen in this context and if fully developed to its logical conclusions, the Ostrom type of institutionalism announces itself as a unique contribution to a broader perspective acknowledging and dealing consistently with the problem of heterogeneity and its consequence, institutional diversity.

Heterogeneity: Findings and Challenges

The definition of heterogeneity used by the Bloomington school institutionalists has come in time to pivot around three dimensions or facets: heterogeneity of capabilities, heterogeneity of preferences, and heterogeneity of beliefs and information (Ostrom and Keohane 1995; Poteete and Ostrom 2004; Poteete, Janssen, and Ostrom 2010). However, the literature defines and operationalizes the concept in multiple and sometimes richer ways and, in reviewing the literature, it is important to look at the entire range of heterogeneities considered relevant by various authors: economic, technological, social, cultural, racial, ethnic, linguistic, gender, community, education, and even personal experience. The Bloomington scholars themselves vacillate between the more constrained and the rather liberal uses. But, irrespective of perspective and definition, the preoccupation with the problem and its many facets has been a result of necessity: the limits of models and theories based on the assumption of homogeneity were a major motivator for such efforts. In the literature, the first-generation models based on the "representative agent" were crucial for the development of an entire family of rational choice theories linking individual decision-making to aggregate data. Yet the notion that aggregate behavior can be explained on the basis of the behavior of a single type of unit, a homogenous "representative agent," was increasingly questioned. That was especially the case in the wake of the birth of a new research agenda: fieldwork having research designs framed by rational choice political economy theories. Pioneers of such studies, the Ostroms pointed toward heterogeneity, diversity, context, and situational logic as critical elements in the analysis of institutions, governance, and collective action. Indeed, very soon heterogeneity was becoming salient for an increasing number of authors.

This salience was also reinforced by the fact that any discussion of size, scale, and numbers in collective action has sooner or later to come to terms with the fact that the problem of the number of actors involved is related to the problem of heterogeneity. Collective action is indeed essentially defined in terms of numbers, of multitudes. The very notion evokes first and foremost the quantitative aspect. However, as those authors studying it rapidly noted, the number and the heterogeneity of actors tend to be related variables. Both have a special place in the studies of collective action and governance, looming large. Yet at the same time researchers noted that in an overwhelming number of instances of collective action, problems of number could be converted, for analytical and normative purposes, into problems of heterogeneity. In a complex, dynamic social system, number and heterogeneity are not independent variables, and for most analytical and normative purposes, it is not number per se that is important, but only its effects on the problem of collective action. By keeping track of heterogeneity, one is implicitly keeping track of the relevant scale aspects and, at the same time, including some other possibilities that might be lost if the focus were just the issue of number. For instance, a focus on heterogeneity brings with it two other important elements that are intrinsic to its very conceptualization: interdependence and the possibility of imperfect information, based on asymmetries between social actors. Setting aside such corollaries, we should simply note that one of the most effective ways the literature deals with the number-heterogeneity issue is by developing the notion of "second-level dilemmas" or "second-level collective action."

The "collective action within a collective action," subgroup segmentation, and self-selection of participants contributing to collective goods are mechanisms by which, ultimately, a problem of numbers becomes (or may be addressed as) one of heterogeneity. Thus, all in all, the theme of heterogeneity comes to be recognized as central.

This interest in heterogeneity has taken two directions: The first has been more radical. In time it led to the thesis that in a "complex system," because of heterogeneity, complexity, and interaction, one cannot explain aggregate dynamics as the sum of the behavior of individuals. Emergence, clustering, thresholds, and nonlinear and discontinuous relationships are the norm (Miller and Page 2007). The aggregate is different from the sum of its parts. Even more, the aggregate in its dynamics may strongly determine individual behavior. This is a new form of holism whose practical implications are more often than not unclear. The relative unpredictably of "emergence" phenomena and the associated processes at the level of "the whole" suggest rather ambiguous normative and policy insights. That is why the attention of the Bloomington institutionalists, whose interests were always strongly driven by the normative and policy side, was on the second, more operational perspective. In this second view, the problems associated with the aggregation of heterogeneous agents are of central relevance, but the holistic and nondeterministic implications are toned down. Agents have asymmetric features and endowments, and the structure of the aggregate process may have a logic different from that of the individual behavior. Yet the discontinuity between the two levels is not assumed to be so massive, prevalent, and inscrutable for immediate practical purposes. Dramatic threshold effects are not a key feature. This is a perspective driven more by case studies, fieldwork, the analysis of events and processes in historical time, surveys, and lab experiments, as well as by concrete case-based scenarios, than by the radical propositions inspired by simulations interpreted through complexity theory and agent-based modeling.

At this stage the question is this: How do we understand heterogeneity and its consequences in the light of recent research dedicated to the issue? What do we know today about the role that heterogeneity plays in various collective action situations? Revisiting the theme of heterogeneity and its consequences, as well as the relevant scholarly developments related to it, what have we learned during the last several decades? What insights have we reached about collective action and governance in conditions of heterogeneity and about the theories that guide our attempts to explain and understand them? What do those lessons entail in terms of the next steps and the future agenda? Are we closer to understanding the design principles able to guide collective action and governance in conditions of heterogeneity? In other words, what are the implications of what we know today for the knowledge base on which institutional theory, institutional design, and normative considerations are to be built? The scope of the exercise is clear: We want to overview some of the key insights that are emerging from the various attempts to explore theoretically and empirically the implications of heterogeneity and thus to provide the background against which we'll be able to appraise in context the relevance of the Ostroms' proposition as well as to address the broader facets and implications of the institutionalist perspective they advance.

At the very beginning two major theses are on the table: on the one hand, the thesis that heterogeneity has negative effects on collective action; on the other hand, the thesis that there are nontrivial positive effects, more precisely, that in many instances, heterogeneity increases the chances of collective action. Let's use as a starting point Lore Ruttan's (2006) attempt to systematize a part of the relevant literature. Her study looks at the effect of social and cultural heterogeneity on collective action and the management of natural resources, and more precisely of the commons. Ruttan organizes the discussion around the two sets of precisely defined hypotheses.

The first originates in the work of Oliver and Marwell (2001; Oliver, Marwell, and Teixeiria 1985). The argument is that "heterogeneous groups would not generally behave the same way as homogeneous groups" and that the emphasis on heterogeneity in model building reveals the phenomena of the critical mass and leadership (defined as "the subset of highly interested and/or highly resourceful people" who play a crucial role in the critical phases of collective action). Heterogeneity is thus seen as a potential facilitator or a precondition of innovation and leadership. Central to these arguments is the use of production functions (the relationship between the effort invested in providing a collective good and the quantity of the collective good). The crucial link between heterogeneity and leadership-entrepreneurial action is determined by the shape of the collective goods production function. Differently shaped functions induce different kinds of actions. Accelerating and decelerating curves determine the dynamics of collective action at different stages and induce different strategies depending on stage. Hence there are phases of collective action that have different properties. In certain stages, entrepreneurs may have the incentive to act either to provide a collective good or to absorb the costs of organizing people to do that. The bottom line is that relatively small groups of people are often at the core of action. The importance of a small initial group leads to the idea of "second order" collective action. This is indeed the logic behind the argument that in the analysis of most collective action situations the problem of number may be reduced in the end to a problem of heterogeneity.

The second set of hypotheses is broadly based on the analysis of the conditions leading to solution to the collective action problem, as developed by Elinor Ostrom's book *Governing the Commons* (1990). Ruttan questions interpretations that take Ostrom's work to mean that homogeneity is a necessary condition for successful outcomes. She suggests the following twofold interpretation: (*a*) Success is most likely when users have similar discount rates, similar views of the resource, and high levels of trust, while (*b*) trust and similarities in cultural view of the resource might be intervening variables. In this case, social heterogeneity may reduce levels of trust and/or create different preferences of cultural views about how the resource is to be used and managed. It is more likely that sociocultural heterogeneity has a negative effect on outcomes.

Ruttan tests these specific alternatives against data on 40 fisheries and 54 irrigation cases contained in the Common-Pool Resource Database. The results, she writes, "do not support the hypothesis that sociocultural heterogeneity is associated with positive outcomes, and in fact, among the irrigation cases, more entrepreneurial activity is observed when there is homogeneity." There is "only very slender support for the idea that sociocultural differences result in heterogeneity in preferences that in turn induces some individuals to take on an entrepreneurial role in facilitating collective action." However, results support the argument that "trust is required for successful outcomes and that heterogeneity can limit levels of trust." Finally, and very important, while engaged in the exercise, she notes an important observation: the evaluation of the impact of heterogeneity depends heavily on how success is defined.

For now let's note that Ruttan doesn't seem to be very surprised by the results. Indeed, she mentions a number of works that, in some sense, have set up her expectations. Baland and Platteau (1996) and Bardhan and Dayton-Johnson (2002) find that differences in economic endowments or in sociocultural attributes of the resource users affect the levels of free riding. The same Baland and Platteau (1999) argue that in the context of economic inequality, the same conditions that lead some individuals to have an increased preference for the collective good lead other individuals to have a diminished interest.

In fact the literature is very generous in presenting studies such as (or those surveyed in) Habayrimana et al. (2009) that conclude that heterogeneity has negative effects, and that trust may mediate the relationship between sociocultural heterogeneity and success. Works such as Vedeld (2003) find that distributional conflict "may occur where resource users have substantially different culture views of the resource," and other field and laboratory results support the idea that reduced levels of trust have negative effects on cooperative outcomes (Ostrom and Walker 2003; Jones 2004; Hackett, Schlager, and Walker 1994).

Going beyond the boundaries of strict commons and natural resource governance studies, one interesting area of research on the impact of heterogeneity on collective action has been the investigation of its consequences for social capital. Once social capital is seen as group participation (volunteering, organizational membership, voting), as strength of network ties (trust), or as community commitment, the direct relevance for the broad equation of collective action becomes evident. Using General Social Survey data, Alesina and La Ferrara (2000) find that organizational membership and group participation are lower in metropolitan areas that feature greater racial and ethnic diversity and higher income inequality. Costa and Kahn (2003) use data from US cities, metropolitan areas, and urban counties to show that "the share of spending on such productive public goods as education, roads, sewers, and trash pickup is inversely related to the area's ethnic fragmentation even after controlling for other socioeconomic and demographic characteristics." Heterogeneity does not increase civic engagement. Diverse communities, with heterogeneous members, participate less, measured in both time and money. In addition their voting, and their willingness to take risks to help others, is diminished. Miguel and Gugerty (2002, reported in Costa and Kahn 2003) find that there is lower school funding in communities that are more ethnically diverse. The list of relevant findings, following Costa and Kahn (2003), is pretty consistent in its results: Public goods expenditures are inversely related to an area's ethnic fragmentation (Alesina et al. 1999). Trust is higher when race and nationality coincide (Glaeser et al. 2000). Support for welfare spending is higher if a greater share of welfare recipients is from one's own racial group (Luttmer 2001). State spending on education is lower when the share of elderly is rising and they are from a different racial group than schoolchildren (Poterba 1997). The census response rate is lower in counties where ethnic fragmentation is greater (Vigdor 2001, reported in Costa and Kahn 2003). And so on...To sum up: civic engagement tends to be lower in more heterogeneous groups, societies, and communities.

The study of cooperation and regimes in international relations is by definition the domain where the assumption of heterogeneity and interdependence in various forms and shapes is central (Keohane and Nye 1977; Martin 1994; Keohane 2002; Snidal 1994). International relations studies are emblematic examples showing how heterogeneity is a real challenge to coordination and collective action. Different authors emphasize different kinds of heterogeneity, from differences of structure and endowments of states as actors, to different types of actors altogether. The more the position of the state as a unit of analysis has been challenged by internal economic developments, by the role of transnational non-state actors and by transnational issues such as environmental problems or terrorism (Janssen et al. 2006; Oberschall 2004) the more the theme of deep heterogeneity and its implications has become a background reference point in international relations theorizing. The result is the widespread acceptance of the notion of a much more heterogeneous international arena, involving not just state actors, but many different private, state, and private-public partners, operating at different scales: "The logic of collective action is becoming a heterogeneous, multilayered logic, derived not from one particular core structure, such as the state, but from the structural complexity embedded in the global arena" (Cerny 1995, 595).

In this context, when it comes to the theme of heterogeneity and number, Arce (2000) is typical when he argues that the success of international environmental protocols is a function of scale but at the same time notes that the entire theory involves a heterogeneous population: "The global diversity of economic development itself is often viewed as a major stumbling block for the formation of regimes." Heterogeneity implies "asymmetric levels of provision (or abatement)" and raises questions about "the ability of international regimes to accommodate differences between various countries of the world" (Arce 2000, 754). It is a very good illustration of the ways heterogeneity reasserts itself as a key variable even when scale is meant to occupy the first stage. The fact is that in a field like international relations theory, it is difficult to diverge too much from the thesis that heterogeneity poses real challenges for global coordination and collective action.

The pattern emerging so far seems to suggest at least skepticism regarding the positive effect of heterogeneity on successful collective action. Yet, overall, the literature dealing with collective action reveals huge gray areas of ambiguity. The final results are more nuanced, and they complicate things by showing how context-dependent and ambiguous are all our findings when it comes to collective action. Baland, Bardhan, and Bowles (2007) note that "the complexities of the relationship between inequality and collective action are in need for more context-specific empirical investigations into different types of alternative mechanisms through which the relevant processes may operate." Hence the existing alternatives are not limited to pessimism and skepticism. After all, one has as a key exhibit Scott Page's work celebrating the "difference" and claiming that heterogeneity is a condition, even a strategy, of success.

Page's book (2010) explains how diversity produces collective benefits, and more precisely, the conditions under which diversity produces benefits. It analyzes problem solving and prediction in collectives of people, the creation of alternative solutions, and the evaluation of possibilities, all crucial for collective action. Page argues that given a set of conditions, diversity trumps homogeneity: "collections of people with diverse perspectives and heuristics outperform collections of people who rely on homogeneous perspectives and heuristics." In addition to that, diversity trumps ability: "random collections of intelligent problem solvers can outperform collections of the best individual problem solvers." At least in theory, cognitive heterogeneity (of perspectives and heuristics) may be in fact a facilitator of collective action solutions.

Thus there are studies that argue strongly in favor of "differences" (Page 2007; 2010), there are studies that report no general effect of heterogeneity (Bardhan and Dayton-Johnson 2002), and there are studies that do suggest positive or at least context-dependent effects (Ruttan 1998; Ruttan and Borgerhoff Mulder 1999; Andersson and Agrawal, 2010; Agrawal 1998; Vedeld 2003). In some cases, the same study gives mixed signals. Baland, Bardhan, and Bowles (2007) conclude that in some settings inequality inhibits collective governance but in other settings the effect of inequality is minor in comparison to other factors. Anderson and Paskeviciute (2006) examine how heterogeneity defined on ethnic and linguistic parameters affects citizenship behavior (measured by cognitive and interpersonal engagement about politics), membership in voluntary associations, and interpersonal trust. They report that their data from 44 countries show that "heterogeneity does affect the quality of civil society in a country." Heterogeneous societies have problems of trust, "but it is linguistic rather than ethnic heterogeneity that reduces trust in less democratic societies." However, "indicators of population heterogeneity do not have uniformly positive or negative effects on individual-level measures of civil society—while they reduce some, they shore up others." Hence, "heterogeneity may be a necessary ingredient for building a vibrant and stable civil society and democratic life rather than being a prime cause of democratic distress" (Anderson and Paskeviciute 2006, 783).

One may think that adding to our inventory further subliteratures that focus on the issue from different angles may change the direction of the assessment. But the fact is that the general haziness of the findings will persist. New perspectives may be brought into the picture by looking, for instance, at the studies focused on heterogeneity as a facilitator of leadership/entrepreneurship. These are studies in which leadership is considered "a noncooperative means to achieve (more) cooperation in social dilemma situations" (Arce 2001). Levati, Sutter, and van der Heijden (2007), for example, focus on leadership and the private provision of a public goods when group members are heterogeneously endowed. Results show that in cases of homogeneous endowments, the average contribution is higher. "Leadership is almost ineffective, if participants do not know the distribution of endowments." However, "the presence of a leader increases average contribution levels." Yet another hint at the complexity of variables in play.

Speaking of endowments, Levati, Sutter, and van der Heijden (2007) mention the research line opened by Warr (1982; 1983) on the impact of income distribution on voluntary contributions to a public good. Warr's initial conjecture was that group contributions should be invariant under redistributions of income. But as Levati et al. (2007) report, Chan et al. (1996; 1999) actually "find that on average, this turns out to be true in a nonlinear setting, although, contrary to Warr's income-neutrality postulate, the rich tend to undercontribute and the poor to overcontribute relative to their endowments." On the other hand, note Levati et al. (2007), Cherry, Kroll, and Shogren (2005) use a linear public goods game to show that "average contributions are lower with asymmetric rather than symmetric endowments." Van Dijk and Wilke (1995, 1–2), using an asymmetric step-level public goods game, find that "participants with a twice as high endowment contributed almost twice as much as low endowed participants." The same Van Dijk (this time with Grodzka, 170–1) (1992) observes "no significant difference between participants with high and low endowments." Aquino, Steisel, and Kay (1992, 665) find "strong support for the hypothesis that inequality leads to decreased cooperation." In the light all of the above, it is plain why Levati, Sutter, and van der Heijden (2007, 813–14) are compelled to conclude that "the evidence on the effect of asymmetric endowments on cooperation levels is thus far from being conclusive."

Before concluding this bird's-eye view on a good sample of insights emerging from the research done in the last 20 years or so on heterogeneity in collective actions, one should bring up Heckathorn's work, not only because of its emphasis on sanctions but also because it illustrates in such a clear way one of the most important insights emerging from this family of research efforts. Heckathorn builds on the already mentioned line of research opened by Marwell and Oliver (1993, 2001), a line of research whose leading conjecture is that heterogeneity is a positive force for collective action for several reasons: It facilitates the organization of uncoordinated individuals; it weakens the cohesion of social groups; and in general it shapes the structure of opportunity costs of collective action that move the groups and individuals along the production function curve regions in areas that may inhibit or encourage action. Heckathorn's work illustrates how sensitive are the results to contextual factors and different models and variables setups. He explores the link between group heterogeneity and collective action in three regimes: "voluntary" systems (domains of unrestricted decision-making, with no sanctions); "compliance" systems (domains with sanctions to enforce cooperation, in which there are norms compelling actors to participate in public goods production); and "balanced" systems (domains in which there are sanctions both for and against cooperation). The findings are both telling and intriguing. When the average/ mean interest is low, heterogeneity increases cooperation in all three types of systems. Cooperation increases most in the compliance systems, least in the voluntary systems, with the oppositional or balanced systems in between. However, there is "a transitional range after which heterogeneity produces even higher cooperation for voluntary compliance systems but produces lower cooperation for compliant control systems and drastically lower cooperation for oppositional control." Resource and cost heterogeneity "improve voluntary compliance when conditions are otherwise unfavorable but have little effect on systems with sanctions" (Heckathorn 1993, 329).

One thus may see how a more nuanced and complex understanding could be achieved with each further specification of the model applied. As Ostrom (1998, 15) put it, "this illustrates how changes in one structural variable can lead to a cascade of changes in the others." A small change "may suffice to reverse the predicted outcome." The context or the regime matters. Yet this volatility and the variability it entails raise serious doubts about the possibility of isolating and charting the code of collective action via the heterogeneity factor. One could get out of such analytical exercises a better understanding of the phenomenon, but no universal key or general model. It would be wonderful to be able to establish a straightforward, plain, linear relationship between heterogeneity and collective action, but the most likely result is the identification of a variety of mechanisms and linkages connecting possible configurations of variables of interest, in various scenarios. We thus come to understand "how difficult it is to make simple bivariate hypotheses about the effect of one variable on the level of cooperation" (Ostrom 1998, 15). This conclusion was reinforced by Oliver and Marwell (2001, 293)—representing the other great line of research on heterogeneity mentioned at the beginning of this section. In collective action and governance studies, they write, "it is necessary to move from simple mono-causal theorizing about 'collective action.'" Things may be even more challenging. In fact, write Oliver and Marwell (2001), it may be the fact that there is no single and unitary social phenomenon under that label. One needs "a disciplined search for the distinctions among different types of collective action and the factors that distinguish them." These are very important conclusions, indeed. Their implications for the way we think about institutional theory and design are considerable. And it looks like the case for pluralism and diversity (or for that matter for heterogeneity), if it is to be made, has to rest on a much more sophisticated line of argumentation than one limiting itself to simple causal analysis and the simple political economy models based on it.

A Set of Preliminary Implications

The preceding overview of a sample of the relevant literature through the lenses of three theses (heterogeneity facilitates the initiation of collective action; heterogeneity impedes the initiation of collective action; heterogeneity can either facilitate or impede collective action, depending on context) shows that reconciling the conclusions of various attempts to confront the theory with empirical reality is difficult. Many of these studies were done under different assumptions, different models, and different variables. Some broad patterns seem to emerge, but we need to recognize that social and institutional arrangements such as those under examination are "complexly organized and that we will rarely be able to state that one variable is always positively or negatively related to a dependent variable" (Ostrom 1998, 16). In these circumstances it should be no surprise that "the kind of theory that emerges from such an enterprise does not lead to the global bivariate (or even multivariate) predictions that have been the ideal to which many scholars have aspired" (Ostrom 1998, 16). That doesn't mean that it is not possible to have theoretical predictions. It means "only that they cannot be simple and global. Instead, the predictions that we can validly generate must be complex, interactive, and conditional" (Marwell and Oliver 1993, 25).

We are now very far away from the broad initial generalizations of the "tragedy of the commons" or the "logic of collective action" of the early literature. In the years that have passed since, social scientists have been increasingly put in the position of reconsidering their efforts to build "the theory of collective action." After all, this seems to be one of those domains in which "it is not possible to relate all structural variables in one large causal model, given the number of important variables" (Ostrom 1998, 14). Today scholars are more than ever ready to acknowledge that "there are many different issues and many different kinds of collective action and that one can shade into the other depending upon the structural characteristics of the situation" (Marwell and Oliver 1993, 25).

Where does all this leave us? What are the implications? The reaction to these conclusions depends indeed on our initial expectations. For those starting with great expectations of finding the "grand theory" and "the solution" to the Problem of Collective Action and Governance, they are indeed disappointing. No grand design blueprint seems to be emerging. On the other hand, those starting with more modest expectations may be satisfied with the fact that at least we better understand the limits of our approaches. It is important to note that these conclusions apply not only to the specific domains focused on by the Ostroms and their associates, but to the broader field of the game-theory-based new institutionalism. In this respect the discussion is indeed, as it has mentioned from the very beginning, a discussion about institutionalism in general and about its future.

Taking a broader stand, let's focus now on a preliminary set of implications and conclusions emerging in light of all of the above. A brief look at theoretical and analytical, applied and normative implications will reveal how this perspective is integrating itself into a broader framework, spanning social scientific prediction and moral philosophy, a framework that points to a particular horizon of epistemological and social philosophy. In brief, one may see that a set of principles (theoretical, normative, and applied) seem to consistently underlie the institutionalist enterprise, as sketched by E. Ostrom, giving it a certain tone and stance, and imprinting on it a certain logic and direction of development.

Let's start with the theoretical and analytical level. One of the most salient implications is that one needs to rethink the aims and limits of our attempts to theorize and generalize in this domain. We are approaching a point in which we need to realign our methodological and epistemological expectations and assumptions to the realities of the last cycle of empirical research. The gap between the theory-building and generalizing ambitions of the initial approach and the ensuing results requires a recalibration. The alternatives suggest a departure from the traveled path. For example, in response to this challenge, Oliver and Marwell (2001, 308) advance the notion of "response surface" as a tool aimed at helping us to think "about the complexities involved in collective action." A response surface is "a k-dimensional graph of an outcome variable as predicted by k − 1 independent variables." Outcome is the variable that one decides defines best the solution to the collective action/good problem in case (the total contribution, the number of contributors, etc.). The independent variables are the standard ones, such as group size, the shape of the production function, the degree of interest and resource heterogeneity, and so forth. There are regions of the response surface in which the values and combination of variables make collective action impossible and regions in which collective action is made possible. "It is obviously impossible to study all possible independent variables at once," argue Oliver and Marwell (2001, 308), "but when we write models, we should be envisioning the location of our model within the full response space, recognizing what is being held constant (and at what level) and what is being varied (and within what ranges)." This, they suggest, is a heuristic strategy that may work better than the current one: "Envisioning the full response surface should be linked with a search for controlled comparisons and thoughtful experimental designs to clarify complex interdependencies. This is all too rare. Instead, most of us seem to approach modeling so that we can say something like, 'See, I can make my model do something different from what your model did.'" The alternative seems therefore superior: "simply explicitly listing the factors held constant and comparing them to other models might more readily call to attention seemingly unimportant operational decisions that turn out to make big differences in the results" (Oliver and Marwell 2001, 308–9).

Recognizing the significance of all of the above, Elinor Ostrom introduces the notion of "theoretical scenarios." An alternative to grand generalizing could be to build scenarios of how "exogenous variables combine to affect endogenous structural variables." Their function is first and foremost heuristic. They are an instrument that facilities understanding. It is possible to "produce coherent, cumulative, theoretical scenarios that start with relatively simple baseline models. One can then begin the systematic exploration of what happens as one variable is changed." The logic of combinations and permutations reinforced by empirical verification would guide the research. The reason behind explanation and analysis reveals something important about the phenomena. But the most important thing is that at the end of the day, one could hence see how this line of research ends up confronting us with, as Ostrom (1998, 15–16) put it, "a world of possibility rather than of necessity." That is to say, "we are neither trapped in inexorable tragedies nor free of moral responsibility for creating and sustaining incentives that facilitate our own achievement of mutually productive outcomes." Possibilism entails pluralism. Institutional arrangements are not predetermined; they are not a mere matter of a combinatorial theory of variables and forces but also a matter of human deliberation, decision, and responsibility. In this respect, human decisions are important not as expressions of mechanical maximizers but of moral agents able to imagine and create alternative rules and bear the responsibility for alternative courses of action. Such conclusions immediately suggest the next dimensions: the applied and normative.

When it comes to the applied level, the first thing to recall is that relaxing our ambitions for theoretical and empirical generalization implies a limitation of our expectations regarding the nature and power of the institutional design principles derivable from our data. Overall, the evidence points toward the idea that, more often than not, heterogeneity impedes collective action. And yet sometimes heterogeneity may facilitate it, depending on various factors and conditions. This conclusion is definitely baffling for practical purposes. Context matters, and institutional design is an enterprise largely driven by context and circumstances. Various configurations of homogeneity and heterogeneity seem to be crucial factors in institutional design, irrespective of what one thinks of the general directions and forms of influence. And heterogeneity brings with it an entire set of problems that remain dormant as long as one is concentrated on merely determining the relation between homogeneous actors and predefined rules.

The message is that irrespective of what we think about theory, when it comes to policy, applied-level work, the configurations of circumstantial variables cannot be dismissed as mere outliers. As Scott Page (2010b, 4–5) has demonstrated, relying on means or averages in policy analysis and design can be misleading. For that reason economists, "especially those interested in policy effects," have reached the conclusion that heterogeneity "pushes back against the tendency towards averaging" (Page 2010b, 4–5). This is a real challenge for any field or project that aims to be relevant for institutional design. Alternatives to averaging need to be further developed. This is to say that scholars who look at scientific results as a basis for social interventions have to rethink in some fundamental respects their approaches and the methodological apparatus supporting them.

Could one simply limit the study to the mere documentation and "lessons learned" from the wealth of institutional design experiments and cases available to us? Or should one try to go beyond that and identify broader institutional design principles? If the second, what would be the basis of generalization for these principles? These are serious questions for a research agenda that has reached the conclusion that a general theory of collective action may be beyond our reach and that the tendency toward averaging in public policy could be seriously misleading. Even more, with heterogeneity (of endowment, of beliefs, of preferences, etc.) taken seriously into account, the empirical and theoretical investigations (especially when they are meant to be relevant for institutional design) force additional dimensions to the forefront. Whether one likes it or not, pluralism of perspectives and of alternatives comes to occupy an important place on the stage. And in these circumstances, the foundational normative dimension, the third set of implications on our list, has to be an important part of the conversation.

Certain normative assumptions and preferences are undoubtedly and inescapably embedded at a very basic and intuitive level in the perspectives advanced by scholars, like the Ostroms, who explore collective action and institutional arrangements. For instance, lurking behind is a problem that has only been alluded to in the discussion up to now: What is the definition of "success," "performance," or "solution" for the variety of collective action problems relevant for institutional and governance analysis? As Ruttan (2006) put it, one must be careful about how "success" is defined. Success may be defined and measured in terms of participation, but this is not the sole criterion. Degrees of provision, the nature of provision, conservation, mobilization, reducing or halting trends, minorities mobilization, and so on, could all be seen as legitimate criteria and/or objectives. Trade-offs, tensions, and incompatibilities matter. As long as we define the "goal" as "saving the planet" or "saving the commons," these things and the complexity of the assessment scale may be lost between the lines. But we should not forget that "outcomes that are positive with respect to resource conservation may not always be positive with respect to equity" or, for that matter, other criteria. It looks like, when it comes to the applied level, collective action and institutional and governance arrangements "must be judged in the context of particular kinds of success, rather than in the abstract"(Ruttan 2006; Ruttan and Borgerhoff Mulder 1999).

"To judge" and to do it "in context": The contextual impact of heterogeneity, the diversity of possible social arrangements emerging from it, and the plurality of perspectives and criteria to be applied to them all matter. In the end it seems that, like it or not, a significant part of the agenda hinges on the normative and applied dimensions and the basic social theory that embeds these dimensions. The agenda advanced by Bloomington scholars seems to be a project that starts solidly in the empirical realm, but the more it advances, the more salient the normative presuppositions of the social theory framework behind it become. And thus the Ostroms' institutionalism looks more and more like a broader intellectual enterprise that belongs to that realm, properly identified by James Buchanan (2000), "between predictive science and moral philosophy."

To sum up, reviewing this set of implications and conclusions, one realizes that the results and directions of the research front on which the Bloomington school has been an important participant during the last decades are in fact setting up the intellectual scaffold for a novel stage in thinking and theorizing about collective action, governance, and institutional arrangements. It is a new stage that displays both continuity and change. The evolutions on this front made clearer and clearer the contours of a new perspective that integrates the varieties of pluralist themes and insights that emerge as a result of the last cycle of research on institutions and collective action. All essential dimensions of a well-rounded paradigm or school of thought—the analytical (theoretical and empirical), the normative, and the applied—are present.

Confronted with this fact, we have two options: (*a*) To deny or neglect the reality that at the end of the current cycle of research on collective action, institutions, and governance, the problems and challenges clustered around the theme of heterogeneity are setting the stage for a thorough reassessment and reconstruction of our approach to institutional theory and analysis as well as to their epistemological and social philosophy foundations; (*b*) to accept that the challenges brought to the forefront by a research agenda that is increasingly pressed to embrace the themes and theoretical lenses of pluralism are creating the conditions favorable to a profound reconsideration of the institutionalist project. The contours of an overhauled intellectual avatar of this project seem in sight. This new version emerging at the end of this cycle of research is, needless to say, the natural extension of previous projects. In brief, the first alternative is to continue to do pretty much what we are doing now, as Oliver and Marwell (2001) put it, to continue to play the game of "See, I can make my model do something different from what your model did." The second choice would be to boldly embrace an effort to rethink some of the dearest and deepest assumptions of our methods, approaches, and theories. It is this book's contention that the Ostroms and their collaborators have made important contributions to opening up the second alternative.

Heterogeneity, Diversity, and Institutional Theory

We have seen so far that an overview of the relevant developments in the study of collective action and governance with a focus on the problem of heterogeneity leads to significant insights regarding the potential broad evolution of the type of institutionalism advanced by the Ostroms. It is also plausible that the developments have already set up the parameters for a new cycle of theorizing and research in social sciences and social philosophy, and hence at this juncture it is appropriate to try to make a first step in outlining some of the most distinctive and interesting contours of the variety of institutionalism that seems to be emerging. As we have already noted, first and foremost, this refurbished institutionalism is strongly rooted in the problem of heterogeneity. The roots are multiple and multifaceted: Although homogeneity is fully considered a key element, heterogeneity and not homogeneity is the premier background condition to be dealt with in social theorizing. The challenge of heterogeneity is foundational and does not lend itself to easy solutions, be they theoretical or normative, such as universal institutional recipes for institutional design. However, although an intrinsic challenge for collective action, heterogeneity may nonetheless also be a resource for collective action and governance, and, from this perspective, diversity should be seen as instrumentally important. Hence the normative implications suggest at the operational level a process able to capture it as a resource, while minimizing its unavoidable drawbacks.

The best way to further specify these synoptic points is to use as a vehicle the very conceptualization of heterogeneity. As previously discussed, one way of sketching it is to focus on three dimensions: heterogeneity of capabilities, heterogeneity of preferences, and heterogeneity of beliefs and information (Ostrom and Keohane 1995). Page (2009) conceptualizes the three dimensions from a slightly different angle: diversity of resources and capabilities (diverse endowment natural resources, diverse economic capital, diverse social capital); cognitive diversity (diverse perspectives, diverse interpretations, diverse heuristics, diverse predictive models); and diversity of preferences (diverse fundamental or end state preferences, diverse instrumental or means preferences.) Such distinctions help us to get a clearer view on the full range of implications heterogeneity has for the way we theorize and design institutional arrangements. Many mixtures of heterogeneity and homogeneity are possible. And these combinations are both building blocks and keys to collective action and institutional order. The bottom line is that each of the various possible combinations poses specific problems for collective action. Each invites or discourages certain processes and institutional solutions.

Taxonomies like those introduced by Ostrom and Keohane (1995) or Page (2009) thus illuminate the broad range of heterogeneity in its polar relationship with homogeneity and the multitude of cases and combinations that reflect it. At one extreme, one may simply imagine a case in which heterogeneity defines all dimensions in play: resources, capabilities, perspectives, interpretations, heuristics, predictive models, fundamental preferences, and instrumental preferences. The other extreme is a case of radical homogeneity: homogenous resources, capabilities, perspectives, interpretations, heuristics, predictive models, fundamental preferences, and instrumental preferences. Once things are seen from this perspective, one understands that such extreme situations are in fact the background and boundary condition of social theorizing. In between these extremes of the conceptual space ranges the entire economic and political theory that uses agents, rules, preferences, and incentives as basic elements and building blocks.

If one adopts this perspective, it becomes obvious that more often than not we are shaping our discussions on a "response surface" improperly defined. Instead of taking into account the full range of dimensions and combinations, we focus only on fragments of it, singled out more or less arbitrarily. Yet, arbitrary as it may seem, there is a bias in all this. More precisely, as Keohane and Ostrom note (1995), we tend to use models in which a lot of homogeneity is assumed, sometimes in regards to the most sensitive features, which are in fact visibly and consequentially characterized by deep heterogeneity.

The global warming / climate change problem is exemplary for the discussions about collective action, coordination, cooperation, and institution building at a global level. For many years, the discussions operated under the postulate that a set of perspectives, interpretations, and predictive models was uniquely valid, and as such (should be) homogenously shared in the communities of interest. An additional assumption was that we knew more or less what the "correct" set of fundamental or end-state preferences was, as well as the "correct" set of instrumental or means preferences. Things were in many cases further simplified by the fact that the problem was implicitly operationalized as a fixed point, a catastrophe threshold, a 1 or 0 situation—a radical trade-off, disaster versus salvation. The variation of temperature vis-à-vis a projected baseline (scientifically determined) was combined with one form or another of the precautionary principle to convey a sense of epistemic closure. From there to the conclusion that all that was needed was to generate a global collective action with an old-fashioned, simple Olson-Hardin situation was just a step. It is no surprise that with all that came packaged the idea of a standardized global solution. The diversity of heuristics, interpretations, and even preferences, as calibrated to different levels, forms, and circumstances of collective action and governance, although empirically real, was conceptually and normatively sidelined. As we know now, there were better alternatives.

Such alternatives involve, as Keohane and Raustiala (2009) have demonstrated, a more nuanced and calibrated approach, for instance, one in which it is acknowledged that in solving these problems, one needs to deal with issues of participation, effectiveness, and compliance as related but distinct issue-areas, each with its own functional, geographic, and political arenas and dynamics, each involving trade-offs. "Solving all three problems simultaneously," write Keohane and Raustiala (2009, 2), "is particularly difficult, since these goals are often in tension." These problems "require careful institutional design," with "careful attention to the realities of world politics" and following in most cases a "bottom up" process. In a similar way, Keohane and Victor (2011) explain that when it comes to efforts to limit the extent of climate change, "there is no integrated, comprehensive regime" governing these efforts. "Instead, there is a regime complex: a loosely coupled set of specific regimes" that could be explored and explained using functional, strategic, and organizational perspectives.

The alternative articulated by such authors is thus not a broad and decontextualized criticism of the standard models or their application. In many cases, they write, the models' application may be legitimate and valid, as their isomorphism (be it formal or intuitive) is warranted. Yet what is suggested instead is that if used as benchmarks, such conceptualizations reflect and take into account just one possible combination of values for the variables in play. Out there is more heterogeneity (of agents, circumstances, and functions) than it is assumed. Complex as they are in comparison with the initial, first-generation models, even the newer frameworks still do not capture the full potential and implications of the challenge of heterogeneity. And thus it looks like the diversity-centered approach to institutionalism, on the lines advanced by the Ostroms' work, is leading toward a special kind of "general theory." It is a theoretical perspective that fully accepts the challenge of heterogeneity and all that this entails in theoretical, methodological, normative, and epistemological terms. The cases or models that assume certain combinations of homogeneity and heterogeneity are to be seen against the background of the whole "response surface," while the response surface is to be seen against the background of a social philosophy able to capture and illuminate both the assumptions and the implications of the theoretical perspective.

The Institutionalism of Heterogeneity and Diversity

And thus we have reached the major point of this argument: The Ostromian brand of institutionalism seems to be an embodiment of a theoretical and methodological discipline dealing consistently with heterogeneity and its consequence: institutional diversity (Munger 2010). The fact that it goes beyond the markets-versus-states dichotomy, or the state-centered perspectives, or the fact that it introduces notions such as "public economy" and polycentricity is not an accident. They are the expression or corollary of a basic intuition and conjecture about the nature of institutional theory seen as the effort to formulate, chart, and analyze the diversity of human institutional arrangements emerging from heterogeneity in its interplay with homogeneity. How do we deal conceptually, theoretically, methodologically with the fundamental problem of heterogeneity? How do people deal, and how should they be dealing with it, in practice so that they can be more effective in their institutional designs? The two themes, heterogeneity and institutional diversity, are two facets of the same problem. Institutionalism is the research program that unites these two facets and confronts the theoretical, empirical, methodological, and policy challenges emerging from this task.

That being said, it is important to admit straightforwardly that the Ostrom brand of institutionalism has a robust normative component. There is in it an implicit embrace of pluralism and diversity, a predilection toward negotiation and commonly agreed solutions. Imposing solutions using force, centralization of decision-making, monocentrism, and compelling consensus and homogenization by design are not regarded as prima facie answers, and when accepted, they are accepted as a mere second best—"Faustian bargains," as Vincent Ostrom put it. Certain normative preferences seem to be embedded in the Ostroms' way of approaching things, either as assumptions or as conclusions, or sometimes as a synthesis of both. However, at the same time we want to acknowledge that by pivoting and functioning as a link between normative and positive theory, this type of institutionalism entails a more nuanced view of the relationship between motivation and obligation in collective action and institution building. What is the individual-level motivation for cooperative behavior in collective action situations? One cannot simply assume that motivation is simply and straightforwardly "flowing from moral obligation" (Muldoon 2009). And we cannot assume that motivation generates simply and straightforwardly moral obligation. Once we realistically accept the widespread reality of heterogeneity, the conundrum of how to base political and moral obligation in motivation becomes even more salient. How is and how should obligation be rooted in motivation in conditions of deep heterogeneity of beliefs and preferences?

The idea is that the issue of how moral and political obligations could follow or could get aligned to an incentive system generated by an institutional arrangement is essential. Humans operate in a world in which incentives, rule-guided behavior, and morality all play their part. When homogenization of motivation is assumed and the homogenization of moral and political attitudes and commitments is factored in from the very beginning, things are relatively easy. This point can get lost between the lines of complex models and arguments. It is evident why an important part of political theory, public choice, and economics, not to speak of institutional theory, is based on (or emphasizes) one version or another of the "normalization," "homogenization" thesis. Yet the empirical and practical presence of resilient and widespread heterogeneity reminds us that this strategy is the easy way out of a real and important challenge with significant practical implications. What happens when normalization is not a viable alternative? There are cases in which achieving normalization (on one facet or another of the relevant variables) is part of the problem, and the social, political, and institutional strategies of reaching it are the first step toward a solution. There are situations in which even the very notion of what a solution is, or the criterion on which it should be evaluated, is far from being shared, situations in which homogenization of this or that key variable or factor remains a distant desideratum. With homogeneity assumed or conceptually manufactured, things are easier. But either to sidestep heterogeneity or to generate homogeneity through arrangements in which individuals (with all their diversity of preferences, information, resources, and capabilities) interact as incentives-motivated strategists and rule-guided and moral human beings—that is the true and real challenge.

This is the juncture where the Bloomington perspective reveals its full relevance. The work done by the Ostroms and their collaborators demonstrates that it is both necessary and possible to deal at both the analytical and institutional design levels with situations in which homogeneity is not assumed via any a priori normalization procedure. In the governance situations studied by the Ostroms and their collaborators in depth, one could see how institutional processes (empirically analyzable, not postulated in their end results) illustrate the complexity and diversity of possible approaches to the problems of governance in conditions of heterogeneity. In this way their views converge with the innovative agenda advanced in social and political theory by a group of authors including Gerard Gaus, Jack Knight, James Johnson, Nicholas Rescher, Scott Page, Chandran Kukathas, Fred D'Agostino, David Schmidtz, and Ryan Muldoon. These authors open—from dissimilar but convergent angles—new ground, challenging (and going beyond) the theoretical universe defined by one version or another of the "normalization/homogenization/consensus" thesis. With all that comes an entire set of issues related to the problems of comparability and commensurability (D'Agostiono 2003). Their work reconsiders, adjusts, extends, and in some cases transcends various themes of the pluralist neo-Berlinian literature associated with such names as William Galston, John Gray, George Crowder, John Kekes, Robert Talisse, and Craig Carr. At the same time it is important to note that, as Peter Lassman (2011, 8) put it, this tradition of research owns much to F. A. Hayek, Raymond Aron, and Karl Popper, who "all subscribed to versions of the view that an appreciation of the reality of plural and conflicting values was an essential component of an adequate understanding of modern politics." The work on these lines opens up the possibility of challenging what the authors advancing it call the "deep strain of utopianism" of contemporary social theory. Diversity and heterogeneity are a fact of life, and it is utopian to base our approaches on the idea that a firmly secured general consensus that homogenizes various beliefs or objectives of the social actors is the key precondition to governance and institutional order. The management of a society's business, writes Rescher (1993, 166–168), "need not root in agreement—and not even in a second-order agreement in the processes for solving first-order conflicts—as long as the mechanisms in place are ones that people are prepared (for however variant and discordant reasons) to allow to operate in the resolution of communal problems." The message is that even without first-order agreement and consensus, without homogeneity of preferences, opinions, goals, objectives, values, and so on, people may nevertheless be able to coordinate and create social order:

> The key consideration for the conduct of interpersonal affairs is that the activities of people can harmonize without their ideas about ends and means being in agreement. It is a highly important and positive aspect of social life that people can and do co-operate with one another from the most diverse of motives.... What is needed for co-operation is not consensus but something quite different—a convergence of interests.

And it is a fortunate fact of communal life that people's interests can coincide without any significant degree of agreement between them (a circumstance illustrated in both domestic and international politics). (Rescher 1993, 180)

This may be indeed a very bold and controversial thesis. But the theoretical and philosophical literature exploring the nature and limits of such theses sets into motion a shift of attention from "abstractly universal and collective basis of agreement" (and for that matter of institutional design) to various ways in which social actors in various circumstances manage "convergence based on concrete, particular commonalities of interest and value" (Rescher 1993, 180). In the end the thesis may be deemed too bold, but its investigation has already led to a shift to concrete institutional mechanisms and processes.

It is noteworthy that such a shift of interest points toward exactly the type of analysis developed by the Ostroms and their collaborators. It draws our attention to the fact that "cooperation among real people is based on the concrete realities of their personal situation" and that in our approaches to institutional theory and design we need "to exploit this fact as best we can in the best interests of the community at large" (Rescher 1993, 180–83, 191). This is indeed convergent with the message regarding institutional design received from our overview of the heterogeneity and governance literature. The basic idea is the same: "Even if we could agree on what ideally rational people would do under ideally rational circumstances," writes Rescher," this would provide precious little guidance as to how to proceed in the real world." Theorizing about "how to play a perfect hand in a card game will not help us to decide how to play the imperfect hands that fate actually deals to us....A theory geared to utopian assumptions can provide little guidance for real-life conditions." We need to forget about universal institutional designs and general "solutions" and to focus on the processes "attuned to the suboptimal arrangements of an imperfect reality," a reality defined by abundant heterogeneity, diversity, and endemic disagreement (Rescher 1993, 178; Levy 2000; Newey 2001; Root 2012; Carr 2010; Schmidtz 2011). This is about a space of "negotiated compromises" (Bellamy 1999), of a "modus vivendi based on working compromises" (Kukathas 1999) reflecting the relative power of parties "that have partially conflicting and partially complementary interests" (Gaus 2003, 57). The trick is, writes Gaus (2003, 230), "to explicate a robust conception of public reasoning—citizens reasoning together—while avoiding making too much a matter of consensus or looking for agreement when none is to be found."

Such an approach that takes seriously and confronts the reality of heterogeneity is more relevant today than ever. The empirically grounded institutional analysis of the possibility of governance and social order in extreme conditions that lack convergence of beliefs, preferences, and values seems to be, like it or not, a priority of the age. We live in a world in which diverse values, identities, principles, and cultures clash in the global arena while emigration, demography, technology, and culture challenge separately or in conjunction governance systems at all levels: global, national, and local. The problem of the impact of diversity on collective action, public goods production and consumption, and their governance imposes itself on the public agenda with an unprecedented intensity. The problem of endogeneity in the emergence of rules, and the dynamics of discovery and choice in institution building and change are indeed an increasing preoccupation in current political and economic theory. The move is unavoidable once heterogeneity is recognized as a key feature of the social reality to be dealt with. This is not merely a discussion about community-based cooperation or natural resources and their governance (although these problems are an important part of the picture). This is a discussion about the fundamental nature of governance (both domestic and international) in the new era. The attempt to determine whether it possible to have a peaceful and prosperous institutional order in an increasing interdependent world of diverse and conflicting views, beliefs, preferences, values, and objectives places us both at the core of the major political and economic challenges of our age and at the cutting edge of contemporary social science and political philosophy.

Beyond the "End State" Perspective

We find ourselves, thus, in a territory in which, again, old themes of constitutional and political theory converge explicitly with the core themes of institutional theory. Yet the emphasis is different. With diverse perspectives and preferences, it is clear why the discovery of institutional solutions is an essentially social process: "There is no possibility of a philosopher sitting in her study, abstractly considering what our shared interests are, proclaiming the common good. Until we actually engage in social interaction with diverse interests, we cannot know whether there will be a convergence" (Gaus 2011, 15). Instead of focusing on static structures and institutional formulae, the attention shifts to the processes by which the normative diversity of perspectives leads dynamically to solutions or arrangements acceptable if not to all, at least to a (super)majority. One is left not with a standard of institutional design, a blueprint for institutional forms, but with an institutionalized process of interaction and discovery. In such processes "the best boundedly rational and good-willed persons can expect" is that they may be able to "eliminate some possible social worlds as clearly suboptimal." It is a relatively open-ended process that is generating solutions that are possible imperfect and potentially clouded by "moral indeterminacy" (Gaus 2011, 14–15), yet, in the end they are solutions that satisfy criteria that otherwise would be elusive and difficult to replicate.

At the same time, the diversity of perspectives and strategies offers a diversity of ways to imagine solutions and arrangements. Social actors will try different approaches; they will combine and recombine in different configurations and arrangements. It is not just a matter of statistical probabilities. This diversity sets into motion social discovery that increases the chances that poor local optima are identified and replaced with better alternatives. A society, hence, moves via a collective process toward better alternatives. "This selection process is an actual collective social choice," writes Gaus. In this respect, "choice by a society takes up where discovery leaves off" (Gaus 2011). In most cases

> this is not an intentional "we-choice"; it is a social choice that arises out of a multiplicity of individual choices. Neither is it an abstract choice from some impartial Archimedean perspective outside our real social world. It is a collective choice that arises out of the social nature of individual choices: each person choosing to do what his perspective recommends given what others are doing. (Gaus 2011, 15)

Or as Rescher put it, we need to seriously consider the fact that a

> political process that is both theoretically valid and practically workable must seek not to abolish divisive self-interest but to co-ordinate it. It must provide for a system of interaction within the orbit of which co-operation of individuals for the greatest common good ("the best interests of the community as a whole") becomes an integral component of the interests of each. And this requires not methodology alone...but substantive mechanisms of co-ordination. (Rescher 1993, 181)

What authors like Gaus and Rescher are describing at the normative-theoretical level, the Ostroms and their associates have been analyzing at the empirical level. Their brand of institutionalism draws our attention to real-life cases of social choice processes in collective action and governance in conditions of heterogeneity. Social interaction, information exchange and negotiation, learning, and adjusting are crucial parts of a process that not only is different from top-down, centralized, technocratic approaches but also does not predetermine the content or specific substance of the solution.

These insights and their corollaries come to support sooner or later, from a new angle, an older distinction between, on the one hand, "end state" (or final outcome) perspectives and, on the other hand, "process" (or chain of causes and consequences) perspectives. End-state social theories, writes Norman Barry (1988, 19), attempt "an understanding of social phenomena through a description of the features of a society at a specified point in time. It is a kind of photograph which reveals such elements as a society's distribution of income, wealth, power, status, the structures of the economic and political arrangements, and so forth." The *static* character of end-state analyses is obvious. On the other hand, process theories focus on the ways end states emerge (Wagner 2007, 56). In a sense, they are rule-oriented and procedural theories; they concentrate on the nature of the rules as well as the actions and decisions of the social actors who follow them. From a "process" perspective, when it comes to the applied level, the question is not so much how we imagine and get the optimal end state X, but how we create the conditions to solve problem Y, aiming, admittedly, to do it in ways that satisfy some normative criteria of fairness and efficiency. From this perspective, political and economic design aims at improving institutional procedures and less at precisely specified end states. The key conjecture is that institutional arrangements that maximize individual choice in conditions of heterogeneity offer better conditions for performance and adaptive strategies. In a word, political and economic design should aim at improvement of institutional procedures and not at end states defined by criteria difficult to operationalize and preconceived outside the social process, as from an Archimedean viewpoint.

While a large part of theorizing in political economy is more or less explicitly "end state" oriented, the Ostroms' research agenda seems to be closer to the "process" perspective. In a sense, the "process" view and the associated social philosophy defining it seem to be the natural companion of this agenda, the two being interconnected by an inner logic, as facets of the same conceptual corpus. That is to say that the Ostroms' institutionalist line of research seems to provide the much-needed empirical and analytical basis of the "process" perspective and its social philosophy, a basis much needed to illustrate and bolster its normative- and applied-level claims.

At this juncture one may have already noticed the fact that the discussion of "end states" versus "process" is traditionally associated with the study of constitutionalism and constitutional political economy—a study that, although most of the time it starts with "end states," goes beyond that and investigates the procedural rules and human interactions that generated it. But this convergence between the logic of applied institutionalism and the logic of normative endeavors such as those associated with constitutionalism and constitutional political economy should not be a surprise. Vincent Ostrom (1998) has already drawn our attention to it. And, after all, we have already established that the type of institutionalism advanced by the Ostroms and their associates offers a broader theoretical framework, spanning scientific prediction and moral philosophy. It is a framework broad enough to accommodate a large part of the mainstream's models but also to transcend them and set the stage for the analysis of rules and choices in conditions of radical heterogeneity, uncertainty, and bounded rationality. In other words, it is a powerful instrument for the study of institutional diversity, seen both as a consequence and as a cause of heterogeneity of resources, capabilities, perspectives, interpretations, heuristics, and preferences.

2

Institutionalism and Polycentricity

IN DEALING WITH the challenge of heterogeneity and pluralism as irreducible and permanent features of the social world, institutional theory has moved on a twofold pathway: The first is better known and has been to study the problems and dysfunctions created by heterogeneity as well as the mechanisms by which people try to solve these problems. The emphasis in this case is on the difficulties of cooperation and coordination generated by diversity. The second has been as important, although usually overshadowed by the first: the study of how heterogeneity and diversity are, not just a source of problems and dysfunctions, but, in fact, a resource. The emphasis in this case is on diversity as a factor helping people to solve problems and better coordinate and cooperate.

The fact that the side focused on difficulties is more salient shouldn't be a surprise. Most of the traditional political economy and constitutional studies literature is dedicated to it. Scott Page himself, the influential student and supporter of diversity as a resource, acknowledges nonetheless that heterogeneity "leads to some sobering observations." His list is hefty: "More diverse fundamental preferences should result in fewer resources allocated to collective goods and projects." Moreover "individuals with diverse preference can form collections that, formally speaking, are not rational." Even when formal social choice procedures are introduced, "the results of votes can be somewhat arbitrary when preferences are diverse." Knowing that "no procedures work perfectly; individuals have incentives to misrepresent their preferences and to manipulate the agenda." All these are amplified when to the diversity of preferences one adds diverse perspectives and heuristics. "Too many solutions combined with diverse preferences can be a lethal combination. When people have diverse preferences, each solution has multiple values, one for each problem solver. This can result in preference cycles, manipulation, and misrepresentation" (Page 2009, 283, 294–95).

Given the fact that heterogeneity is a fact of life, these and similar problems are inescapable. Utopian formulas of homogenization and consensus aside, one has to deal with them at both theoretical and practical levels. Like it or not, the heterogeneity of views and preferences (not to speak of that of endowments) and their impact on the emergence, choice, and change of institutional arrangements require a high level of effort invested in both positive and normative approaches. One may want to avoid a revamped confrontation with the basic problems of social choice, public choice, and constitutional political economy, but they are forcefully reemerging at the very cutting edge of the agenda, even if one insists on the strictest terms of positive institutional analysis.

That being said, it is important to stress that the full relevance and distinctiveness of heterogeneity-and-diversity institutionalism is not entirely appreciated without understanding the second dimension in play. This approach to institutionalism not only acknowledges the reality of diversity and tries to cope with its challenge, but does that by seeing it as a potential resource, exploring the ways to capture and employ it. What is distinctive about the Ostromian proposition is that it does not theorize institutions as mere remedies to problems of coordination, cooperation, or perverse incentives created by heterogeneity, interdependence, and information asymmetries. It also tries to look at heterogeneity and pluralism and their institutional consequences from a more hopeful and constructive angle.

In this respect, the Bloomington perspective dovetails with significant developments in political economy and political philosophy, developments that all try to reconsider traditional problems of social and public choice from a novel angle. One simple way of presenting the substance of this convergence is to see the various problems of collective action institutional theory is called to deal with (be they at the local or global level) as optimization problems. Each institutional arrangement has a certain potential: it could maximize or minimize some values, preferences, or options from a given heterogeneous set existing in a given society. The potential to minimize as well as to maximize is part of the same institutional package. The optimization model thus allows a unified approach to the problem of institutional choice, combining the "challenge/problem" side and the "opportunity/resource" side of diversity. Obviously, it is difficult to optimize when you have different values, preferences, and perspectives. Total social satisfaction is a bundle of values, and the values are not additive. Moreover, the preferred solutions or institutional arrangements differ. Total social satisfaction varies from institutional arrangement to institutional arrangement. A variety of combinations is possible. This creates a rugged landscape of options. On each segment of the landscape there are local optima that dominate each other, and each such optimum could be achieved through at least one institutional arrangement. And there is at least one general optimum point. How does one find out the optimal when in most cases there is no Archimedean perspective from outside the social system? Is it possible to optimize over all the dimensions of the common solution (i.e., all the fundamental interests involved)? How does one improve the total social satisfaction when the agents are bounded rational actors with imperfect knowledge and subjective preferences? How does one move society in the direction of optima that dominate the current one, even if that optimal point is not the general optimum? These questions are truly crucial and have substantial consequences at the applied level, as they lead to the pivotal problem of institutional choice, the core of political economy.

Our problem, writes Gaus (2010, 3), a major contributor to this emerging literature, "is that we are trying to find the global optimum in a rugged landscape. If we all had a God's eye perspective, and so could scan the entire landscape, we may know what to do, but boundedly rational individuals cannot survey all possibilities." Institutional choice is a lot harder in such conditions. Is institutional arrangement A or institutional arrangement B the optimal (or optimizing) solution in this or that specific area of the landscape? How could one determine that? The solution cannot be a priori. Identifying and moving toward (local) optima cannot be other than contextual and determined by the social, cognitive, and institutional parameters of the specific segment of the landscape in which the decisional and institutional processes are taking place. What authors like Gaus are doing is to build one end of a theoretical bridge from political philosophy toward the Ostroms' type of institutionalism. On it the institutionalism and social philosophy sides converge in an attempt to show how and why people may be able to endogenously overcome, as a group, the predicament of uncertainty and heterogeneity and produce institutional arrangements able to find solutions and generate improvements in given circumstances.

As mentioned, the noteworthy fact in this convergence is that diversity is indeed a problem to be accommodated but also a resource to be exploited. Developing an argument whose logical complement seems naturally to be a theory of institutional diversity and institutional selection, Gaus demonstrates that "rigid normalization so that all *really* share the same perspective" it is almost certain to ensure "that we will be caught at a local optimum that falls short of the global optimum." Cognitive homogeneity or preference homogeneity has a blinding and narrowing-down effect. However, in a realistic vein, the downside should be acknowledged too. There is always the problem that, warns Gaus, "if we allow diversity, whatever benefits it may produce will be swamped by...dispute in which each party vetoes the favored social worlds of others, leaving us with an empty set of mutually acceptable social worlds" (Gaus 2010, 9–11). All depends on the ways the interaction and interdependence between the parties is set up to take place in specific circumstances, between given agents, with given beliefs, values, preferences, and perspectives.

One way or another, the discussion leads to the notion that governance and the institutional choice principles implied in it are both in their will and substance "the outcome of a social process, partly a process of discovery and partly an outcome of social choice." The link with the Ostromian brand of institutionalism is obvious. The accent is moved from grand principles and general designs to social processes and contextual analysis. Institutional arrangements grow out of a real social processes: "it is not a social contract in the form of an imaginary agreement, but a dynamic process of social discovery and choice that creates an actual social and moral fact" (Gaus 2010, 17). We are increasingly taking distance from the Rawlsian and Habermasian hypothetical arrangements or the neoclassical economics models and their assumptions. A unique combination of social philosophy and social science is starting to crystallize.

The "Second-Order Task" of Institutions: The Institutionalization of Institutional Assessment and Change

The perspective outlined above puts us in a position to take a step further in depicting how Ostrom-inspired institutionalism is positioned in the emerging research program exploring methodically the consequences of heterogeneity and pluralism. We have established that increasing attention is being given to (real, historical, empirical) social process associated with institutional choice, or to put it another way, institutional choice as a social and institutional process. This theme marks the point where another strand of the innovative institutionalism literature becomes relevant for the current argument. Having identified the move from an ideal, principles-based, and acontextual view of institutional assessment and choice, toward a contextual approach based in social processes, we are now in the position to use one of the most constructive and challenging modes of conceptualizing the issue in the current literature.

In *The Priority of Democracy* (2011), Jack Knight and James Johnson integrate the new pluralist theme of the social process approach to institutional assessment and selection, into the older literature, while at the same time creating the conditions for the transition to a novel, upgraded framework. Their effort systematizes and redefines in several critical ways institutional theory as the capstone of modern political economy—the overarching framework that encompasses both traditional economics and political science. Part and parcel of this strategy is their elaboration of the distinction between the "first-order functions" and the "second-order functions" of institutions.

The "first-order task" of institutions refers to the ways in which a specific institution solves the particular economic, social, and political problems it is meant to solve as its primary function. For instance, in the case of democracy, its first-order function is the facilitation of collective action regarding substantive policy issues, the capacity to bring people together in pursuit of common projects and to generate if not consensus at least commonalities, while legitimizing the decisions taken. Democracy is in this respect one among many institutional forms that help social actors to coordinate their activities. In a similar way, one may look at market arrangements, courts, and so on, through the lens of their first-order functions.

"Second-order tasks" are different, in the sense that they are meta-level phenomena. They concern the monitoring and management of the entire institutional set of a society. This involves an "ongoing process of selecting, implementing and maintaining effective institutional arrangements," in brief, the institutionalization of the process of evaluation and institutional choice in identifying failures, dysfunctions, externalities, and coordination problems as well as remedies to them (Knight and Johnson 2011, 19). A strong feedback function, monitoring the performance of the institutional mix defining a certain society at a certain moment is required, as well as capacities to influence its workings. An institution may be effective as a first-order mechanism but dysfunctional as a second-order one. Needless to say, the effectiveness of first-order mechanisms is structurally enhanced by a effective second-order mechanism. The role of the second order for the overall performance of an institutional system can hardly be overestimated.

Setting up the discussion in these terms, Knight and Johnson put on the table a key question: What is the institutional form(s) best suited for second-order tasks? (and by implication, what are the functional, structural, and normative criteria that need to be satisfied by such an institution?). A large part of their book is dedicated to answering these questions, arguing that "the set of institutions" called "democracy" has "an important priority among the available institutional alternatives." Hence the title of the book. Through an impressive tour de force through political science, economics, and institutional theory, they try to demonstrate that although in a world of heterogeneity and pluralism one cannot claim that democracy (or for that matter any institutional arrangement) is the best first-order way to coordinate all social interactions, democracy comes to fore as a second-order facilitator of effective institutional choice. This suggests a shift from seeing democracy as a mechanism of consensus and commonality to seeing it as an institutional mode of "addressing the ongoing conflict that exists in modern society," a mechanism of accommodating "tensions that in any event do not lend themselves to any principled and lasting resolutions," and a social instrument able to "decide in any particular moment how best to resolve specific problems and issues" (Knight and Johnson 1996; 2011, 20).

While making their case for democracy, Knight and Johnson outline the features that should be used to describe, analyze, and assess second-order institutional arrangements. Given the importance their approach has in understanding the Ostromian contribution to the new institutionalism of diversity and pluralism, it is necessary to briefly delve into them. The features identified by Knight and Johnson (2011, 169) cluster around the notion of "reflexivity." More specifically, three functions are central: "(1) to coordinate effective institutional experimentation, (2) to monitor and assess effective institutional performance for the range of institutions available in any society, and most importantly, (3) to monitor and assess its own ongoing performance." These are institutional functions that require mechanisms through which members of a society "can collectively assess the interrelationship of conditions and consequences over time." Their systemic tasks are greatly assisted by establishing and maintaining "an experimental environment that can enhance our knowledge of the relationship between different institutional forms and the conditions under which they produce good consequences." All this leads to the normative priority of democracy over alternative institutional forms, both decentralized and centralized: the reflexive structure of democratic decision-making is "the distinctive benefit of this centralized form of coordination." The Knight and Johnson case for the second-order priority of democracy rests thus "on the comparative claim that democratic decision making has properties other institutional forms either lack or possess to a lesser degree." Precisely because of "its emphasis on reflexivity, democracy is uniquely structured to provide, under the proper conditions, an effective framework for these complex and often contentious tasks" (Knight and Johnson 2011, 20).

The dismissal of the market and all decentralized mechanisms as possible contenders to the position of primacy is an important element of the argument. Knight and Johnson consider their interpretationcontrary to more prevalent views (although this prevalence may be debatable when one goes beyond the boundaries of mainstream economics and political economy). In any case, they challenge what is generally considered to be the current default presumption in political economy: the priority of the market, the market as the ultimate reference point and mechanism for institutional effectiveness. A comparative analysis, they write, shows that "democratic institutions are most effective when decision making is properly strategic and reflective." Markets "do not facilitate the types of communication necessary for the tasks of institutional assessment and monitoring."It is first of all a market failure argument. More precisely, a failure of markets to provide the much needed reflexivity. In markets, "communication between actors is about particular exchanges and not about the general functioning of the market itself." As communication extends to other types of issues, markets tend toward imperfection and inefficiency. This and other similar lines of comparative criticism are extended to all decentralized mechanisms (Coasian bargains, community-based cooperation, technocracy, incentive-compatible rules). The primacy currently given by scholars to decentralization among the available institutional alternatives is not warranted. Centralized democratic mechanisms "will do a better job of facilitating the various tasks of institutional choice than will decentralized mechanisms" (Knight and Johnson 2011, 52).

Setting aside possible diverging interpretations and claims of primacy, the vital point is that in articulating the problem of the second-order institutional arrangements, Knight and Johnson draw attention to one of the most important and most neglected issues in institutional analysis. Institutionalism is not only about this or that specific institution and its specific functions and performance. It is also about the overall capacity of a human society to monitor, assess, calibrate, adjust, and change, via institutional tools, the diverse set of institutional arrangements defining it. This is an institutional function in itself. To discuss it in mere theoretical terms is unproductive. It would mean remaining blocked at the level of analytical and ideal theory. To escape that predicament, we need to ask important questions: What devices do social agents and their societies have available to evaluate, design, and optimize their institutions? What are the conditions in which the mechanisms of institutional emergence and change operate? What is the relationship between spontaneous and designed change? How are preferences, relative power, and principles reflected in the process of change of institutions? What processes define the institutional structures involved in change? Are there systemic features that make one society more prone than others to adaptive institutional improvement? Knight and Johnson not only raise such questions but also advance the discussion, exploring the institutionalization of institutional choice in modern complex societies defined by diversity and pluralism. They favor democracy as the primary institution in this respect, but they favor it based on clear criteria and a comparative analysis.

All these points are relevant for the current discussion because only when we understand the stakes of the "second-order task" theme do we have a grasp of the context in which the Ostroms' perspective should be seen. The question is: Is decentralization indeed a dead end and is democratic centralization the institutional formula able to fulfill the crucial functions identified by the authors of *The Priority of Democracy*? Are there alternative ways to respond to the challenge they identify? Bloomington institutionalism might offer such an alternative.

At this juncture it is important to highlight what probably has already become apparent: an outcome of the Knight and Johnson project is an ingenious redefinition of the traditional political economy debate between centralization and decentralization. They do not deny the merits of decentralized arrangements. They not only allow but encourage decentralization and institutional pluralism as a first-order best in certain areas. However, on the bottom line, they reassert the overall primacy of centralization, via "the set of institutions" called "democracy." Thus they create a conceptual and thematic framework for the future debates on traditional themes of markets versus the state, and on decentralization versus centralizationx. It is in this framework, and under a certain interpretation, that the preeminence of democratic centralization is reestablished. This is a powerful argument, especially if seen from a perspective that still operates under the spell of what James C. Scott (1998) has called "seeing like a state." But if one turns to the Bloomington side and uses the Ostroms' theoretical lenses, a different perspective opens up. Without denying the merit of democracy (agreeing, in fact, with many of the qualities identified and emphasized by Knight and Johnson), Ostromian institutionalism develops a distinct angle in the light of which the case for decentralization gets restated. This is not a return to a version of older arguments, but an innovative view.

The idea of polycentricity (tentatively defined as a social system of many decision centers having limited and autonomous prerogatives and operating under an overarching set of rules) developed and explored by the Ostroms and considered to be pivotal to their work, can be seen as a response to the sophisticated anti-decentralization challenge on the lines advanced by the authors of *The Priority of Democracy*. It is important to remind readers that the debate in this case is not part of the cycle of conventional disputes between elementary theories of centralism and elementary theories of decentralized spontaneous order, or of the "markets versus states" literature preceding the institutional revolution, but it is an argument between two perspective that are inspired by and define the most up-to-date thinking in the field. We are talking about versions of centralism and decentralism that have incorporated the problems of heterogeneity, pluralism, and institutional diversity (both centralization- and decentralization-based) as well as most of the theoretical and empirical discussions in the relevant disciplines.

That being said, the Bloomington school reaction to the Knight and Johnson thesis has to be based on three elements: first, to acknowledge and embrace the general conceptual framework Knight and Johnson develop, as well as the basic agenda-driving questions they frame; second, to applaud the analysis of (and the emphasis on) democracy and especially its pluralist, epistemic-communicative and coexistence-against-conflict functions; third, to note that given that framework and the very institutional functionality criteria the authors outline, democracy fares less well than they claim. The major issue is that their assessment of democracy as an institutional form and its conditions of operation does not recognize the public choice problems identified by the Buchanan and Tullock Virgina school of public choice (Brenner and Lomasky 1989). While social choice problems are preeminent in the Knight and Johnson discussion, the structural dysfunctions of democracy discussed in the public choice literature are absent. But these are exactly the type of dysfunctions that raise serious doubts about democratic institutions' ability "to coordinate effective institutional experimentation," to monitor and assess "the effective institutional performance for the other institutions," and democracy's ability "to monitor and assess its own ongoing performance." For that matter, neither Mancur Olson's doubts about the structural dynamics of democratic systems and their flexibility are considered, although they are extremely relevant for an argument that makes reflexivity and flexibility the pivot of its case. The vulnerabilities of democracy, the topic of Vincent Ostrom's last book, deserve to be confronted up to the end. These observations in themselves are a powerful invitation to reconsider democracy's merits as a second-order institution, and they deserve a separate discussion.

However, our attention will be dedicated to a fourth element of the Bloomington reaction, the most important in the context of this book: advancing a theory of polycentricity. When it comes to decentralized, federalized, multijurisdictional governance structures Knight and Johnson's argument neglects the insights resulting from the Ostroms' investigations on polycentric orders. The Ostroms' insights regarding community-based cooperation have led to broader observations regarding the nature of governance in conditions of diversity, heterogeneity, and pluralism. These insights orbit around the notion of polycentricity. In other words, the Ostroms' variety of public choice and institutionalism leads to an alternative response to the challenge identified by Knight and Johnson under the label of the second-order tasks of institutional arrangements. Thus, a close overview of the notion of polycentricity and the research program associated with it at Bloomington becomes mandatory. Only in the light of such a close review can one assess its potential and limits as a solution to the problem of "second-order tasks" as well as its relationship with other central institutional arrangements such as those of the market and democracy. In doing that, we also better and clearer establish the place that Ostromian institutionalism occupies in the current landscape.

Polycentricity: Initial Developments

The concept of polycentricity was first envisaged by Michael Polanyi in *The Logic of Liberty* (1951). From there it diffused to law studies, thanks to Lon Fuller (1978) and others (Chayes 1976; Horowitz 1977), to urban networks studies (Davoudi 2002; Hague & Kirk 2003), and, even more importantly, to governance studies, thanks to the Bloomington school of institutional analysis (McGinnis 1999a,b, 2000; Wagner 2005; Sabetti et al. 2009; Aligica & Boettke 2009; Toonen 2010). Although the concept is often recognized as important, not much has been done to clarify and elaborate it, beyond the work of the aforementioned authors. This is why we'll start by introducing the concept as advanced by Polanyi and developed by Elinor and Vincent Ostrom, then continue by introducing possible instances of polycentricity and related notions, elaborating the concept through a concept design approach that systematically applies the logic of necessary and sufficient conditions. Based on that, we'll be able to return to the problem of institutional assessment and selection and its institutionalization through the second-order function of institutions.

Michael Polanyi's original development of the concept of polycentricity was the outcome of his interest in the social conditions preserving freedom of expression and the rule of law (Prosch 1986, 178). His approach was original in that he based his social analysis on an analogy to the organization of the scientific community. This was facilitated by his antipositivist approach to the philosophy of science, as he considered the success of science to be the outcome of a certain kind of social organization, rather than of scientists following a rigidly defined "scientific method" (Polanyi 1951, 1962).

Polanyi argued that the success of science was mainly due to its "polycentric organization." In such organizational systems, participants enjoy the freedom to make individual and personal contributions, and to structure their research activities in the way they consider fit. Researchers' efforts don't usually dissipate in unproductive directions because they share a common ideal, that is, their freedom is utilized to search for an abstract end goal (objective truth). Polanyi's key point is that such an abstract and underoperationalized ideal cannot be imposed on the participants by an overarching authority. Thus, the authority structure has to allow a multitude of opinions to exist, and to allow them not just as hypotheticals, but as ideas actually implemented in practice. The attempt to impose progress toward an abstract ideal is doomed to failure, as progress is the outcome of a trial-and-error evolutionary process of many agents interacting freely. Polanyi argued that the same analysis applies to art, religion, or the law, because these other activities are also polycentric in nature and driven by certain ideals (beauty, transcendent truth, and justice).

Polanyi did not stop at these observations. He used the concept of polycentricity as a tool particularly well suited for addressing the well-known socialist calculation problem (Mises [1922] 1981; Lange 1938). His arguments about the impossibility of economic calculation in a socialist system were closely related to Hayek's, yet they also benefited from the more general perspective provided by the concept of polycentricity. The market, he wrote, should be seen as approximating a polycentric system involving many agents who constantly adjust their behavior to the decisions made by others. Socialism implies the transformation of the system into a monocentric one. To make his point, Polanyi draws an analogy between scientists trying to discover the truth and entrepreneurs trying to discover the best way to make a profit. In some sense, the market can also be said to have an ideal, namely to deliver the optimal distribution of goods and the optimal production processes (i.e., to reach a Pareto equilibrium), and real markets always fall short of this ideal, as agents lack perfect information and human activities often involve externalities.

The socialist system is an attempt to reach (Pareto) economic optimum states faster and better than the market by means of a command-and-control strategy. That is supposed to reduce the misallocation of resources, something supposedly inherent and unavoidable in a polycentric market system. In other words, centralized socialism was expected to work better than the free market and to deliver faster economic growth. However, the Pareto equilibrium ideal is not easy to operationalize. First of all, preferences are subjective, and thus the demand for any good or service cannot be guessed from an outside vantage point. It is only revealed by the actual behavior of agents. Second, the amount of information required to manage all the production processes is enormous and cannot possibly be gathered and analyzed in a centralized fashion.

Consequently, in a monocentric-socialist system, the economic ideal can neither be derived nor imposed by central authorities. The system has to be allowed to move toward the "optimum" (ideal) by trial and error. In the same way that scientific progress cannot be guided by an authority (or by some rigid method), economic growth cannot be delivered using a command-and-control strategy.

[S]elf-coordination of independent initiatives leads to a joint result which is unpremeditated by any of those who bring it about. Their coordination is guided as by an "invisible hand" towards the joint discovery of a hidden system of things. Since its end-result is unknown, this kind of co-operation can only advance stepwise, and the total performance will be the best possible if each consecutive step is decided upon by the person most competent to do so.... Any attempt to organize the group...under a single authority would eliminate their independent initiatives and thus reduce their joint effectiveness to that of the single person directing them from the centre. It would, in effect, paralyze their cooperation. (Polanyi 1962, 62)

This argument is obviously related to Hayek's, but Polanyi parted ways with Hayek in regard to one important aspect, namely, social justice. The difference is important for our current understanding of polycentricism. While Hayek (1976) argued that the concept of social justice is literally meaningless, Polanyi was concerned that the market system comes into conflict with certain religious or secular moral values and that it may actually generate incentives undermining moral behavior (Polanyi & Prosch 1975). This way of reframing the issue of market and morality by reference to individual behavior avoids the types of collectivist arguments that Hayek tried to debunk, while keeping the issue of morality on the table.

Nonetheless, Polanyi's epistemic brand of moral relativism also meant that he believed that any attempt to impose morality by a central authority was not likely to succeed. Moreover, as a side effect of centralized enforcement, such attempts would only diminish freedom. In this regard, Polanyi argued that socialism was not an economic theory, but a moral system and that its claims to scientific status were a rhetorical device meant to facilitate the spread of the system. To his economic critique of socialism Polanyi added the argument of moral relativism, that is, the idea that justice itself is an ideal one can only hope to approach by means of a gradual trial-and-error process. This idea, and Polanyi's concept of polycentricity in general, proved to be an inspiration in legal studies.

Lon Fuller (1978) remarked that many problems that judges are called to settle are polycentric in the sense that disputes often involve many decision centers and the network of cause-and-effect relationships is not understood very well. This makes any decision not only more difficult but also a source of unintended consequences. Therefore, attaining justice can be a remote ideal. Fuller argues that when problems appear in polycentric systems, many of the affected parties are not called to express their point of view in court.

Many unrepresented parties are affected by the most conventional forms of litigation. Significant losses under a contract can close businesses. A criminal conviction can wreak havoc on an entire town.

A finding of negligence, products liability or fraud can bankrupt a business and send shock waves throughout a large network of contracts. Likewise, a contractual dispute concerning the management of a city's water and sewage system could affect millions of people, without the justifiability of any issue being called into question. Constitutional law questions, human rights, and statutory interpretation routinely involve settling legal questions with incalculable implications for unrepresented parties. Furthermore, the fact that judicial decisions affect the rights of parties not before the court is not only a collateral effect, but a fundamental responsibility of the courts. They are to clarify the applicable law for all to follow. (King 2006)

Given this existing complexity, Fuller (1978, 354–55) asked the following question: Which issues should be settled in court, which should be settled by political means, and which should be left to the market? As a general rule of thumb, Fuller argued that when there are many parties affected by an issue, the probability of judicial error increases because of the impossibility of avoiding unintended consequences. For that reason, there should be a threshold, defined by the level of polycentricity in a system, beyond which courts should not rule, but leave the matter instead either to markets or to the political process. Polycentric nonjuridical processes could offer better solutions (Fuller 1978; King 2006).

In other words, Fuller makes out of polycentricity a key element (i.e., an operational criterion) in his system of justice. Both Polanyï's and Fuller's approaches highlight the contours and relevance of the concept. However, the work of Vincent and Elinor Ostrom that operationalized it and gave it empirical substance.

Political Economy, Polycentricity, and the Metropolitan Reform Debate

The Ostroms became interested in polycentricity in the 1960, in the midst of a heated debate on the nature and objectives of the public administration reform in American metropolitan areas. However, their work transcended the "metropolitan governance" debate and evolved in two directions: The first was foundational—a social theory or social philosophy of social order built around the concept of polycentricism. The second was empirical and applied, focusing on case studies that acquired new relevance once seen through the lense of polycentricity.

The conventional wisdom in the 1960s was that in order to be organized optimally a metropolitan region should be one large community, functionally integrated by economic and social relationships through a centralized administrative system. However, despite this normative ideal the functional unity of these regions was artificially divided administratively by what many authors considered to be ad hoc governmental units. A metropolitan region had, thus, no unitary administrative identity. Instead, there were many state and federal governmental agencies, special districts, counties, and cities. Each had its separate jurisdiction, in most cases overlapping and subverting other jurisdictions. Mainstream authors argued that such a state of affairs made efficient administration impossible. The disparate units acted autarchically and were thus unable to perform the functions they were meant to perform. Deprived of an overarching coordination center, each unit of local government acted in its own interest, with no regard for the public interest of the rest of the metropolitan community (E. Ostrom [1972] in McGinnis 1999b; Institute for Local Self-Government 1970). Out of this diagnostic grew an entire literature converging around the idea that the "problem of metropolitan government" was that "the multiplicity of political units" made governance in metropolitan areas "a pathological phenomenon." There were "too many governments and not enough government" and as a result, a "duplication of functions" with confusing "overlapping jurisdictions"—in brief, an "organized chaos." Interestingly enough, these arguments were, at a deeper level, similar to the traditional claims for the economic superiority of central planning over free markets.

Vincent and Elinor Ostrom and their associates responded by challenging one of the basic theoretical tenets of the "reformers." (For an extended discussion, see Aligica and Boettke (2009)—on which this section is based.) Their main argument pointed to the fact that the optimum scale of production is not the same for all urban public goods and services. That is to say, some services may be produced "more efficiently on a large scale while other services may be produced more efficiently on a small scale" (E. Ostrom [1972] in McGinnis 1999b; Oakerson 1999; Ostrom, Bish, & Ostrom 1988). Therefore, the emergence and persistence of multiple agencies interacting and overlapping, far from being a pathological situation, "may be in fact a natural and healthy one." This duplication is a natural expression of the fact that different services requires different scales to be efficiently provisioned and that principles of division of labor (such as cooperation and exchange) function in the public sector, too.

> Duplication of functions is assumed to be wasteful and inefficient. Presumably efficiency can be increased by eliminating "duplication of

services" and "overlapping jurisdictions." Yet we know that efficiency can be realized in a market economy only if multiple firms serve the same market. Overlapping service areas and duplicate facilities are necessary conditions for the maintenance of competition in a market economy. Can we expect similar forces to operate in a public economy? (Ostrom and Ostrom 1965, 135–36)

The Ostroms explained that the variety of relationships between governmental units, public agencies, and private businesses, emerging, coexisting, and functioning in a public economy, "can be coordinated through patterns of interorganizational arrangements."

> Interorganizational arrangements, in that case, would manifest market-like characteristics and display both efficiency-inducing and error-correcting behavior. Coordination in the public sector need not, in those circumstances, rely exclusively upon bureaucratic command structures controlled by chief executives. Instead, the structure of inter-organizational arrangements may create important economic opportunities and evoke self-regulating tendencies. (Ostrom and Ostrom 1965, 135–36)

The insights produced by applying the standard political economy perspective were remarkable and illuminating. Yet they were not considered analytically sufficient. In order to be adapted to a phenomenon that was, in the end, quite different from standard market-based phenomena, the political economy conceptual framework needed several adjustments. Certain concepts and insights derived from the private economy had a direct application. Others needed further adjustments. But one idea was clear: Once things are seen from the political economy perspective, there is no reason to assume a priori that competition among public agencies is necessarily inefficient (Ostrom, Tiebout, & Warren 1961; Wagner & Warren 1975; Bish 1971).

To advance in in the analysis it was not sufficient to note the differences between the metropolitan reform and political economy approaches to metropolitan governance and to suggest that one is better than the other:

> With basic differences in theoretical perspectives, scholars will adopt quite different orientations to their subject matter, will use different concepts and languages, and will pursue their inquiries in quite different ways. These differences will not be resolved by discussion and deliberation alone. Instead, ... we can attempt to undertake critical tests

where divergent theories imply contradictory conclusions. The theory that has the weaker explanatory capability presumably would give way in the course of time. (Ostrom and Ostrom 1965, 135–36)

The Ostroms suggested having an empirically grounded debate that went beyond ideological and theoretical parameters. What was required was to specify in empirical form the claims that otherwise remain implicit in the literature on metropolitan reform. Once the key propositions under consideration became plain, empirical analysis was possible. The strategy was then simple—pairing up propositions such as (1a) "Urban public goods and services are relatively homogeneous and similarly affect all neighborhoods within a metropolitan area" versus (1b) "Urban public goods and services differ substantially in regard to their production functions and their scale of effects." Or, (2.a.), "Urban voters share relatively similar preferences for urban goods and services" versus (2.b.) "Individuals with relatively similar preferences for public goods and services tend to cluster in neighborhoods; preferences will tend to be more homogeneous within neighborhoods than across an entire metropolitan area." It was a two-step approach. First, two sets of propositions were created. Second, the two parallel sets of propositions were matched, taking advantage of the empiric comparisons thus made possible (E. Ostrom [1972] in McGinnis 1999b, 148).

To explore the issues, a concrete empirical agenda was put together by the Ostroms and their team. One key theme of the metropolitan debate focused on how the size of the governmental unit affects the output and efficiency of service provision—that is, the impact of the size of a government producing a service. The Ostroms' team decided that instead of speculating, they should get out into the field and collect the data needed to measure the relationship. They attempted, first, to test the opposed theories of urban governance focused on the size of governmental units and, second, to focus on the number of such units in a metropolitan area.

Their studies on police services are in these respects exemplary. They began in Indianapolis, with a comparative analysis of independent, small police departments that served neighborhoods adjacent to and similar to those served by the larger Indianapolis City Police Department. The Ostroms then extended the study to the Chicago Police Department; the St. Louis metropolitan area; Grand Rapids, Michigan; and the Nashville–Davidson County area of Tennessee; and then replicated it in Indianapolis. They also tested for external validity, using a large survey of citizens living in 109 cities with populations of more than 10,000. The findings challenged the notion that larger urban governments produced superior public services: "The presumption that economies of scale were prevalent was wrong; the presumption that you needed a single police department was wrong; and the presumption that individual departments wouldn't be smart enough to work out ways of coordinating was wrong," Ostrom wrote. On the whole, "polycentric arrangements with small, medium, and large departmental systems generally outperformed cities that had only one or two large departments" (E. Ostrom [1972] in McGinnis 1999b, 148; Ostrom, Parks, and Whitaker 1973c; 1978; Ostrom and Parks 1973a; 1973b; Bish 1999).

The result of all these efforts was not only solid empirical research but an entire new domain. It is in this context that the outstanding work on common pool resources was later to emerge, as well as the tools of institutional analysis that have become well known and a trademark of the Bloomington school (Sabetti 2011; Vanberg 2011; Kliemt 2011). But the most important thing for this discussion is that the inquiry into the two models of metropolitan governance and their policy recommendations revealed that the differences between the two were not simply theoretical and methodological. A deeper and more profound difference of vision (political economy vs. traditional public administration theory; individualism vs. holism) was revealed. The competing vision seemed to be defined by a paradigmatic pair of correlate concepts: "polycentricism" and "monocentrism." Exploring and understanding their nature and the differences between them emerged as crucial for the debate. Even more important, developing them and their implications was not a task of "normal science"—that is, an effort to apply an existing model or concept to an additional domain. Instead, the research required a change of paradigm. In following and articulating the Ostroms' logic, a new domain was to be defined. That required an new conceptual framework.

> By conceptualizing metropolitan areas as polycentric political systems, we were suggesting that a system of ordered relationships underlies the fragmentation of authority and overlapping jurisdictions that had frequently been identified as "chaotic" and as the principal source of institutional failure in the government of metropolitan areas. We identified a polycentric political system as having many centers of decision making that were formally independent of each other. A "system" was viewed as a set of ordered relationships that persists through time. (V. Ostrom [1972] in McGinnis 1999b, 53)

It is significant that the two notions defining the conceptual space are interlinked. That is to say, any approach to the study of polycentricity is also a study of monocentricity. Moreover, the relation is not only logical—the two being

logically correlated—but also empirical. "A predominantly monocentric political system need not preclude the possibility that elements of polycentricity
may exist in the organization of such a system." Conversely, "the existence of
a predominantly polycentric political system need not preclude elements of
monocentricity from existing in such a system" (V. Ostrom [1972] in McGinnis
1999b, 52).

It was clear that reformers and the mainstream political scientists were
missing something important by insisting that the fragmentation of authority and overlapping generated chaos. Patterns of order were present, and that
become clear once appropriate theoretical lenses were used. The problem of
polycentricity and chaos (defined as lack of order) and more precisely its eluci-
dation was thus central to advancing the Ostroms' agenda. The challenge was
to identify, chart, and analyze the patterns of order underneath the apparent
chaos associated with polycentricity as a social phenomenon.

It became clear that at stake was nothing less than a theory of hidden order,
a theory of an "invisible hand" directing the "social mechanism." If articulated,
such a theory might be applicable to many instances of social order, in different arenas and at different social levels. The fact that polycentricity was applicable to a large range of social phenomena was foreseen by Michael Polanyi.
That is to say, a discussion of polycentrism in political-administrative systems
was only out of many possible ways to approach the issue, using an empirical
example as a vehicle. If polycentric systems of government in metropolitan
areas are just one case of polycentricism, if metropolitan areas are just one
instance in which polycentric order may be detected, then that specific case
could be used for a working definition or general account of the phenomenon.
That is to say, polycentricity raises fundamental theoretical, empirical, and
normative challenges that have ramifications well beyond the governance of
metropolitan areas.

Specifying the Concept: The Ostroms' Perspective

In specifying the concept of polycentricity, the issue of power, more specifically
its use and its monopoly, is a major element. One of the key features in defining a polycentric—or for that matter, a monocentric—order is the legitimate
exercise of coercive capabilities. On the one hand, in a monocentric political
system the prerogatives for determining and enforcing the rules are "vested
in a single decision structure that has an ultimate monopoly over the legitimate exercise of coercive capabilities." On the other hand, in a polycentric
political system "many officials and decision structures are assigned limited
and relatively autonomous prerogatives to determine, enforce and alter legal

relationships" (V. Ostrom [1972] in McGinnis 1999b, 55–56). In a polycentric system no one has an ultimate monopoly over the legitimate use of force. The "rulers" are constrained by a system of rules whose ideal expression is the "rule of law." The factors creating and maintaining the system of rules may be wide-ranging, from cultural to a balance of power, from power bargaining and (self-)interest to norms and moral codes. Significantly, such factors may not be independent of the nature and function of the other elements defining the polycentric system.

The bottom line is that polycentric systems function under something close to (or tending toward) a "rule of law." That is why in defining a polycentric system the notion of "rule" is as important as "legitimacy," "power," or multiplicity of "decision centers." Ostrom, Tiebout, and Warren (1961) considered it the major functional principle behind the phenomenon. The multiplicity of decision centers was a meaningful way of defining polycentricity only under the assumption that a broad set of rules (even if informal and tacit) was in operation. There are many forms of organization that might seem analogous to a polycentric order. Yet they did not have the attributes associated with polycentricity if they lacked an encompassing system of rules that had substantial sway over the decision centers.

While exploring the meaning and conditions of polycentricity, Vincent Ostrom and his associates realized that the study of polycentricity (and even more precisely the problem of whether the government of a political system can be organized in a polycentric manner) had a considerable history. It was no historical accident that Alexis de Tocqueville made his observations about democracy and the invisible mechanisms of social order while studying America. According to Ostrom, the American Constitution could be viewed as an experiment leading to polycentricity. At he same time, federalism could be seen as one way to capture the meaning and to operationalize one aspect of this type of order. And, in light of that insight, polycentricity seems to be a necessary condition for achieving "political objectives" such as liberty and justice. The dispersion of decision-making capabilities associated with polycentricity, wrote Ostrom, "allows for substantial discretion or freedom to individuals and for effective and regular constraint upon the actions of governmental officials." As such, it is an essential characteristic of democratic societies (Ostrom 1972).

The historical and normative note is important. It suggests that if one is interested in the conditions preserving and enhancing the aforementioned "political objectives," one needs to better understand what makes polycentric systems so special. The conclusion was that a polycentric arrangement has a built-in mechanism of self-correction. Self-correction is the crucial functional or operational feature of polycentricity that explains an important part of its performance.

> While all institutions are subject to takeover by opportunistic individuals and to the potential for perverse dynamics, a system that has multiple centers of power at differing scales provides more opportunity for citizens and their officials to innovate and to intervene so as to correct maldistributions of authority and outcomes. Thus, polycentric systems are more likely than monocentric systems to provide incentives leading to self-organized, self-corrective institutional change. (E. Ostrom 1998)

The study of the US constitutional experiment as an experiment in polycentricity leads to other interesting insights. For instance: if polycentric systems depend on the value and culture of the individuals creating them, then whether or not a significant number of individuals share or aspire to those values is critical for the operation of the system. Thus, the Ostroms' exploration led to the conclusion that the discussion on polycentricity is not just about multiple decision-making centers and monopolies of power. Such a discussion has unavoidably to deal with rules, constitutions, fundamental political values, and cultural adaptability in maintaining them.

Discussing polycentricity leads sooner or later to the issue of the spontaneous processes and spontaneous order. From the very beginning Polanyi used the term *spontaneous* as synonymous with polycentric. He implied that the attribute of spontaneity is, in a deeper sense, an additional defining characteristic of polycentricity (or at least something that is hypothetically related to it). In his attempt to advance a more robust concept of polycentricity, Vincent Ostrom ([1972] in McGinnis 1999b, 60) elaborated Polanyi's point. He explained, for instance, that spontaneity means that "patterns of organization within a polycentric system will be self-generating or self-organizing" in the sense that "individuals acting at all levels will have the incentives to create or institute appropriate patterns of ordered relationships." In a polycentric system, "spontaneity" is a function of self-organizing tendencies occurring, under specific conditions, at several different levels. Outlining these conditions is a further step in specifying polycentricity as seen from the Ostromian perspective.

The first condition for "spontaneous self-organization" is freedom of exit and entry in a particular system. The establishment of new decision centers under the existing rules must be easy to accomplish. If such nodes are blocked, then one cannot expect a polycentric order to emerge. Freedom of entry ensures the spontaneous development of the system (V. Ostrom [1972] in McGinnis 1999b, 60). The second necessary condition is related to the enforcement of general rules of conduct. These are the rules that provide the legal framework for a polycentric order. "If individuals or units operating in a polycentric order have incentives to take actions to enforce general rules of conduct, then polycentricity will become an increasingly viable form of organization" (V. Ostrom [1972] in McGinnis 1999b, 60). Finally, the third condition is that spontaneity should be manifested as the revision of the basic rules that define the framework of a specific order. Individuals must be free not only to play the game within the given rules and have incentives to enforce those rules but also to change them. That alteration, however, should take place in an orderly way.

These three conditions imply two prerequisites. One is procedural. There should be rules on changing rules. The other is cognitive: a specific understanding of the relationship between particular rules and their consequences under given conditions. "If conditions were to change and a particular set of rules failed to evoke an appropriate set of responses, rules could then be altered to evoke appropriate responses" (V. Ostrom [1972] in McGinnis 1999b, 60). This has important implications for the relationship between spontaneous order and design. Learning from experience and the enhanced understanding that comes with it are the vectors of an ongoing process of knowledge integration in the institutional system and the prerequisites for adaptations to the changing environment. In other words, institutional design (seen as the application of our understanding of rules and consequences and the conditions that determine their interplay) is part and parcel of spontaneous order and not inimical to it. That is, design and spontaneous order are not irreconcilable. Design is possible (and takes place overwhelmingly) within the overarching rules and within the broader process of the ever-evolving spontaneous order. The connection between the two is given by the notion of knowledge and an entire set of correlate concepts such as learning (V. Ostrom [1972] in McGinnis 1999,b 60).

Finally, one of Ostrom's most interesting conjectures was that the structure and dynamics of a polycentric system is a function of polycentrism in the governance of the other adjoined systems. The basic social functions and institutional domains of a society can be organized in various degrees under a polycentric order: polycentricity in the structure of governmental arrangements, in economic affairs, in political processes, in judicial affairs, and in constitutional rule (V. Ostrom [1972] in McGinnis 1999b, 56; McGinnis 2005). The relationship between these domains is important for descriptive, analytical, and normative reasons, but one has to keep in mind a multiplicity of angles in approaching the issue. McGinnis's (2011) inventory of levels and domains as seen from various angles is telling for the polymorphism of both the phenomenon and possible conceptual approaches:

> Multi-Level: Local, provincial, national, regional, global units of governance; Multi-Type: general purpose nested jurisdictions (as in traditional federalism) and specialized, cross-jurisdictional political units (such as special districts; Multi-Sectoral: public, private, voluntary, community-based and hybrid kinds of organizations; Multi-Functional: incorporates specialized units for provision (selection of goals), production (or co-production), financing (taxes, donors), coordination, monitoring, sanctioning, and dispute resolution. (McGinnis 2011, 171–72)

Ostrom thought that studying the cases of polycentric order (in economy, law, and politics) reveals that a polycentric order is more than just a series of different centers of decision operating in competition with each other in a specific domain or area. Polycentricity is a complex system of powers, incentives, rules, values, and individual attitudes, all combined in a complex system of relationships at different levels. One may detect very interesting dynamics at work. Market polycentricism seems to entail judicial polycentricism. Judicial polycentricism entails political polycentricism, and in its turn political polycentricism entails constitutional polycentricism. Accepting the existence of such a systemic logic, one may visualize the entire social system as defined by underlying currents originating in pulsating polycentric domains. Polycentric order in one area entails and produces polycentricism in other areas. A tension is created, pushing change in the direction of more nodes of decision-making.

However, at the same time, one can imagine monocentricity operating under a similar pattern. The result of the ongoing tension between the two principles is a dynamic, unstable coexistence. One area or domain opened to polycentricity encourages polycentricity in another area. One area or domain under monocentricity drives monocentricity in other domains. Capturing, conceptualizing, and analyzing the entire dynamics of the field of tensions and friction between monocentrism and polycentricity becomes important analytically. Thus, it is easy to understand why building the proper conceptual apparatus for this task was declared the priority of polycentricity scholarship. As Vincent Ostrom put it:

> Penetrating an illusion of chaos and discerning regularities that appear to be created by an "invisible hand" imply that the tasks of scholarship...will be presented with serious difficulties. Relevant events may

occur without the appropriate proper names being attached to them. Presumably events implicated by definitions used in scholarship may deviate from conventions that apply to the use of proper names. Patterns and regularities which occur under an illusion of chaos may involve an order of complexity that is counterintuitive. (V. Ostrom 1972, 20)

Ostrom argued that the monocentric vision dominated political sciences for such an extended time because scholars missed the correlation between the concepts of polycentricity and monocentricity. A proper language and concepts needed to map, describe, and analyze polycentric systems were lacking, but even worse, the existent language in political science was embedded with a monocentric vision. Perceiving polycentricity through the conceptual lenses of a monocentric vision, using a vocabulary growing out of that vision, was doomed to distort and mislead the analysis. The conclusion was straightforward: the existent conceptual frameworks, and the associated vocabulary, and theories based on them needed to be reconfigured in ways that would make their limits and preconceptions explicit.

At the same time, the Ostroms were aware that conceptual development alone wouldn't lead far without an expansion of the empirical agenda. There was a tension and a trade-off between these two desiderata. The result was that the much-needed elaboration of a conceptual framework was stalled. And thus, although the point to which the concept was brought had considerable potential, it has yet to be theoretically explored. "Polycentricity" as developed by the Bloomington researchers is no longer a mere mixture of intuitions and functionalist descriptions. The Ostroms' work offers a clearly articulated reference point for further developments (Sabetti 2008; Sproule-Jones et al. 2008; McGinnis 2011). Mike McGinnis has recently synthesized the topic as follows: polycentricity is "a system of governance in which authorities from overlapping jurisdictions (or centers of authority) interact to determine the conditions under which these authorities, as well as the citizens subject to these jurisdictional units, are authorized to act as well as the constraints put upon their activities for public purposes." Based on that summary, let's take as a starting point the notion of polycentricity as developed by the Ostroms and try to take several steps further in exploring its conceptual space.

Related Concepts and Further Elaborations

Before any attempt to elaborate the concept of polycentricity, it is useful to revisit examples that illustrate the notion. While we consider these examples we also need to look at some references that, although they don't use the term "polycentricity," do illuminate or emphasize phenomena akin to polycentricity.

Any list of real-world examples used at one point or another to exemplify or to illuminate polycentricity cannot omit the following: science (Polanyi 1951; Feyerabend 1975), representative constitutional democracy (V. Ostrom 1972; Wagner 2002), free markets (Polanyi 1951), and common law (Hayek 1973; Fuller 1978; King 2006). (It is noteworthy that the high regards Knight and Johnson have for democracy are vindicated from an Ostromian perspective, except that democracy in the latter view is worthy to the degree that it is an instantiation of polycentrism). The diversity of the phenomena on the list is evident. For instance, in some cases the decision centers are nonterritorial (they have overlapping jurisdictions), in some cases they are territorially delimitated, and in some cases they are both. Hence the underlying crucial question: Do all these phenomena indeed share some feature? Is that common element really something called "polycentricity"? Or are we talking about a series of overlapping "family resemblances"? Either way, even a mere list of phenomena that are suspected of polycentrism makes for a challenging research agenda.

To this list we should add examples of notions that are related, in the sense that they point to processes related to polycentrism as defined in the Polanyi-Ostrom tradition. These are notions that, once defined and elaborated, display many features associated with polycentricity (but also some significant differences): polyarchy (Dahl 1971), multiplism (Lindblom & Woodhouse 1993), market-preserving federalism (Weingast 1995), and federation of liberty (Kukathas 2009).

A final item on the list of phenomena and notions that are (or could be) associated with the themes of polycentricity and which deserve a special note is anarchy as a social phenomenon (Tullock 1972; Stringham 2005; Powell & Stringham 2009). This attention is needed because there is a potential for confusion between the two ideas. The best-known literature on anarchism (from Godwin to Rothbard) is *normative*. These normative theories have been accused of being impossible to realize in practice (Nozick 1974; Buchanan 1975). The field of *positive* anarchy (as opposed to the normative strand) emerged with the goal of testing scientifically the validity of Nozick-and Buchanan-like intuitions and, consequently, gauging the general importance of institutional enforcement for the creation and maintenance of social order in large groups of quasi strangers, as opposed to the culturally mediated spontaneous order (Boettke 2005; Coyne and Lemke 2011).

The preliminary conclusions of such "positive anarchy studies," especially the empirical efforts, are threefold. First, just as there are many varieties of states, there are also many possible varieties of anarchic systems, based on different rules and modes of enforcement of those rules, and these varieties are widely divergent in terms of peacefulness and security. Second, there are cases in which the Hobbes and Buchanan form of pessimism about peaceful anarchy is unjustified, as the emergent social order is preserved in the absence of a monopoly of force or even, in certain cases, *despite* the existence of a monopoly of force acting contrary to the preservation of peace and failing to promote prosperity. Third, not all anarchic organizations are peaceful and promote prosperity; in certain cases the Hobbes-Buchanan intuition proves entirely correct (Aligica and Boettke 2009).

Positive anarchy studies overlap to a certain extent with the literature on polycentricity, as anarchism involves by definition multiple centers of decision-making. The connection between the two fields has two aspects. On one hand, one can view some of the positive anarchy studies as studies of the dangers of polycentricity, of how multiple centers of decision-making can degenerate into social chaos. Although anarchy presupposes multiple centers of decision-making, not all anarchic systems are instances of polycentricity. It is important to keep in mind that polycentricity involves multiple centers of decision-making *within an accepted set of rules*. In other words, only certain variants of anarchy are polycentric, as these variants are peaceful precisely because rules exist and function (albeit in the absence of a single enforcer having a monopoly on force). In turn, the concept of polycentricity provides the theoretical branch of positive anarchy studies a comprehensive way of modeling the boundary between peaceful anarchy (i.e., polycentricity) and chaotic and violent anarchy.

On the other hand, one can see positive anarchy studies as studies of the most fundamental aspects of polycentricity, namely, how social order originally emerges out of the interactions of individuals. While one can, of course, study polycentric institutions that are already strongly embedded in a system of rules, the analysis is not really pushed to its natural end unless we understand how and why these systems of rules came about. Moreover, and most importantly, such understanding is not just of historic interest. Just as in biology ontogenesis is not just the process by which an adult living being develops from a single cell, but also the day-by-day process at cellular the level by means of which the living beings maintains their structural integrity by being constantly rebuilt, positive anarchy studies describe a form of social ontogenesis—the historic process by which the complex social order of contemporary societies developed is also an ongoing, pervasive process responsible for the day-by-day functioning of those complex social orders. These original social forces are still present, and they constitute the raw material out of which the complex social order is built, and they are merely constrained and modeled by modern culture and institutions. For these reasons, positive anarchy studies provide important data for understanding contemporary social phenomena.

All of the above points allow a better understanding of polycentricity. Polycentricity emerges as a nonhierarchical institutional and cultural framework that makes possible the coexistence of multiple centers of decision-making with different objectives and values, and which sets the stage for an evolutionary competition between the complementary ideas and methods of these different decision centers. The multiple, overlapping centers of decision-making may act on the same territory or may be territorially delimited in a mutually agreed fashion. With the above overview in place, we are now in a position to restate an important point. Implied in the effort to elaborate the concept of polycentricity is the crucial assumption and expectation that it provides a unified conceptual framework for analyzing and comparing different forms of social self-organization as special cases of a more general evolutionary phenomenon. This phenomenon is manifested in social groups and networks made up of different kinds of actors (from scientists to entrepreneurs to politicians to judges to urban planners to military leaders) and relative to different kinds of overarching goals (such as truth-seeking, maximizing economic profits, gaining and maintaining political power, seeking justice, or maintaining social order). Understanding these social phenomena as special cases of polycentricity may make it easier to draw informed analogies from one field to another.

Moreover, it may be the case that, as the Ostroms' conjecture suggests, in the real world many of these different cases of polycentricity are not independent of each other but in constant interaction. Thus, the concept of polycentricity may provide a better foundation for understanding the interactions between, say, economic order and democratic order, and for analyzing possible social changes (such as the possible transition from a market-based democracy to a centrally planned dictatorship, Hayek's well-known "road to serfdom"). Thus, Polanyi's and the Ostroms' original goal in defining the concept—the facilitation of useful and productive analogies among various cases of spontaneous order—can be extended. In the end, whether or not all or only some of the above examples, and others like them, will be accepted as instances of polycentricity depends in large measure on (*a*) whether the polycentric conceptual framework provides useful insights about their functioning and, conversely, (*b*) whether they in turn provide useful insights into other already accepted cases of polycentric phenomena. The bottom line is that, at this point, the literature has not yet reached a sufficiently robust and rigorous level of analytical development for such questions to be constructively addressed. This is the context in which one should consider our subsequent goal, that is, to move closer to an analytical development of the concept able to serve such investigations.

Polycentricity: Conceptual Structure and Boundaries

The preceding brief overview of potential examples of polycentrism, as well as of related notions, leaves us in the position to ask again whether it is possible to identify a core common element. The end of the preceding section outlined a basic conceptualization of polycentricity as it emerges from the assumption that the examples provided do indeed share common features. Let's push the matter further. Although several directions of development are possible, it is natural to use the one outlined by the Ostromian perspective.

The fundamental dilemma in elaborating a concept for operational and analytical purposes is whether one is dealing with "core elements" or with "family resemblances" or with neither. In most cases involving complex notions, such as those used to address problems in social science, it is difficult to define a concept in the traditional Aristotelian genus-differentia fashion. On the other hand, Wittgenstein's "family resemblance" approach ([1953] 1999), based on the idea that various empiric instances of a concept may not all share a set of fundamental "essential" properties, offers no intrinsic criterion for establishing a concept's border, a criterion for keeping the concept from becoming utterly vague. This is when the solutions offered by Gerring (2001) and Goertz (2007) become important. First of all, they provide a formalized approach to the issue of family resemblances, allowing researchers to map exactly how various instances of a concept morph from one to another as certain attributes change. Second, Gerring (2001) provides several pragmatic criteria for establishing the legitimate boundaries of a concept: resonance and relevance, parsimony, coherence and boundedness, commensurability, and operationalization.

Goertz (2007) develops a simple, yet powerful, framework for refocusing the analysis from difficult–to-measure attributes toward more clear-cut indicators. A concept is defined by means of its attributes (basic features), and those attributes are further explicated by means of more detailed empiric indicators. Goertz thus proposes a three-level framework for concepts (2007, 50–53). At the first level is the *concept* we are trying to define, in our case polycentricity. The second level contains the *attributes* in terms of which we are defining the concept. In our case, these are the basic features of polycentricity outlined by the definition in the preceding section, features emphasized by the Bloomington school, namely (1) many overlapping centers for decision-making, (2) a single system of rules (be they institutionally or otherwise enforced), and (3) a spontaneous social order as the outcome of an evolutionary competition between different ideas, methods, and ways of life. The third level contains *indicators* with which we make the definition more operational and empirically powerful. The possible values of those indicators are incorporated in a general logical formula involving both conjunctions and disjunctions. (The traditional Aristotelian approach allows only the conjunction of attributes/indicators, hence its limitation.) This logical formula opens the path to an analytic, rigorous definition of the concept.

We may now make a step further and try to determine the logical structure of polycentricity in terms of deeper indicators, rather than just in terms of the three basic attributes. The output of this logical analysis is the ability to map the conceptual space of different kinds of (hypothetical or real) polycentric systems. In order to accomplish this step, we need to perform an initial analysis of the candidate cases for polycentricity, based on the conceptual guidelines emerging in the previous discussion. The following set of features summarizes the Bloomington school's perspective on polycentricity (note that this delineation is tentative and that alternatives are possible): many centers of decision-making; ordered relationships that persist in time; many legitimate enforcers of rules; an over-arching system of rules; overlapping centers of power at different organizational levels; spontaneous order resulting from free entry and exit; an alignment between rules and incentives (rules are considered useful); and public involvement in rule design (rules about changing rules, connection between rules and consequences relatively transparent). In order to encompass a more general perspective, one needs to further elaborate the concept.

As far as our analysis of polycentricity is concerned, we have to decide whether the candidates for polycentricity mentioned in the previous section (municipal governments and urban networks, science, representative constitutional democracy, free markets, common law) should indeed be classified as such. The only way to approach this determination is treat the examples *as if* they truly are cases of polycentricity and see what happens. In other words, we should see (1) whether the resulting concept has counterintuitive or objectionable consequences and (2) whether it provides us with useful insights into the workings of the phenomena it is meant to capture. As we shall see, the resulting concept does indeed offer intriguing insights, for instance, into the conditions under which polycentric order breaks down (into either authoritarianism or violent chaos). Moreover, it allows us to better understand the manner in which spontaneous order phenomena fit within the larger framework of social order, that is, how such phenomena interact with other social phenomena (be they polycentric or monocentric). Thus, there are solid grounds to consider that the examples are indeed different manifestations of the same general phenomenon of polycentricity. Finally, there are other potential examples, such as international law, which have not been considered, but which nonetheless seem to fit the definition of polycentricity. Thus, the resulting concept seems to have traction outside the original empiric cases used in its creation.

The first step in concept design is to map more explicitly the detailed attributes and indicators characterizing the different paradigmatic cases of the phenomenon (Gerring 2001; Goertz 2007). This allows us to determine the necessary and sufficient conditions for polycentricity and to detail the family resemblances. In the previous sections we have already presented insights about what attributes are relevant and why. We are now building on these insights. Analyzing the real-world possible examples of polycentricity mentioned in the previous section according to those attributes leads to a tentative synthetic picture of the cases.

The result of this analysis can be summed up as follows. Polycentricity has three basic features that are to be explored in more detail in the following way: (1) The *multiplicity of decision centers* is analyzed in terms of those centers' ability to implement their different methods in practice (what we call the "active exercise of different opinions"), in terms of the presence of autonomous decision-making layers, and in terms of the existence of a set of common/shared goals. (2) The institutional and cultural framework that provides *the overarching system of rules* defining the polycentric system is analyzed in terms of whether the jurisdiction of decision centers is territory-based or superimposing, in terms of whether the decision centers are involved in drafting the overarching rules, in terms of whether the rules are seen as useful by the decision centers (regardless of whether they are involved in their drafting—i.e., the alignment between rules and incentives), and in terms of the nature of the collective choice aggregating mechanism (market, consensus, or majority rule). (The idea is that the general rules cover all subunits within a polycentric system. But that does not mean that the many subunits in a polycentric system all have the same rules regarding the relevant action situations.) (3) Finally, the spontaneous order generated by evolutionary competition between the different decision centers' ideas, methods. and ways of doing things is analyzed in terms of whether there exists free exit, in terms of whether the relevant information for decision-making is public (available to all decision centers equally) or secret, and, finally, in terms of the nature of entry in the polycentric system—free, meritocratic, or spontaneous. That is to say, in case of "free entry" a decision center can *decide* to enter the polycentric system, and existing decision centers cannot prevent it from doing so, while in case of the "spontaneous entry" no formal decision is involved—either on the part of the newcomer or of the existing decision centers—but the entry happens naturally and more or less unavoidably).

The idea of "an overarching system of rules" deserves further clarification. We have already summarized in the previous section the Ostroms' analysis of the system of rules, an analysis elaborated in the context of the debate about the meaning of federalism and the nature of metropolitan governance. At this juncture, another point should be added. The idea of an "overarching system of rules" has the function of an operational criterion that distinguishes between the members of a polycentric system and its outsiders. Outsiders are agents who are not subjected to the same system of rules as insiders. This might be the case by design, with a clear functional role in mind (e.g., it creates the possibility of impartial arbiters), or it may be the result of failure and systemic imperfections (e.g., due to outsiders' lack of commitment and will, their institutional inability to integrate, or the inability of enforcers to integrate them). The outsider might have additional rights (as in the case of an arbiter) or fewer rights than the members (as in the case of an agent that fails to integrate and commit to the system of rules, which can bring various disadvantages). In a polycentric system one may be a outsider to an unit but insider to another and thus ultimately part of the overarching system.

This idea of identifying the members of a polycentric system based on the broad system of rules to which they are subjected should be seen in direct relationship with the Institutional Analysis and Development (IAD) framework (Ostrom 1990; 2005; see chapter 3). According to the "institutional factors" component of this framework, the institutional positions (or roles) can be identified by looking at how the rules regulate access and other rights to resources and information. That process not only creates structures of authority but at the most basic level separates insiders from outsiders. In addition, one of the important tasks in such an approach is to identify nested structures of authority. These nested structures correspond to the relationships between different polycentric systems that coexist and interact. Thus, when one identifies the outsiders of a polycentric system, especially those that act as outsiders because they have additional rights, one often identifies the connection points between different polycentric systems. For example, the judge in a commercial dispute can be seen as the connection point between two polycentric systems: the market and the juridical system. Last but not least, it is also important to mention that when we refer to the members of a polycentric system, we mean not flesh-and-blood individuals but institutional roles within the system (i.e., the institutional rules consisting of a bundle of rights and obligations attached to an individual). This is noteworthy because the same individual may act in different circumstances and at different moments as part of different polycentric systems.

With this catalogue of relevant attributes and indicators in place, we are in the position to analyze each candidate for polycentricity to see how it fares in terms of each characteristic. The most important task is to define tentatively the necessary conditions for polycentricity, that is, indicators that are found in all cases:

- Active exercise of diverse opinions and preferences (denoted "P_1" below). "Active exercise" means that the opinions (methods or ideas about how to carry out an action) are implemented by at least one decision center, rather than just being announced (i.e., existing merely as a proposal or a hypothesis).
- Incentives compatibility, the alignment between rules and incentives (P_3). The rules are considered useful by the agents subjected to them, and the consequences of the rules are relatively transparent. If the alignment between rules and incentives is very limited, the case is less likely to be an instance of polycentricity, even if a multiplicity of decision centers actively exercise their opinions and preferences (as we shall see below, this corresponds to a case of polycentricity degenerating into violent anarchy).

These two essential conditions for polycentricity are in line with the Ostromian, Bloomington school definition we have already presented in a previous section. In other words, although the Ostroms focused on a rather small number of cases, they developed a definition that is of far greater generality than one might expect.

An important aspect of defining polycentricity is the problem of decision-making levels. One could easily make a distinction between hierarchical and nonhierarchical cases, that is, structures in which *prima facie* there are multiple layers of decision-makers and structures in which there is a loose ensemble of decision-makers. In this vein, one could legitimately view a supposedly hierarchical polycentric system as a bundle of two or more nonhierarchical polycentric systems. Here the concept of "subsidiarity" may provide help. Thus, we suggest that autonomous decision-making layers are also part of the essential attributes of polycentricity:

- Autonomous decision-making layers (P_2). The different overlapping decision centers make operational decisions autonomously from the higher level.

Hierarchy in polycentricity is definitely more complex than this (see, for instance, the problem of overlapping and nestedness in Sproule-Jones 1993). However, the lack of steep and intrusive hierarchies coupled with "subsidiarity" rings truer than potential alternatives. But one should recognize the ambiguities and complexities involved, especially because an intriguing point about polycentric systems is the fact that rule enforcers are in many cases outsiders (a different type of agent), and thus a polycentric (sub)system depends either on the functioning of another system or on recognized mutual interest.

Once the core area has been outlined, we move to the differences between the various instances of polycentricity. A tentative list such as the following advances the argument by highlighting nonnecessary conditions and thus maps varieties of polycentricity. First, related to *decision centers and how they work*:

(A$_1$) Common/shared goals and (A$_2$) individual goals.

To these conditions one should add P$_1$ and P$_2$ conditions:

(P$_1$) Active exercise of diverse opinions and preferences and (P$_2$) autonomous decision-making layers.

Second, related to *the characteristics of the institutional/cultural framework (the overarching system of rules)*:

(B$_1$) Territorial jurisdiction of decision centers or (B$_2$) nonterritorial jurisdiction of decision centers.

(C$_1$) Agents directly involved in rule design or (C$_2$) rules designed by outsiders.

(D$_1$) Consensus or (D$_2$) individual decisions or (D$_3$) majority rule

To these conditions one should add the P3 condition:

(P$_3$) Incentives compatibility: alignment between rules and incentives

Last but not least, *related to the spontaneous order process—how the mutual adjustments and evolutionary competition works, and how information flows in the process*:

(E$_1$) Free entry or (E$_2$) merit-based entry or (E$_3$) spontaneous entry.

(F$_1$) Free exit or (F$_2$) constrained exit.

(G$_1$) Public information or (G$_2$) private information.

We have now the elements needed to articulate a logical structure of polycentricity (fig. 2.1).

$$\underbrace{P_1 \text{ \& } P_2 \text{ \& } (A_1 \# A_2)}_{\substack{\text{multiplicity of} \\ \text{decision centers}}} \text{ \& } \underbrace{P_3 \text{ \& } (B_1 \# B_2) \text{ \& } (C_1 \# C_2) \text{ \& } (D_1 \# D_2 \# D_3)}_{\substack{\text{insitutional/cultural framework} \\ \text{(overarching system of rules)}}} \text{ \& } \underbrace{(E_1 \# E_2 \# E_3) \text{ \& } (F_1 \# F_2) \text{ \& } (G_1 \# G_2)}_{\substack{\text{spontanous order,} \\ \text{evolutionary competition}}}$$

FIGURE 2.1 The logical structure of polycentricity
Symbols key:
= Or (Exclusive)
& = And

If one takes as parameters the features used in our tentative analysis, the logical structure derived from the paradigmatic cases considered allows for 288 possible types of polycentric systems (there are 288 possible combinations of the basic indicators permitted by the above logical formula). Needless to say, as in any formal typology, some of combinations exist, while others are purely conceptual and hypothetical. As is true in any typology of this sort, it remains open to readings in which the accent is put on the *degree* in which polycentricity is present, as opposed to absolute presence versus absolute absence. In addition, it is important to remind readers that even if one does not subscribe to the approach outlined (be it on logical grounds or because of the key attributes and indicators selected), any alternative will come sooner or later to deal with the same descriptive and analytical structure. One cannot avoid the selection of certain attributes from a rather well-defined set and cannot avoid the logic of necessary and sufficient conditions. When all's said and done, the current exercise retains its illustrative and propaedeutic virtues even if elements of the construction or the use of logical operators may be a matter of debate.

One of the most interesting applications of this approach is to explore the pathologies and breakdown of polycentric systems. If one accepts outline of conditions presented above, there are nine fundamental ways in which polycentricity may break down:

- Multiplicity of decision centers breakdown:
  - Non-P_1: active exercise of diverse opinions eliminated
  - Non-P_2: the system becomes hierarchical
  - Non-(A_1 or A_2): the activity becomes considered meaningless (the goals disappear; the polycentric system disappears because it no longer serves a function)
- Overarching system of rules breakdown:
  - Non-P_3: rules no longer considered useful by agents
  - Non-(B_1 or B_2): agreement about territoriality disappears (decision centers fight over territorial authority)

- Non-(C_1 or C_2): no agreement about rule design (rules are no longer considered legitimate, and their enforcement becomes difficult or impossible)
- Non-(D_1 or D_2 or D_3): the rule of law breaks down into power-based decisions (authority rule)
- Spontaneous order breakdown:
  - Non-(E_1 or E_2 or E_3): no entry (monopoly)
  - Non-(F_1 or F_2): the constituency of the system is unclear (some decision centers accept X as part of the system while others do not)
  - Non-(G_1 or G_2): no available information relevant to decision-making (random decisions, relation between consequences and rules unclear, spontaneous order turns into drift).

Polycentricity may give way either to a monocentric system (authoritarian or not) or to chaotic, violent anarchy. It is clear that certain versions of polycentricity are more vulnerable to these breakdown conditions than others. It appears that the following attributes make the polycentric system more vulnerable: A_1, B_1, C_2, D_3, E_2, F_2, G_2. These attributes are closest to the corresponding breakdown condition described above. For example, if rules are designed by outsiders (C_2), it is more likely that they will be seen as illegitimate. Likewise, majority rule (D_3) is closer to power-based decisions than consensus or individual decisions; a system based on shared goals (A_1) can lose meaning (if the sense of common purpose is lost) more easily than one based on individual goals. Needless to say, differences in the relative robustness of systems may prove important for the field of positive anarchy studies, as peaceful anarchy may come about from violent anarchy via the same attributes. For example, peaceful anarchy may appear as interacting agents develop a sense that certain rules are mutually useful (Leeson 2005; 2009).

The implications of this analysis go even further. Proposed reforms of existing polycentric systems often involve changing the value of one of the six nonnecessary attributes. For example, critics of the free market system often argue that in the case of certain goods or services (such as education or healthcare) the D attribute should be changed from D_2 to D_3 (i.e., individual decision-making should be replaced by majority rule). Similarly, in regard to other issues such as banking, libertarians argue that the existing D_3 attribute should be changed to D_2 (i.e., interest rates should be determined not by the central bank but by individual banks). Advocates of market regulations, such as licensing, propose that the E_1 attribute of the market be changed to E_2 (i.e., free entry should be replaced by merit-based entry). As yet another example, advocates of human rights propose that the B_1 attribute of international law be changed to B_2 in certain instances (i.e., that certain rights should be independent of territory). Finally, there has been a historic transition of the juridical system from C_1 to C_2, marking a separation between the juridical power and the legislative and executive powers (i.e., ideally, the rules that constrain executive power are no longer designed by the executive itself), and the separation between constitutional rules and common law. Similarly, it is usually considered undesirable when firms and corporations determine, mainly via lobbying, market regulations; that is, the C_2 attribute of the market (agents are not involved in rule design) is considered desirable, and, historically, the transition from mercantilism to modern capitalism may be seen as a transition from C_1 to C_2. However, in the case of democracy, the transition from C_2 to C_1 was of crucial importance (citizens are no longer completely separated from the process of rule design), and C_1 can be considered the essential attribute of a democratic system (and, as a parenthesis, a key element in the Knight-Johnson interpretation of democracy).

To sum up, the framework provided by a conceptualization and analysis on the lines introduced above has the potential to illuminate not only polycentric systems but also the design of social systems in general. The concept of polycentricity, as developed in the Polanyi-Ostrom tradition and elaborated above, is not only useful as an analytical framework but also for drawing analogies between different complex systems. At the same time, it makes possible interesting analytical and normative speculations based on the comparative analysis of different forms of polycentric arrangements and governance systems.

Thus, a polycentricity framework of description and analysis on the lines defined above provides the beginning of an analytical structure for the study of complex social phenomena. However, there is more to it: it provides a method for drawing *analogies that are not ad hoc* between different forms of self-organizing, complex social systems, as well as a means to bolster our institutional imagination. These analogical insights have to be tested, and *if* many of them turn out to be correct, *then* the concept of polycentricity is indeed useful in additional ways. In light of previous work by the Bloomington scholars and others, it seems likely that it can generate interesting new lines of inquiry, as well as shed new light on existing debates. In the end, if this approach is correct, one can identify not one but many multifaceted forms of polycentricity. A goal of this approach is improve the functioning of different configurations and complex social systems by means of drawing analogies between them. Different complex systems have weak and strong points. The challenge is how to transfer the strengths from one area into another in order to bolster its weak points. The classic approaches have usually drawn upon analogies with markets (a technique criticized by Knight and Johnson); for example, the Ostroms' idea of market-like interorganizational arrangements or of public entrepreneurship brings market-like attributes to public administration; Hayek's emphasis on common law and Weingast's market-preserving federalism bring market-like attributes to the evolution of legal systems. On the other hand, most advocates of market regulation propose to make the market more like democracy. Unfortunately, most of these arguments lack an overall supporting conceptual framework. At minimum one needs a more systematic approach to drawing analogies between complex institutional systems. Polycentricity can be utilized as a conceptual framework not only for drawing inspiration from the market, but also from democracy or any other complex institutional arrangement incorporating the simultaneous functioning of multiple centers of governance and decision-making with different interests, perspectives, and values.

The "Second-Order Task" Revisited

An analogical and comparative look at democracy and markets as coexisting and competing institutions marks our return to the origins of the present discussion. As a reminder, the preceding overview of polycentrism has as a background the Knight and Johnson–inspired (2011) framing of the "second-order tasks" of institutional arrangements. The question, however, is neither conceptual framing nor general research directions emerging from it. The question is in what measure Knight and Johnson's assessment of democracy and, implicitly, of decentralization is warranted. The preceding discussion of polycentrism suggests that a decentralized formula, on the lines sketched by the Ostroms, may be an alternative, an encompassing solution that better satisfies the criteria articulated in *The Priority of Democracy*.

Such a thesis, assuming that is valid, doesn't detract from the merits of democracy and what Knight and Johnson (2011) have written on it. The issue is whether democracy has the priority granted by the Knight and Johnson thesis. Is it indeed an institution uniquely able to coordinate "the ongoing process of selecting, implementing and maintaining effective institutional arrangements"? Is it an unparalleled institutional arrangement able to "establish and maintain an experimental environment that can enhance our knowledge of the relationship between different institutional forms and the conditions under which they produce good consequences"? (Knight and Johnson 2011, 19). Or are there are other ways of conceptualizing the structures and processes by which second-order problems can be responded to? Knight and Johnson assert that reflexivity is the most important element in the normative priority of democracy. The reflexive structure of democratic decision-making is, they write, "the distinctive benefit of this centralized form of coordination." They reject alternative institutional forms both decentralized and centralized because they lack precisely this feature (or they do not have it sufficiently). Yet the account given in this chapter indicates that the decentralized system of polycentricity has the features needed to carry out second-order tasks.

First of all, a polycentric system is the embodiment of institutional pluralism. Although it is essentially a decentralized structure, it doesn't preclude elements of centralization. The two principles operate in tension, but one does not exclude the other. In a polycentric system diverse institutions, decision centers, and units coexist in dynamic, interdependent (both competitive and cooperative) ways. The strengths and limits, the advantages and disadvantages of each institutional arrangement (be they centralized or decentralized) are tested, captured, channeled, moderated, reinforced, and so on, by an unending and mostly spontaneous process of reciprocal counterbalancing. Ongoing adjustment, bargaining, and communication take place between the diverse units and decision centers, at various levels and scales. Polycentricity is thus intrinsically dynamic and pluralist.

The pluralism of institutional forms ensures a variety of responses to a variety of circumstances. If experimentalism is a central issue, as Knight and Johnson (2011, 6) argue, and if "institutional experimentation is a useful instrument for generating knowledge about the effectiveness of institutions in various contexts," then one can hardly think of a better arena for experimentation than polycentricity. It is a system of reciprocal monitoring and assessment in dynamic interdependence. The various units and decision-making centers depend on each other or compete with each other or both. They must stay informed about (and to be prepared to adjust to) the evolutions of other units. A system of "reciprocal monitoring and assessment for the range of institutions available in society" is thus put spontaneously in place, but in addition a system of broad checks and balances emerges. The viability of institutional choices is constantly checked by the very mechanics of competition and cooperation operating naturally within a polycentric system. Deliberation and assessment are reinforced by a wide range of paraphernalia: price signals, voice, individual exit, Tiebout effects, secession, loyalty, contestation, and so on. In brief, reflexivity is a systemic feature in a more diverse, broad, intense, and complex way than in any possible form of democracy (and for that matter, market), and a strong feedback function is ensured via multiple and diverse channels.

In addition, in a polycentric system democracy is always at home, and a polycentric is able to retain all the major features of democracy as described and praised by Knight and Johnson. Democracy may function as a part of polycentric system in the typical form or as a principle induced in the internal operations of units, institutional domains, and decision centers (Wagner 2011; 2007). It may also operate at various levels and between various units and decision centers. Democratic institutional arrangements can better monitor and assess their own performance when they are part of a polycentric system. Other institutions, such as markets, provide signals, checks, and balances that shape the dynamics, deliberation, and decision-making in the overall adjustment of democratic centers' operation and structures. Similar considerations apply to markets. If one of the intrinsic problems of the market is its lack of reflexivity regarding the very institutional structure needed to support its effective functioning—or as Knight and Johnson put it, "the communication between actors is about particular exchanges and not about the general functioning of the market itself"—then polycentricity offers more robust and reliable meta-level mechanisms to maintain and enhance markets. In brief, it seems that by all accounts, polycentricity retains the value of democratic feedback, coordination and legitimization, and even more, it enhances them.

The Knight and Johnson argument brings to the fore the essential but underexamined matter of the conditions required for institutional performance. Many institutional analyses, they warn, focus exclusively on the structure and operations of the institution of interest (or its ideal model), neglecting the fact that "any form of institution will operate effectively and will generate normatively attractive outcomes only under particular...conditions." However, the effectiveness of institutions is "a function of the extent to which these conditions in fact obtain" and "may well be a function of social and cultural norms that characterize any particular society" Knight and Johnson 2011, 6). Therefore, a systematic analysis of the preconditions of effective performance of an institution should be mandatory in any institutional analysis. Accordingly, Knight and Johnson investigate the conditions required by both markets and democracies for their effective performance in first- and second-order tasks. Their assessment of second-order tasks makes possible a comparison with the conditions revealed in our overview of polycentricity.

Prima facie observation leads to the conclusion that the sheer combinatorial number of features makes polycentricity look flexible, adaptable, and viable, requiring a less stringent environment for effective functioning. The preconditions for a functional polycentricity appear to obtain more easily than the preconditions for functional markets and democracy. A functional polycentric system can grow and persist within a larger range of options and scenarios than efficient markets or a fully functional democracy. Moreover, one cannot avoid the insight that our success in creating markets and democracies may be in large part conditioned by the degree of polycentrism of the social

environment in which their specific institutional arrangements are embedded. This polycentric social environment may be a significant factor in the
genesis, performance, and explanation of democracies and markets.

That is to say, markets, democracies, and polycentricities are the result of
a combination of spontaneous evolution and human deliberation and design.
Yet polycentricity seems to have an unmistakable preeminence, not only in a
realist view that acknowledges the social fact of its existence and specific nature,
but also from a normative perspective. Institutional theory, historical observations, and combinatory calculus suggest that an approximation of "polycentrism" may be a viable alternative to Knight and Johnson's "democracy" as an
encapsulating institutional framework able to solve second-order tasks.

In addition, let us note that following the Ostromian perspective, one may
make a step further to what McGinnis calls—following insights sketched in
V. Ostrom (1998)—a "third-order problem." The problem is whether or not
the institutions set up to solve the first two tasks "do so in a way that tends
to instill in the participants a set of moral values and practical incentives that
support the continued operation of these same institutions. This test is likely
to be failed if democracy is interpreted as centralized and if citizens do not
learn practical skills of self-governance but instead come to rely on representative elections" (McGinnis 2012). In the end, polycentricity seems to display a
unique combination of, on the one hand, spontaneous features of order and,
on the other hand, elements that make room for deliberation, design, and
relative control. The two aspects in conjunction make it a second-order mechanism able to lead via reflexivity and self-correction to better performance of
the system, and a precondition for a constructive approach to the third-order
problem. Markets are needed for efficiency, democratic arrangements for the
effective governance of markets according to criteria and values other than
efficiency, but polycentrism is needed for both to be fully functional and
sustainable.

All this may sound counterintuitive. Polycentricity, even more than other
decentralized systems, looks intricate, difficult to handle, and less prone to
control. In comparison with the simplicity and clarity of the mainstream models of markets or democracy, polycentricity seems a highly wrought system,
full of combinatorial possibilities, polymorphic, and difficult to comprehend
in its multiple facets and metamorphoses. However, in many respects these
are precisely the attributes noted by Hayek when he invited social scientists
and policymakers to assume a humbler attitude about their ability to grasp
the complexity of social order emerging from human intentions. These complex decentralized systems emerge in time, shaped by their evolutionary logic
and historical accidents punctuated by human deliberation, strategies, and

blueprints, and it is a matter of pragmatic realism to acknowledge the cognitive and practical limits of what one can understand and control in such systems.

The Ostromian theme of polycentrism is thus consistent with a powerful intellectual tradition that has consolidated its distinctive domain at the intersection of social sciences and social philosophy. This tradition evokes, as Kukathas (2009, 3) put it, a vision of "a society of societies which is neither the creation nor the object of control of any single authority; though it is a form of order in which authorities function under laws which are themselves beyond the reach of any singular power." As its instantiation in polycentric institutions demonstrates, this is a vision of an open, evolving, pluralist order. The overlapping jurisdictions and multilevel, multifaceted, dynamic, and polymorphic features of polycentricity are the reflection in political economy and institutional theory of a social philosophy that understands that "the principle of a free society describes not a hierarchy of subordinate and superior authorities but an archipelago of competing and overlapping jurisdictions" (Kukathas 2009, 4).

These are, therefore, the elements of the broad intellectual context in which the discussion of second-order tasks should take place. Looking at democracy from the perspective of this pluralist social philosophy, William Galston (2002), notes that if one takes pluralism seriously, "it becomes more difficult to accord democracy the unquestioned normative priority it typically enjoys in both ordinary and philosophical discourse." Seen from a pluralist point of view "the scope of democratic political authority is restricted" and "certain alternatives to democracy within the sphere of politics must be taken more seriously than they usually are." That is indeed consistent with a view of governance in which

> our social life comprises multiple sources of authority and sovereignty—individuals, parents, associations, churches and state institutions among others—no one of which is dominant for all purposes and all occasions. Non-state authority does not exist simply as a concession or a gift of the state. A well-ordered state recognizes but does not create other sources of authority....A theory of multiple sovereignties does not imply the existence of separate social spheres each governed by its own form of authority. Political pluralism is consistent with the fact of overlapping authorities whose relationship to one another must somehow be worked out. (Galston 2002, 36)

These remarks and the tentative conclusions about polycentricity we have reached contrast up to a point with the Knight and Johnson thesis, according to which democratic centralization takes preeminence and other institutional arrangements, both centralized and decentralized, operate under the second-order umbrella of this *primus inter pares*. The qualifier "up to a point" is important for two reasons. First, Knight and Johnson embrace a version of pluralism, too: their notion of democratic centralization allows more degrees of freedom and more flexibility than is suggested by the echoes of the traditional, standard usage in academic and common language. Second, their assessment of democracy is largely based on criteria that also apply to polycentricity. Looking through the theoretical lenses of polycentricity, one observes that democracy may be seen as one form of polycentricity. In fact, in Vincent Ostrom's own work the two notions (polycentricity and an idealized model of "bottom-up," deliberative democracy) are sometimes used interchangeably. Thus, in the end, the gap between the Ostromian perspective and Knight and Johnson may be not so large. In fact, as we'll see in chapter 6, a pragmatist social philosophy permeates both. In any case, for the purposes of this chapter's argument, the important thing to note is that we have seen how the Ostromian idea of polycentricity comes to occupy a central position in the new cycle of research on institutional diversity, pluralism, and governance, to the launching of which Knight and Johnson's book has made an important contribution.

3

Institutional Mapping and the Institutional Analysis and Development Framework

THE CHALLENGE OF institutional diversity and polycentricity is not just theoretical, normative, and philosophical; it is also a challenge of method, approach, and analytical framing. The notion of polycentrism spawns a range of analytical and methodological questions: Is there a systematic way to deal with the complexities inherent to the overlapping and multilayered institutional arrangements specific to polycentric systems? How can one find the order in basic patterns and social mechanisms to make them analytically navigable? How can one identify the operating dynamics specific to this or that particular case of polycentricity? In this respect one is reminded of the old distinction in comparative economics between the case and the model, between the empirical phenomenon and the theoretical framework. When it comes to polycentricity, a general conceptual framework (and the ability to articulate combinatorial models) is a good starting point. However, we need to address the empirical challenge of mapping concrete, real-life cases. How do we define the dynamics of specific systems and individual actors' actions in various situations, and the different institutional arrangements composing a certain polycentric system? The challenge is the same for any form of institutional analysis: to develop a methodical manner to investigate concrete cases in order to identify the factors and drivers of the ecological rationality.

The Ostroms' response to the challenge has materialized in a knowledge-systematization, heuristic, and analytical instrument that has demonstrated a proven relevance for research and policy: the Institutional Analysis and Development (IAD) framework (Blomquist and deLeon 2011; McGinnis 2011; Boettke 2010). A discussion of the IAD framework is important because it is both central to the Bloomington school and the object of many misunderstandings. In a literature where technical sophistication is sometimes taken for analytical or explanatory relevance, the deceivingly simple instrument advanced by the Bloomington scholars has not yet received the appreciation it deserves. Hence this chapter will introduce the IAD framework and at the same time will advance its case by trying to articulate a theoretical sense of its significance, nature, and functions. Placing it in the context of broader discussions in the literature, we can bring to the fore novel arguments regarding its epistemic and methodological legitimacy, providing nuance to the very idea of social and institutional mapping. Moreover, this chapter will show that this ingenious conceptual tool, with its array of epistemic functions, invites a reconsideration of several influential and often taken-for-granted epistemological and philosophical assumptions about the nature of social research, a theme that will be pursued in the next chapters.

To fully understand the distinctiveness of this tool and what it portends for thought about the nature and tasks of social research, one needs to start with the basic challenge: institutional diversity. If we tentatively define, along with Elinor Ostrom, institutions as "the prescriptions that humans use to organize all forms of repetitive and structured interactions," from families and neighborhoods to markets, firms, churches, and governments "at all scales," we realize that their diversity is daunting. We don't need to introduce a composite structure like polycentricity in order to make this case. Even if we use a more constraining definition, like that implied in Williamson's (1985) "economic institutions of capitalism," sooner or later we reach similar conclusions. Moreover, institutional diversity is multifaceted, as there are many levels of institutions, many layers of rules and incentives affecting individuals' behavior, actions, and outcomes. Adding in the variety of social actors' interpretations, decisions, and strategies, all leading to possible new institutional configurations, we start to grasp the huge range of possible combinations in their evolving dynamism. To make things even more complicated, institutional diversity is both structural and functional. Sometimes the same institutional arrangement has several functions; sometimes the same function is performed by different institutional structures. This is the reason why a discussion about institutional diversity should not limit itself to a monofunctional perspective. The temptation of such reductionism is huge. After all, some of the most influential forms of institutionalism are rigidly monofunctionalist (see, for instance, transaction costs economics, as practiced by the mainstream), and in general the entire field operates under the shadow of strong and naive functionalist presuppositions. Yet all we know about tinstitutional diversity, from a variety of fields, from history, and from experience, advises us to resist such simplifications. Thus, institutional diversity is a real challenge in our attempts to conceptually capture and analyze institutional order and change.

The very nature and extent of institutional diversity raise the problem of the limits of generalization in institutional theory and design. Indeed, even a cursory overview of the literature reveals that the number of empirical studies of institutional arrangements is massive, but generalizing from them doesn't seem to be easy. First, "the number of specific variables involved in each of these empirical studies is very large." But even more important, "the special values of variables involved in any one study (or one location in a study) differ from the specific values of variables involved in another study" (Ostrom 2005, 9). Thus, the many relevant variables (each with different values), the immense number of combinations of these variables, and the configurations and constellations of situational factors affecting them generate "one of the perplexing problems haunting systematic empirical testing of social science theories," the "sometimes true theories"—those "likely to hold under specific conditions and not under others" (Coleman 1964 in Ostrom 2005, 9).

It is not that generalization is impossible. The problem is in what measure the types of generalizations that one can usually reach are meaningful or relevant. Whether we like it or not, this situation requires that we rethink the assumptions behind the methodologies and epistemologies we have been taking for granted. This is not a purely academic issue. When it comes to applied policy, the problem of diversity is even more salient. Hence a series of questions: With what specific epistemic perspective and with what methods and instruments should we approach institutional analysis, given the full implications of institutional diversity? How should we frame and analyze institutions, in all their contextual variety, so that our approach is relevant for the purposes of institutional design?

At the outset we need to recall that mainstream views more often than not tacitly embrace an idealized "research method." Centered on procedures of justification of the truth value of given propositions via an explanation-prediction model, it consists of a set of quasi-standardized methodological recipes. These techniques and countless technical refinements of them have become dominant and are more or less taken for granted as a standard of good practice, without too much thought given to their originating context, for instance, their relationship with a particular interpretation of the nature of science rooted in positivist epistemology. Such canonical approaches may work well in many cases, but what does one do when the data push the researcher far from the textbook model? What happens when the questions asked and the answers needed, or the cognitive procedures required, do not fit the prescribed procedures?

Such cases are neither rare nor trivial. As we have seen in studies of collective action, heterogeneity is almost a guaranteed presence in such situations. In that case, argues Ostrom, "While verifying the empirical warrantability of precise predictions has been the guiding standard for much of the work in political economy, we may have to be satisfied with an understanding of the complexity of structures and a capacity to expect a broad pattern of outcomes from a structure rather than a precise point prediction" (Ostrom 2005, 10–11). Identifying patterns and configurations may be the best one can do: "An outcome consistent with a pattern may be the best verification we can achieve in settings of substantial complexity" (Crutchfield and Schuster 2003 in Ostrom 2005, 11). Transferring attention from the empirical warrantability of prediction to identifying patterns and configurations may look like a mere shift of accent, but it is not a trivial move. It implies a major challenge: When it comes to institutional phenomena, what if the standard goal of explanative and predictive power is secondary, and identifying patterns and mapping configurations is in fact the primary thing? Thus, we realize that identifying configurations and patterns may occupy a more important position than we thought.

The Bloomington scholars' response to this challenge was to set aside the philosophical and epistemological discussions and to simply try to build a different approach, under the assumption that elaboration of the foundational and philosophical component of theory could be dealt with later. The result was an inventive analytical and heuristic device "composed of nested sets of components within components" aimed at mapping diverse institutional arrangements, described by Ostrom (2005, 7) as "a consistent method for overtly analyzing the deeper structures that constitute any particular action situation." The idea was simple. Even if relevant general and systemic patterns are difficult to identify, one can nevertheless identify some "basic units" that are similar in all cases. These are the "elements" that are composed and recomposed in various configurations. In fact, one can speak of configuration and patterns only because of them. They are the foundational building blocks of institutional order, as well as of its analysis and interpretation. In brief, the Ostrom strategy aims to identify these basic building blocks and then to reconfigure conceptually the different levels of combinations and arrangements of interest for the case in point.

If the basic blocks are predefined, all becomes a matter of separating the relevant from the irrelevant: to cut through complexity and retain enough elements to make the conceptual framework realistic and relevant for the situations under consideration. First and foremost, the task is to identify the behavioral model or the parameters of what Vernon Smith (2007) has called the "ecological rationality" in case. "The challenge for institutional theorists, writes Ostrom (2005), is to know enough about the structure of a situation to select the appropriate assumptions about human behavior that fit the type of situation under analysis." That means reducing the complexity of the social field to the essential elements that allow us to orient ourselves within the maze of the intrinsic institutional diversity. In the end, this is a task of calibration, how to get "just enough variables to enable one to explain, understand, and predict outcomes in relevant settings" (Ostrom 2005, 7).

As one may expect, game theory lends itself as a useful starting point. Indeed, the very notion of a "game," versatile and yet theoretically robust, seems appealing. Its components—actor, rules, incentives—easily play the role of analytical basic building blocks. Yet, notes Ostrom (2005, 7), there is a problem. Many situations—especially those in which "rules are the object of choice"—are too complex to model as a simple game. What is needed is a broader conceptual framework able to capture both simple patterns of the game-theoretic type and more complex configurations.

These challenges seem to have led Elinor Ostrom to a framework able to map the institutional reality, something meant to have mainly a heuristic and operational role. The instrumental objective is to be able to chart any institutional domain of interest, to identify structures and situations that define it in ways that are both systematic and allow a high degree of intercomparability. The ultimate objective is to create good, functional maps of various institutional realities. The analogy with geographical maps is telling: "The advantage of a good set of geographic maps is that after centuries of hard work, multiple levels of detailed maps of most places are available and are nested in a consistent manner within one another. Most of us recognize that there is not one optimal map that can be used for all purposes. Each level of detail is useful for different purposes" (Ostrom 2005, 8). The heuristic and pragmatic nature of the approach is evident: Ostrom is not looking for "The Map" of institutional reality but for a map-making "instrument." That is to say, her concerns were part of a far-reaching methodological discussion.

The "instrument" the Ostroms and their associates put forward is both a conceptual framework and a manual for operating it, that is, an institutional mapping procedure. Called the Institutional Analysis and Development (IAD) framework, it has been designed "to provide a language" for describing the institutional configurations of various social systems and their "inner workings." It consists of "a series of nested conceptual maps of the explanatory space that social scientists can use in trying to understand and explain the diversity of human patterns of behavior" (Ostrom 2005, 8). A social agent-based tool integrating insights on how institutions shape incentives and consequently individuals' behavior, it is meant to describe both institutional structure and institutional change (Ostrom 2005, 8; Ostrom and Kiser 1982). Its viability, explains Elinor Ostrom, is not a matter of speculation: "Our confidence in the usefulness of the IAD framework has grown steadily in light of the wide diversity of empirical settings where it has helped colleagues identify the key variables to undertake a systematic analysis of the structure of the situations that individuals faced and how rules, the nature of the events involved, and community affected these situations over time" (Ostrom 2005, 9).

In brief, a discussion of the IAD framework is a discussion both about the epistemic and theoretical challenges of social mapping and about an instrument validated by research practice. As Ostrom (2005, 8) insists, we need to keep in mind that this is not a discussion about a methodological recipe able to deliver results mechanically or algorithmically and that the analogy with geographical maps has obvious limits: "Learning to use a set of conceptual maps and determining the right amount of detail to use is, however, itself a skill that takes some time to acquire, just as it does with geographic maps."

Institutional Mapping

Institutional mapping is not an arcane epistemological and methodological discussion of mere academic relevance. The literatures on applied, practice-oriented policy—irrespective of paradigm and normative orientation—abound with references to the mapping and analysis of institutions and stakeholders. That richness reflects the importance of the problems it is meant to deal with. Indeed, initiatives to change institutions or implement policy need, for strategic and tactical reasons, to take an inventory of the institutions involved and identify key players and their interests, relationships, and relative power within that internal configuration. An initiative has to more or less systematically assess the incentives in place and the potential support or opposition induced among players, while highlighting the relevant institutions' roles and the interinstitutional linkages. In other words, it has to carry out an orientation in the field, developing a conceptual picture that captures the key variables of the case in order of relevance (Morgan and Taschereau 1996; Brugha and Varvasovszky 2000). Such an orientation is crucial to understanding the potential roles of social actors and institutions, identifying potential coalitions of support for the project, building scenarios and strategies, and assessing their relative risks. If carried out with the direct participation of stakeholders, the procedure can also build legitimacy and policy ownership. When it comes to practice, stakeholder mapping and institutional mapping (which are two faces of the same coin, two dimensions of the same formula) are not only analytical, investigative tools but also indispensable strategic instruments.

However, although this approach is widely employed in policymaking and institutional development, its theoretical and epistemic foundations are not well understood, and its legitimacy is yet to be fully granted, by the academic community. In their effort to synthesize and elaborate it, the Bloomington scholars thus draw our attention to an overdue task. Their effort is the more significant because their procedure is neglected by theorists and academic researchers who consider it second best to more reputable approaches to social reality. Advancing the IAD strategy, the Ostroms and their colleagues encourage us to develop a better mapping framework but also to investigate the theoretical foundations of institutional mapping. As it turns out, the two are intrinsically connected. One cannot understand the nature and significance of the IAD framework without a detour through the theory of mapping as a cognitive process.

Such an excursion is needed for an additional reason. In the end, at stake is the very status of the IAD framework. As I have already mentioned, though apparently simple, this instrumental metatheoretical framework is puzzling for many. Is it really a viable instrument? How seriously should it be taken? What is its epistemic nature? What is the basis of an approach that gives special attention to configurations, combinations of elements, context, even accidents? How should we understand it in relationship to better-known methodologies? Indeed, the notion of framing used as a heuristic device combined with a "building blocks" approach challenges the mainstream mindset for which one version or another of the hypothetico-deductive method is second nature. Thinking through the assumptions and implications of IAD leads to a unique and innovative perspective on conceptualization in the social sciences. Modest as it may seem, IAD signals a real departure from (and complement to) mainstream methodological and epistemological views. Why that is the case will become more transparent in the next section, which introduces mapping as a cognitive process and explores the structural similarities between maps and theories. It identifies the basic elements of mapping as a cognitive procedure and, based on foundation, outlines the optimal features of possible metatheories as applied to policy-oriented institutional mapping.

Mapping as a Cognitive Process, Social Theories, and Institutional Mapping

To outline the basic features of mapping, one can start with a simple and widespread scheme of cognition processes consisting of two elements: the real world and the mind able to generate simplified models of the world. The dynamics of mind and external reality are well captured by the distinction between the "cognized environment," consisting of all the information modeled in the mind, and the "operational environment," that is, the real world (Rubinstein, Laughlin, and McManus 1984 quoted in Azevedo 1997, 86–87). In understanding the relationship between the two, the key word is "isomorphism." Isomorphism means that "the elements and relations between the elements of one system completely map the elements and relations between the elements of another system" (Azevedo 1997, 68; Gordon 1991; Clarke and Primo 2012). However, it is important to note that "isomorphism" is always imperfect and that the cognized environment is only partly isomorphic with the operational environment. Cognitive modeling is always selective, and even more noteworthy, it is interest or value driven (Rubinstein, Laughlin, and McManus 1984 quoted in Azevedo 1997). Consequently, the cognized environment comprises many representations shaped by various interests, values, and idiosyncrasies and varying in their degree of abstractness, cognitive content, and isomorphism. These representations often take the literal form of maps, that is, they are presented visually rather than linguistically (Turnbull 1989; Monmonier 1993; Azevedo 1997). But the cognitive structures associated with the idea of maps are more complex and go beyond the notion of "visual representation." Mapping is in fact one facet of "adaptive isomorphism" at work.

Of special interest for an argument on the Ostroms' view of institutions is the structural similitude between maps and theories and an exploration of those similarities. Following Azevedo's (1997) argument, whose outstanding discussion of mapping and social theory inspires this section, the key fact is that theories can be seen as a special class of maps—isomorphic, generalized, abstracted representations of a body of information on some aspect of social reality: "A map is not just an accumulation of data. Rather, it is a necessarily abstract representation. It selects certain features and represents them in a schematic form that is generally quite unlike the original except in terms of the mutual relationships between the elements" (Azevedo 1997, 104; for a similar discussion see Clarke and Primo 2012). In a similar way, scientific knowledge is more than the aggregation of observations on reality. Rather, "scientific theories abstract regularities from the world and produce explanations of them in terms of the relationships between entities and/or phenomena. Scientific theories, like maps, are necessarily abstractions and are quite unlike the world they map except in terms of the relationships that they represent" (Azevedo 1997, 104).

The diversity of conceptual structures that are part of the "maps" family is thus daunting. Besides geodesic maps, hydrographic maps, authority maps, mathematical maps, maps of processes, and geographic maps, cognitive structures such as organizational charts or social theories can also be seen as a species of maps: maps of social reality. The variety of the family is determined both by the object of each specific member of the class and by its principle of composition. Although there is great variety even among geographic maps and it is a simplification to speak about "geographical mapping" as a unitary genre, this type of map is best known and emblematic for the entire family, and so a discussion of map naturally turns to them as examples and reference points. Therefore, in the discussion of institutional mapping and social theory it is natural to implicitly use geographic mapping as the default reference point in order to illuminate how various cognitive features associated with typical maps apply to institutional maps as well.

As it has already been mentioned, one of the most important features of mapping is that it may take place from different perspectives, inspired by different objectives and employing different techniques. Consequently there is no single or uniquely correct map of a particular "territory." One may have different and incomplete representations of a particular territory that are equally accurate as maps. The repercussions of this diversity for institutional theory and policy research are not insignificant. The idea that there is one privileged way of mapping a social space—that there is one privileged conceptual structure that gives a comprehensive account of a phenomenon—is naive. If that is the case, and "universalism" and "comprehensiveness" are out of consideration, then the instrumental functions become the main arbiters. The content and validity of maps and theories are directly related to the interests of their creators. The purposes for which they are constructed dictate their structure. Maps reflect reality, but they are not merely mirror images. They are instrumental human artifacts; they share these attributes with the political economy and institutional theory:

> When a cartographer or surveyor sets out to make a map of some particular territory, she starts with the purposes of the prospective map in mind, a body of theory about projections, and so on. She then has to choose a baseline, orientation, scale, method of projection, and system of signs. These choices will relate both to the purposes of the map and to the body of background theory, and will determine the sort of map produced. But the fact that these choices must be made does not make the map less correct relative to the purposes for which it was constructed. Indeed, there is no way that a map can be made without such choices. Map making requires a body of prior theory, and interest-related decisions must be made over the choice of appropriate construction tools. (Azevedo 1997, 105)

What is true about cartography is true about institutional mapping and theorizing. The objectives assumed and the choices of tools are interest-related and affect the type of conceptual structure produced. Therefore, if institutional maps and institutional theories are designed to be guides to action and decision-making, the choice of a specific mapping approach and the assessment of its quality/validity should be made in terms of how well it achieves its objectives, that is, "according to its relevance to the problems it is intended to solve" (Azevedo 1997, 124; Clarke and Primo 2012). A certain map may be a perfect guide to crossing a river but useless for finding an ore deposit.

To be more precise, if the goal is to identify a viable strategy to produce institutional reform in a specific community, no description of reality in general formal terms, irrespective how sophisticated, will help crafting a reform coalition. Instead what the map should capture are key actors, their interests, their interrelations etc. If the problem is to generate solutions in a common pool resource situation (tragedy of the commons), then using prisoner's dilemma and collective action formal models to investigate the situation would not lead very far. Instead, identifying actors, rules in use, decision nodes, and the specific context offers clues about the parameters that, once modified, may change the entire situation (Ostrom 1990).

An important corollary of this discussion is that not only the content of a map but also it form is interest related, shaped by the problems, intentions, and objectives defining the content. Topologic maps differ in form from topographic maps. A map of rules and actors, including the key decision-makers in a community, differs from a map of the relationship between education and income, or of age and social structure. If the objective is policy-oriented and implies institutional change, the information represented by the latter two types of maps is important, but the information contributed by the first type is essential. A map is good insofar as it enables us to complete the activity the map is designed to guide. In many cases, "more general and abstract maps may be better than highly detailed and accurate maps, by virtue of the very fact that they leave out irrelevant detail, thus making the task of following them easier" (Azevedo 1997, 123–25; Clarke and Primo 2012).

In brief, in an institutional map not only what but also how to portray is determined by the task at hand. When the task is to generate strategies for institutional change, the emerging map will differ from the one inspired by the task of building a general social theory. The measure of validity of an institutional map is given by its ability to guide strategic decision-making. In due course the typical themes associated with this functionalist and practice-oriented approach surface and become dominant. The tenor of the discussion is clearly pragmatist, and one can already see how the general epistemic contours start to change once the pragmatist element becomes salient.

That becomes even clearer in the light of an additional observation: not only the form, content, and validity of mapping but also the methods used to produce a map are interest-induced. Mapping methods are explicitly connected to the purposes for which the map is intended. But even more than that, they are shaped by background assumptions regarding the "territory" (Turnbull 1989). In other words, a map or a theoretical model is a function not only of the object but also of meta-level assumptions regarding the object and the way it should be approached and depicted. Given the interests of the user, a theory of what data are appropriate is required. And given the purposes for which the map is to be used, "there must be a theory of what relationships an appropriate map for that purpose is required to represent, to what degree of accuracy, and in what form" (Azevedo 1997, 110; Monmonier 1993). This is true irrespective of the nature of the territory or discipline. For instance, writes Azevedo (1997, 111), in geography there is a trade-off between the accuracy of shape against the accuracy of scale. "The construction relationship between the map and the data cannot be seen merely as a relationship-preserving mechanism." That is to say, "the data selected for mapping, the form and scale of the map, the degree of accuracy required, and even the projection theory itself, are directed by the fact that the value of the map lies in its ability to guide actions relevant to purposes in the area of interest." In short, "these meta-theoretical features of a map are as important in determining its validity as is the relationship between a map and its domain" (Azevedo 1997, 111).

To sum up: (1) The process of mapping involves three dimensions or levels: (*a*) the territory or the phenomenon to be mapped, (*b*) the map itself, and (*c*) the metatheory of mapping. Each level reciprocally determines the nature and dynamics of the others. The first belongs to what is called the operational environment, the last two to the cognizant environment. (2) Although institutional maps, like other maps, are shaped by interests, specific problems, and objectives, the validity of a map may be objectively evaluated by public assessment. Assuming commonality of interests and objectives, a particular institutional map created for guidance in a specific area should be as useful for one person as for another. A map is a guide to action, that is, it is used as a prediction tool: telling an individual with precision that certain features of social space or territory will be encountered at one point or another. So ultimately the validity of maps is of a predictive nature and by implication practical or pragmatic. (3) Maps may be tested via prediction, which is in fact a measure of their ability to guide action in pursuit of particular interests. The other assessment criteria are subservient to prediction. Explanation and coherence that enable to explain or identify general connections among the data are secondary or instrumental. The final test of an institutional map, as an element of the cognizant environment, is as a guide for the actors through the social space mapped, that is, the operational environment. (4) The notions of what data are appropriate to a particular map, and of what kind of method, form, and so on, should be employed, belong to the metatheory level. The metatheoretic level includes notions such as the sort of background theories applicable, concepts of what an appropriate map for a particular purpose should consist in, the standards of accuracy required of the particular map, and other standards that may apply to the validity of maps in general. In other words, each map is a representation of data, selected and organized by the principles of the metatheory of mapping.

If that is the case, then a great deal hinges on the metatheory. And here we have reached a point of maximal relevance for any discussion of the IAD framework. Indeed, once placed in the context of this discussion, it becomes clear that the IAD framework does not claim to be a (theoretical) map of the institutional reality. To think that it was meant to be a general theory of institutional reality is an evident error. Its nature is different. It is in fact a metatheory of institutional mapping. Epistemologically speaking, it functions not so much in the context of verification as it in the context of heuristics and discovery as well as in that of what Nicholas Rescher (1979) has labeled "cognitive systematization." The metatheory determines the selection of a specific mapping technique and method, defines the criteria for excluding the irrelevant elements, and provides the working link between objectives and domain in the mapping process. The IAD framework is thus both an organizing principle and a heuristic device. It is an instrument indispensable in producing "maps" (or for that matter theories) of various institutional configurations. Hence one should not confuse the instrument with the final product, the IAD framework with the result of its application.

The IAD framework is not the sole possible metatheoretical heuristic device and tool for knowledge systematization. One needs simply to evoke the pragmatist principle to see why. Given the importance of the metatheoretical level, the obvious question is: What are the best metatheories of institutional mapmaking? What are the meta-theories that should shape the process of mapping the special domain of social institutions? There are two answers to this question. The first is anything that serves a given set of intentions, policy objectives, and so on. There is no single theory that fits all purposes. The best map is the one that best orients the social action or policy of interest. The nature of the task at hand determines what is the best metatheory.

The second answer has a slightly different angle and is more precise. If one is interested in human interaction within rules-structured situations, in strategic decision-making, and in managing institutional change, then one needs a map that has specific features. It should be able to capture the essential elements of the strategic space: the actors, the rules of the game, the processes set into motion with those rules. Therefore in terms of metatheoretical design, one needs to look at a theoretical perspective that (*a*) emphasizes social actors rather than disembodied properties of those actors; (*b*) gives a special attention to the interpersonal relations, roles and processes; (*c*) focuses more on the analysis and interpretation of institutions, situations, and events than on general laws, regularities, and variables and (*d*) takes into account social change and tries to captures the dynamics of change in real historical time. In other words, one needs a framework that looks at actors, institutions, and histories first and only subsequently at other sets of variables, factors, and features of the phenomena of interest. In this respect, the IAD framework seems indeed a rather good fit.

Mapping Social Fields

The discussion so far has clarified the epistemic nature of institutional mapping, placed it in the context of a broader social philosophy, and identified the metatheory of mapping as a separated epistemic entity. Thus its somewhat puzzling nature is becoming clearer: A framing, heuristic, and knowledge systematization device, a member of the broad family called "theory," yet a member of a particular nature. As one may expect, one can elaborate such a device in various forms. Different schools of thought, paradigms, and worldviews can be incorporated and different degrees of specificity and elaboration can go into this "metatheory." Hence, one should see the IAD framework suggested by the Bloomington scholars as one alternative among many. But before we focus on it, it is useful to look at an alternative approach that may be thought a precursor. This will allow us to get a better sense of the distinctiveness of the Ostromian contribution and highlight some of the underlying themes of a more metatheoretical approach to social and institutional mapping.

With its focus on social actors, social interactions, and social situations and the pivotal position given to contextuality and processes, the approach developed by the Chicago school of sociology (Ernest Burgess, Louis Wirth, Robert Park, and their students and followers) represents one of the earliest perspectives capturing what we have called the metatheoretical level of institutional mapping procedures. Abbot (1997; 1999), one of the most knowledgeable historians of this intellectual tradition, whose interpretation of the school I follow in this section, makes a convincing case in this respect. In his view, the strengths of the Chicago school were its ability to avoid problems that result from decontextualization of the object studied and that plague social research once its is reduced to a "variable approach": (1) failure to capture the subjective ambiguity of the situation and (2) the denial of contextual determination in causality in general, of which the subjectivity problem is merely a part (Abbott 1997).

The basic relevance of the Chicago approach for social mapping is precisely its effort to avoid abstractions, aggregated indices and variables, and fiddling with the construction of regularities or general laws whose analytical relevance is necessarily limited. Instead, the strategy is to start and end by focusing on a specific community or a certain social/policy issue and to capture it in its context, identifying the actors, their connections, their histories, and their interests and to reconstruct the structures of power and the nodes in the network of influences (Faris 1967; Bulmer 1984). However, this interest in specific places, situations, and events and their careful documentation didn't mean that the Chicago approach limited itself to pure description. As Abbott (1997, 1160) explains, Chicago research "focused on the locatedness of social facts and the importance of contextual contingencies," but that didn't mean it lacked interest in causal theory. "This theoretical commitment entailed the Chicago mixture of methods, for if the effects of causes were so shaped by environing factors that no causes had uniform effects, specific theories must be theories about constellations of forces, not theories of individual causes." Multiple methods, interdisciplinarity, and case studies are all part and parcel of the same approach:

> The fastest way to discover such constellations of forces was by case study, since the sheer combinatorics made studying the matter at the aggregate level difficult. And more generally only the eclectic combination of ethnography, statistics, life history, and organizational history could do full justice to the multiple layers of spatial and temporal contexts for social facts. (Abbott 1997, 1160)

All of this entails an important assumption about how things work in reality, that is, about the connections between actors, conditions, and consequences— in other words, about social causality. Thus a closer look at the Chicago school shows that when it comes to social mapping, assumptions about the nature of social causality are crucial because they infuse the metatheories used and thus the very way mapping proceeds. For instance, one may think of causality as combinations of necessary causes governed by universal laws, a set of relations between abstract variables. That way of conceptualizing causality may determine the selection of a specific metatheory and consequently of a specific technique of mapping the social phenomenon in question that will try to identify in a given field precisely those laws and correlation. In some cases, given the objectives, that might be a viable approach. However, if one considers that (either in general or in the particular case one is dealing with) the relevant causality structure depends fundamentally on context, then one needs to "situate facts" and replace "a particularly simple version of the variables approach with a much more nuanced contextualist approach" (Abbott 1997, 1160). This is absolutely mandatory if the objective of the investigation requires not empirical generalizations—broad, abstract, universal maps lacking the contextual determinants—but the identification of concrete configurations of institutions, communities, and networks of decision-makers in a dynamic process defined by uncertainty. In other words, if one wants to find out why and how and in what context particular social or policy problems occurred and how to solve them, then a localized approach is the way to go.

The notion of "field" (and the implicit idea of "mapping" of the "field") becomes essential and with it the idea of dynamics and change. Hence arises the notion of "interactional field," a social situation/space defined by its contextualities, a cluster of actors and processes with geographically, socially, economic, and politically defined boundaries. It is noteworthy that all these are processes and as such are to be understood in their temporal contexts. That point invites a look at social spaces and their dynamics in time. In other words, a temporal process is dependent on social contexts, but at the same time, spatial or social structures are dependent on the temporal context. This notion captures a fundamental aspect of institutional mapping: it can never be static. The idea inherent in the mapping procedure is not only to capture the actors' positions, resources, preferences, and institutional context but also to build on them in identifying their principles of motion or action, and with that, the dynamics of the entire interactional field.

Following the path opened by the Chicago school, two types of processes can be distinguished: On the one hand, some of them belong to "natural history." A natural history is "a temporal pattern that follow[s] a relatively predictable course." It can be diverted or shaped by contextual factors, "but its general sequence [can] be understood as a whole, beyond the contingent details. They might be diverted or reshaped. They might fail. But the general logic is regular" (Abbott 1997, 1154; 1999). On the other hand, there are processes that evolve with no identifiable regular logic, totally open to contextual influence. One may call defining points on their trajectories "path dependent" or "historically contingent" or call them "accidents" or "tipping points," but irrespective of the label, the basic idea is that they define the dynamics of an interactional field as much as general laws, natural histories, structural and configurational factors, and so on, do (Abbott 1997, 1154; 1999). When it comes to both descriptive and analytical purposes, both types of processes need to be considered along with the more evident and easier to identify elements.

To sum up, the Chicago school suggest that institutional mapping has built into it an appeal to two dimensions: one static and one dynamic. A comprehensive institutional mapping procedure should be able to outline not only actors, resources, interests, and institutions but also at least some elements of the logic of acting of the actor, the trajectories, laws of motion, "natural histories" and accidents and contingencies hinging on a specific case. Although the traditional Chicago school never managed to recover fully from the "revolution in social sciences" brought by "variable thinking," and universal social laws obsessed schools of thought mushrooming in the 1950s, its program retains the same message of viability and significance it had seventy years ago (Abbott 1997; 1999). As such, this brief overview becomes a very good standpoint from which one may approach the IAD framework.

The IAD Framework

The roots and inspiration of the IAD approach to institutional mapping are to be found in the experience gained in the study of social dilemmas and common-pool resources at the Indiana University Workshop for Political Theory and Policy Analysis (Ostrom 1990; McGinnis 2000; Aligica 2003). As has already been discussed, the previous literature addressed the problem of the commons and collective action in general using models and meta-phors that were misleading. Without being opposed to the use of models in policy analysis, Elinor Ostrom became skeptical of models like the "prison-ers' dilemma" or the metaphor of "the tragedy of the commons" as ways to depict concrete situations and cases. Extensive fieldwork raised questions about their universal application by demonstrating that the conclusion that the participants in a commons dilemma are trapped in an "inexorable process from which they cannot extract themselves"—a conclusion predicted by such models—is not supported by evidence. Again and again, field studies in vari-ous countries and societies revealed that local groups created a wide variety of institutional arrangements for cooperating over common-pool resources. These studies also found multiple cases where people failed to organize. The diversity of situations was strongly correlated to the diversity of institutional solutions.

Hence, research need to find out the specific differences accounting for variations in arrangments. In this case, general and abstract models like prisoners' dilemma were far from helpful. Needed was a comparative method of assessing the specific institutional arrangements, the specific environment within which each specific common-pool resource problem was dealt with in particular communities. This is the context out of which emerged the IAD framework (McGinnis and Walker 2010; McGinnis 2011; Kiser and Ostrom 1982). As McGinnis (2011, 169) describes it, the IAD framework

> encapsulates the collective efforts of this intellectual community to understand the ways in which institutions operate and change over time. The IAD framework assigns all relevant explanatory factors and variables to categories and locates these categories within a foundational structure of logical relationships. The IAD framework has evolved through a long and continuing process of engagement and contestation among scholars with different areas of expertise as well as predispositions towards diverse modes of research. As such, it is itself a dynamic institution and [any] overview serves as a snapshot of its current form.

Even though in time the initial framework was elaborated, calibrated, and refined, its basic structure is simple. Whether the most elaborated and sophisticated rendition, such as that advanced by McGinnis (2011), or one of the earlier versions, it pivots around a set of core elements. From the very beginning, central in the IAD approach to institutional analysis is the identification of a unit called an action arena and the analysis of configurations of actors and institutions and their change within its parameters. Let us use as a vehicle one of the initial versions advanced by Ostrom, Gardner, and Walker (1994).The action arena is the focus of examination, mapping, and prediction and has two components: an action situation and an actor. Action situations refer to the social space where individuals "interact, exchange goods and services, engage in appropriation and provision activities, solve problems, or fight" and is determined by a set of factors—the rules organizing interindividual relationships, the attributes of a physical world, and the nature of the community within which the arena is located (Ostrom, Gardner, and Walker 1994, 28). The IAD approach tries to develop a unified framework composed of the same set of elements for all cases explored and

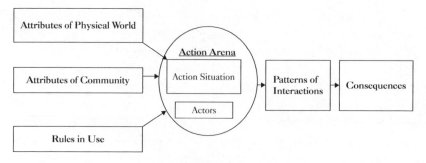

FIGURE 3.1 A framework for institutional analysis
Source: Based on Ostrom, Gardner, and Walker (1994).

applicable to any social space (see fig. 3.1). Thus the institutional mapping procedure tries to capture conceptually the basic form of an action arena, composed of an action situation involving participants who have preferences, information-processing capabilities, selection criteria, and resources. Behind all these considerations is the idea that actors must choose among diverse actions in light of the information they possess, and those actions are linked to potential outcomes and the costs and benefits assigned to actions and outcomes.

At the minimal level the working parts of an action situation are predefined in the IAD framework by several key parameters:

Participants: the actors who are involved in a situation

Positions: placeholders that associate participants with a set of authorized actions (employee, voter, judge, monitor)

Actions: "nodes in a decision tree," particular positions taken at different stages of a process that identify actions that make an essential difference for the entire process in their consequences

Potential outcomes: the results of individuals interacting with one another in a regularized setting (quantities of output, interpersonal relations, changes in rules, externalities etc.)

A function that links inputs to output—in the case of voting, for instance, "the transformation function takes the symbolic actions of individuals and produces a collective decision"

Information: the data about an action situation and its implications

Payoffs, positive and negative weights assigned to the outcomes and the actions leading to outcomes

When it comes to actors the same logic applies. Four key elements are mapped out: actor's preferences regarding certain actions and outcomes; the way actors acquire, process, and use information; the decision criteria actors use regarding a particular course of action; and the resources that they bring to a situation (Ostrom, Gardner, and Walker 1994; McGinnis 2011; Polski and Ostrom 1999).

The same logic applies to rules, physical conditions, and community. The procedure prepares the way by identifying how rules combine with a physical and cultural world to influence the way the elements of an action situation generate particular types of situations and processes. Thus, the institutional analysis looks at these factors while identifying "some of the typical action situations that result from particular combinations of these factors" (Ostrom, Gardner, and Walker 1994, 37). It is important to note that the approach offers a mapping method not only for stakeholders and institutional structures but also for the processes involved. A change in any of these elements produces a different action situation and may lead to very different outcomes. More complex situations are mapped by adding new layers to the complexity of the elements; each of these elements may be further elaborated and specified as a function of analytical needs. The framework stresses a universality of working parts, but at the same time it also enables investigators to analyze unique combinations and to capture the specificities of a contextualized situation.

It should be no surprise that in a perspective that defines institutions using the notion of rule-structured interactions, rules have a central position. Much attention is dedicated to them, both theoretically and empirically. Rules are seen as "prescriptions that define what actions (or outcomes) are required, prohibited, or permitted." The importance of discovering and mapping the rules is hard to exaggerate as rules provide information not only about the actions an actor "must" perform, "must not" perform, or "may" perform but also about the nature of sanctions that result from failure to follow them (Crawford and Ostrom 1995 in McGinnins 2000, 117–18). In addition, the attributes of the relevant physical world matter. The same "rule configuration" may yield different types of action situations, patterns of interaction, and outcomes depending upon the configuration of the physical environment. The IAD approach places a special emphasis on the nature of goods that are the objects of human action. Goods that are subtractive in nature, such as common-pool resources and private goods, affect outcomes in a different way than goods that are not subtractive, such as public goods and toll goods. The same logic that applies to the physical

environment applies to the attributes of the community: its size and structure shape how rules affect the action arena, patterns of interactions, and
final outcomes.

In brief, the filling in of the "actor" and the "action situation" boxes in
the framework (the mapping of an action arena) is the pivotal stage of the
mapping effort. The procedure takes one by one all the predefined elements of the framework, including the rules organizing interindividual
relationships, the attributes of a physical world, and the nature of the
community in which the arena is located and tries to identify the relevant configuration of factors for the case in point, not only looking at
the input and output sides but also at the links between different action
arenas (Ostrom, Gardner, and Walker 1994; McGinnis 2011; Polski and
Ostrom 1999).

Last but not least is the problem of nestedness: the layers or levels of institutions, that is, the idea that action arenas are linked across several levels.
Recognizing that a social event or process rarely if ever occurs in one action
arena, the IAD approach looks at various linkages and levels of analysis. Rules
cluster in hierarchical systems. Sets of rules are nested in other sets of rules
that define the nature and way of changing the first set of rules. The rules
used at one level are always interconnected with other sets of rules. As the very
notion of polycentricity reveals, most of social reality is composed of multiple
arenas linked sequentially or simultaneously. Although for analytical clarity
the focus is usually on one arena at a time rather than on the entire set, one
has to deal in many cases with clusters of arenas in conjunction. At this point
one can see more clearly how the issue of polycentricity can be addressed via
the IAD framework.

The way the IAD approach conceptualizes multiple institutional levels deserves a special note because it is a distinctive feature of its mapping
metatheory. Three levels of rules cumulatively affect any setting: the operational level, the collective-choice level, and the "constitutional" or "constitutive"
decisions level (see fig. 3.2) (Kiser and Ostrom 1982; Ostrom 1986; McGinnis
2011). Constitutional or constitutive decisions are about rules governing future
collective decisions—about the rules to be used in crafting other decisions.
They also determine who, is eligible to do that crafting and how and when.
The collective choice level specifies the basic framework within which actions
take place, and how it is to be enforced or altered. The operational level is
the level of day-to-day actions in everyday, concrete circumstances. Its sphere
of action is established by the higher levels. Although these actions have in
turn an impact on higher levels, most of the time they do so in an indirect

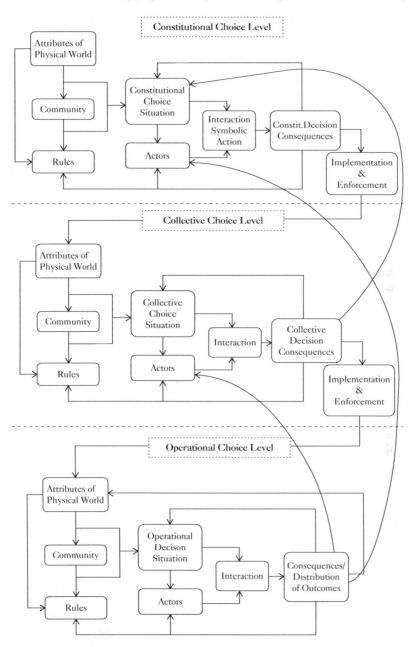

FIGURE 3.2 The three decision/institutional levels through IAD lenses
Source: Based on McGinnis (1999a).

and aggregate way (Ostrom 1986; Crawford and Ostrom 1995; McGinnis 2011; Polski and Ostrom 1999). The analytical structure of the approach is nonetheless identical at all three levels.

One should also note at this juncture two important elements highlighted by McGinnis (2011, 173; 2012) in his comments and elaboration of the framework in what is the most sophisticated discussion of the issue. The first is the notion of "level-shifting strategy": "if participants in one arena of choice feel their interests are not well-represented in that context, they may seek to move the question to consideration at an adjacent level (or arena)." The second is the distinction between (a) "micro-constitutional choice," a "term used to emphasize the general relevance of constitutional choice processes to the construction of all kinds of collective entities, from very small to nation-states and beyond," and (b) the "meta-constitutional level of analysis," which "encompasses long-lasting and often subtle constraints on the forms of constitutional, collective, or operational choice processes that are considered legitimate within an existing culture; many of these factors may not be amenable to direct change by those individuals under the influence of these cultural predispositions, but these cultural factors do change over time, in part as a consequence of changing patterns of behavior."

To sum up, the IAD mapping process is built around three steps: (1) Identifying and mapping the action arena (action situation and actors); (2) identification of factors determining the action arena (the rules, the attributes of a physical world, and the nature of the community); (3) elaboration or projection of how (1) and (2) once put together (sometimes linked sequentially or simultaneously with other areas) generate patterns of interaction and specific outcomes over multiple action arenas.

That being said, it is important to note that the validity and usefulness of the institutional mapping procedure is determined by the objectives and intentions of the investigator. Hence the IAD framework is one among other possible metatheories that could be applied by the institutional analyst. Although its roots are shaped by the specific origins in the research program on governance and collective action, it is easy to imagine that it could be applied to map a variety of situations and processes. As Elinor Ostrom puts it, the confidence of the Bloomington scholars in the usefulness of the IAD framework "has grown steadily in light of the wide diversity of empirical settings where it has helped colleagues identify the key variables to undertake a systematic analysis of the structure of the situations that individuals faced and how rules, the nature of the events involved, and community affected these situations over time" (Ostrom 2005, 9).

The IAD Framework: Some Further Notes

The previous section has presented IAD by identifying it as a social mapping metatheory, by placing it in a comparative context with the Chicago school, "social field" approach, and by broadly describing its structure and application. Such an overview invites several further elaborations. Three of them seem to deserve a special attention: the difference between institutional frameworks, theories, and models; the accommodating nature of IAD to a variety of theoretical perspectives, and, last but not least, the central issue of the nature and function of the "basic units," the building blocks around which the entire approach is constructed.

One of the most important sources of misunderstanding regarding IAD is the confusion between institutional frameworks, theories, and models. In social sciences the common practice is to use these terms almost interchangeably. However, Elinor Ostrom cannot afford to accommodate that practice. The legitimacy and the status of the IAD framework depend on not being confused with the standard theories and models. Therefore, Ostrom (2005, 27) finds it necessary to specify the place of these terms on a continuum of "a nested set of concepts" that "range from the most general to the most detailed types of assumptions made by the analyst." Each level—whose definition and identification are always a function of a given problem—has a certain degree of epistemic and methodological specificity. The researcher, in accordance with the case and circumstances, focuses on one level or another and, by implication, deals with certain degrees of specificity and generality using the appropriate conceptual apparatus.

Seen in this light, a framework is mainly a heuristic device. Its function is to help "identify the elements (and the relationships among these elements) that one needs to consider for institutional analysis." As we have already seen, it is a tool that organizes "diagnostic and prescriptive inquiry" operating at a rather general level. In a word, having an instrumental nature, frameworks are modes to orient research using "the most general set of variables that should be used to analyze all types of settings relevant for the framework" (Ostrom 2005, 28). Theories are more specific. They operate within a framework. Theories "enable the analyst to specify which components of a framework are relevant for certain kinds of questions and to make broad working assumptions about these elements." They are targeted toward a subset of the framework, and their function is explicit: "to diagnose a phenomenon, explain its processes, and predict outcomes." Empirical research at this level has as a main role to "narrow the range of applicable theories over time by showing the superiority of the remaining theories to explain data" (Ostrom 2005, 28).

Last but not least in Ostrom's classification are models. Models are based on theories and are strongly related to them, as they use theoretical assumptions about variables and relationships between variables. They capture a limited set of parameters and variables as well as the relationship between them. Hence, in this scheme, they represent the most specific level, with a limited coverage but with higher contextual adjustability.

As one may see, even after this descriptive effort the distinction between institutional frameworks, theories, and models still retains some areas of ambiguity where the differences are a matter of interpretation. However, the broad contours are pretty clear. IAD (and for that matter any framework that works as a functional equivalent) stands in its own class and should not be confused with a model or theory. This becomes more evident in the light of Elinor Ostrom's remark that not just one but several theoretical perspectives are usually compatible with any framework. That is even more true when it comes to IAD, a general framework able to accommodate a wide range of theoretical perspectives (Ostrom 2005, 27–28; McGinnis 2011).

The example of how neoclassical economics may be accommodated is illustrative. The various nodal elements in the structure of the framework should be seen as placeholders. For instance, the actor's role may be taken by *homo economicus* (a fully informed, fully rational maximizer) in an action arena characterized by a minimal set of rules and incentives. The patterns of interaction are written in the maximizing logic, operating in the "stylized facts" of the environment. Out of this parsimonious setting, neoclassical economic theory is able to diagnose, explain, and predict in a surprisingly large number of cases. However, the framework invites further specification. Starting with the basic, not very rich construct of actor and action arena, one may add new features. Still retaining the neoclassical postulates, new elements may be introduced into the picture. The actor's characteristics and endowments can be elaborated on various lines. Rules can be further contextualized. The criteria for isomorphism can be made tighter and push the conceptual construct close to the richness of the reality under investigation.

Even further steps may be made. One may be able to think beyond the neoclassical horizon to "broader theories that assume individuals are fallible learners trying to do the best they can in the long term by using norms and heuristics in making their immediate decisions" (Ostrom 2005, 7). In other words, maintaining the IAD framework intact, one can move from neoclassical—standard maximization—rational choice to a behavioral, satisficing, bounded rationality as described by Herbert Simon. From there one can make a step further to a situational logic, a Weber-Popper mode of conceptualizing social action. The various elements of the framework are thus dressed new clothes. Introducing flexible "situational logic" as the basic form of rationality of the actor, one has traveled the road from the descriptions of standard economics to something closer to sociology and anthropology. This means that interdisciplinarity is possible in a methodical way, and even more important, a pluralist, comparative assessment between different takes within the same framework is possible. Not just the tension but also the complementarities between various disciplinary approaches are thus illuminated. The bottom line is that one may see IAD as a general framework, able to accommodate a wide range of perspectives, from hard core rational choice to situational logic praxeological approaches via behavioral theory, or any other theory of relevance.

This indeed, as Groenewegen (2011, 15–17) notes, raises the issue of the compatibility of different theories in one overarching framework, that is, "how theories from different paradigms, like the NIE and OIE, can be compatible and probably combined in one framework." The solution requires a change from a perspective centered on paradigm and theory to one centered on problems and problem-solving. Groenewegen and Vromen (1995) propose a strategy of "different theories for different questions" in which "some theories are better for answering specific types of question than others" but in which "different theories can live happily together under the umbrella of a uniting framework." The analytical decision requires a balancing act between theories, framework, and conditions. "Different theories are compatible with one framework when the theories are relevant for different conditions." This argument converges with Ostrom's own take. Her remark that "the challenge for institutional theorists is to know enough about the structure of a situation to select the appropriate assumptions about human behavior that fit the type of situation under analysis" (Ostrom 2005, 7, 28–29) implies a strong role for the conceptual lenses through which theorists look at the situation in question.

That being said, one has to emphasize again that IAD and the heuristics and analytical process associated with it are predicated on the existence of "basic units," elementary building blocks. That is why the affirmative answer to the following questions is the basis of the entire project: "Can we dig below the immense diversity of regularized social interactions in markets, hierarchies to identify a set of basic components that structure all these situations? Those elements that could frame the large diversity of situations of humans' structured interactions? Can we use the same components to build an explanation for human behavior in a variety of situations?" (Ostrom 2005, 5–6). That is to say, the elemental task of the researcher is to identify an underlying set of universal building blocks. They are the main source and reference points of comparability and analytical insights. As Ostrom (2005, 28) puts it, the existence of these units creates the possibility of "a metatheoretic language that is necessary to talk about theories and that can be used to compare theories." In brief, they are the referential basis of comparison and they frame and inspire the leading questions in an analysis.

We have already seen that the notion of "action arena" emerges as a possible answer and as a focal point. Action arenas, explains Ostrom (2005, 13–15), exist everywhere in neighborhoods, in communities, households, and regional, national, and international levels, and in markets and hierarchies. Using the conceptual lenses provided by this notion within the IAD framework helps to capture and map a wide variety of social situations. This strategy is not new, and Ostrom (2005, 29–30) notes that such an approach aimed at identifying a core unit of analysis in the working parts "contained in many diverse environments" is far from unique in the sciences in general. For instance, in biology, "for all of the complexity and multiple levels, there is a large amount of similarity of underlying factors. . . . it is somewhat amazing that there is only a small proportion of the genes that differ between an elephant and a mouse." At our turn, in institutional analysis, "if we develop the logic of institutions further, we will see that many situations that have the surface appearance of being vastly different have similar underlying parts." And hence "our task is to identify the working parts, the grammar, the alphabet of the phenotype of human social behavior as well as the underlying factors of rules, biophysical laws, and community" (Ostrom 2005, 30).

This approach is far from a mere imitation of natural sciences. Social sciences have an impressive tradition in exploring this strategy. The list of related efforts compiled by Ostrom (2005, 14) is indeed telling: social action and interaction settings (Burns and Flam 1987); collective structures (Allport 1962); events (Appleyard 1987; Heise 1979); frames (Goffman 1974); logic of the situation (Farr 1985; Popper 1964; 1976); problematic social situations (Raub and Voss 1986); scripts (Abelson and Schank 1977); transactions (Commons [1924] 1968); and units of meaning (Barwise and Perry 1983; Raiffa 1982). In light of this list, it is difficult to claim that the IAD framework is radically novel. Yet, on second thought, it is clear that its potential has not been fully explored and developed. Especially in the context of mainstream economics and political sciences in the 21st century, it comes as a fresh suggestion about how one should approach institutional analysis.

One may get a glimpse of how far one may go by taking a brief look at hints made by Ostrom regarding ways to elaborate a framework for institutional analysis. While elaborating the concept of a "basic unit," she introduces an intriguing notion that outlines a clear departure from the mainstream path. Ostrom (2005, 11) notes that "like good geographic maps, the IAD framework can be presented at scales ranging from exceedingly fine-grained to extremely broad-grained" and that one may see "layers upon layers of cognitive structure on top of the biophysical components." At the same time, one may see how building "on top of the single individual are structures composed of multiple individuals—families, firms, industries, nations, and many other units—themselves composed of many parts and, in turn, parts of still larger structures." The crucial observation in this respect is that "what is a whole system at one level, is a part of a system at another level." These are parts that, on a closer look, reveal that they are systems in themselves. At the same time, there are systems that on a closer look reveal themselves as being parts of a larger whole.

The argument (which will be echoed in chapter 4 in the discussion of panarchy) goes back to Arthur Koestler (1973), who called these "nested subassemblies of part-whole units in complex adaptive systems" *holons*. Koestler, invoked by Ostrom (2005, 11–12), was a pioneer in exploring the idea of "hierarchically organized whole." It "cannot be 'reduced' to its elementary parts; but it can be 'dissected' into its constituent branches on which the holons represent the nodes of the tree" (1973, 291). Although underconceptualized, the idea of "the nested part-whole units of analysis" and the idea that "the parts used to construct a holon are frequently not descriptive of the holon they have created" seem indeed congenial to the Ostromian framework, including the effort to deal systematically with multiple institutional levels in polycentric systems. The layer upon layer of structures (as in polycentricity, discussed in hapter 2, or in panarchy, discussed in chapter 4) confronts researchers with a challenge. Is a problem specific to one level, to a certain scale, or does it go beyond that? Does a phenomenon manifest itself across a broad range of scales? What is the location of the phenomenon in the multilayered social reality, and how is it structured to function there? The notion of a holon and the strategy of "dissecting" complex systems "into composite holons that are then dissected further" may help us to address such questions, but at the same time warns us that the answers to these questions are far from easy.

The Epistemology of the IAD Framework: Heuristic and Institutional Analysis

The discussion so far has emphasized the distinctiveness of IAD framework in terms of both structure and function. Insisting on its description as an institutional mapping instrument and evoking its pragmatic and problem-oriented dimension invites a further note on its distinctive epistemological profile.

As has already been mentioned, to fully understand its nature, one has to reconstruct the philosophical assumptions and implications that give it its full meaning. Only in this way can the main sources of confusions surrounding it be avoided.

That being said, a first step is to simply place the IAD framework in the landscape of standard philosophy of science. Philosophers of science often talk about the "context of discovery" and the "context of justification," distinguishing between, on the one hand, the process and procedures by which observations and propositions regarding reality are reached, and on the other hand, the procedures by which the truth value of these propositions is tested empirically. The rules of justification of hypotheses are different from the rules that guide researchers in identifying and formulating hypotheses. In other words, the distinction is between the process of discovery of relevant facts and the methods (in a wide sense) of justification (or testing) of their truth claims. The two sets of questions are, first, how do we reach relevant statements of fact, or hypotheses? How do we identify and select them? And, second, can a statement be empirically justified, and how? Is it testable, and how? Or, to put these alternatives differently, the first is, how can we identify plausible statements about social reality, statements whose likelihood of being true goes above a certain threshold of probability? The second is, how do we test a plausible statement and verify or falsify the knowledge claim and thus either increase the likelihood or push it beyond the threshold?

Both sets of issues and questions are relevant. From an operational perspective, in both cases the choice is about what methods and procedures are needed to identify, generate, test, or justify knowledge claims. In this sense, the discussion lies at the core of modern philosophy of science (Popper [1934] 1959; 1963; Lakatos 1976;1970; Zahar 1983; Laudan 1981; Nickles 1987; Clarke and Primo 2012). However, for various reasons, in contemporary social sciences the emphasis has been on the second set of questions—the context of justification. Hence the first set, which may be broadly associated with the notion of heuristics (procedures, methods leading to learning and discovery) has been neglected. The relevance of the conceptual instruments and of the cognitive strategies using available data to identify hypotheses and propositions that are potentially true and relevant for the case in point has been systematically downplayed. At the same time, the justificationist side has been overplayed, leading to the neglect of the crucial complementarity between the two facets of the research process. This imbalance was identified long ago as a problem (Nickles 1987; Clarke and Primo 2012).

For the purposes of argument all we need to note is that the distinction between heuristics and epistemic verification creates the setting to correctly place the Ostroms' IAD framework. From their perspective the framework belongs first and foremost to the "context of discovery." It is mainly a procedure that deals with the identification and articulation of propositions that are both meaningful and empirically plausible in the given research context of institutional theory and analysis. Second, the IAD framework is an instrument of knowledge systematization (Rescher 1979), and only third is an instrument of epistemic justification.

Of course, once we have introduced the crucial clarification, one may see more clearly the source of confusion plaguing research. Many scholars, used to see things exclusively from a "context of justification" standpoint, have been unable to correctly identify the nature of the IAD framework and have exclusively applied to it to the context of justification and not to the context of discovery. But once the bias in favor of the former is eliminated, one realizes that the relationship between hypothesis generation and hypothesis validation, between heuristic power and epistemic warranty, via knowledge systematization, is complex and critical for all aspects of social research.

The strong assumption that novel prediction should be the only source of empirical support in science and that, hence, the manner in which scientific claims are (or can be) generated never furnishes epistemic support, is indeed one possible position to take on the epistemology of the social sciences. Yet the IAD framework reminds us that there are other options on the table and that they are equally legitimate. Some of them are better positioned to accommodate in a realist way the complex nature and dynamics of the research process. For instance, the arguments and the evidence strongly support the view that certain modes of generating (constructing) a claim provide empirical support for it. An entire philosophical literature is built around theses that recognize the epistemic significance of the mode of construction (Nickles 1987). This is yet another reason that the Bloomington school research illustrated in this chapter through the IAD framework is more than a contribution to institutional theory narrowly defined. It is in many respects a challenge to orthodoxies of the day, including those rooted in widespread philosophical assumptions of the mainstream about the very nature of the research process and its instruments.

One may here take a final step. Even if we focus narrowly on the problem of justification, there are additional perspectives that may be helpful in restraining the inclination to dismiss the epistemic significance of the IAD framework on the grounds that it falls short of the hypothetico-deductive criteria of the *malgré soi* Popperian mainstream. Indeed, the Popperian approach to truth determination is based on the claim that the product of the scientific endeavor (thesis, proposition, theory) is preeminent and that the "production" side is secondary. It is the most influential example of the focus on knowledge theses or claims, independent of the method that generated them. But the alternatives are naturally obvious. One of them is that the justification of knowledge claims may come not by direct focus on the theses but on the method and procedures we rely on to accept the thesis in question. In this view, a scientific effort is essentially methodological, an attempt to identify, create, provide a method, a procedure that can be used by any other researcher and with which anybody can verify the truth content of the thesis. We are talking, hence, about an instrumental approach, in which the pragmatic element is crucial. As Rescher puts it, "working well—that is manifesting effectiveness and efficiency in discharging the tasks for which it is designed—is the key standard for the rational evaluation of methods" (Rescher 1977, 71).

In Rescher's work we find an extended explanation of why that is the appropriate standard: Our knowledge is more than just a matter of knowledge (propositions, theses). At a deeper level it is also a matter of *how-to* (of ways of doing things). If we escape the spell of the fashionable doctrines of the day in social sciences, we realize that how-to is primary, more fundamental than *knowledge-that*. At the same time, the criterion of how-to is efficiency, success. We approach propositional knowledge from the direction of its methodological source. The pragmatic criterion (success) is not applied to theses (propositions). The relationship is "indirect and mediated": "A specific knowledge claim is supported by references to a method which in turn is supported on pragmatist lines" (Rescher 1977, 71).

The preceding argument provides another context in which one can place and judge the IAD framework and by extension the Ostromian institutionalist experiment. If the IAD framework is to be seen as an approach, an instrument for putting in order and investigating the protean institutional diversity surrounding us, then the criteria of its assessment should obviously be aligned with this function, not with the dictates of one doctrine or another that happens to be influential at the moment. If we follow this logic to its end, a discussion about the IAD framework is a discussion about how-to more than about knowledge-that—or it is as much about one as it is about the other. In what measure do we treat it as a how-to and in what measure as a knowledge-that? By creating this difficult-to-categorize (and yet apparently very effective in practice) conceptual entity meant to serve as an instrument for the analysis of institutional diversity and complex systems characterized by heterogeneity and pluralism, the Ostroms and their associates confront us with a fascinating intellectual challenge.

4

Institutional Resilience and Institutional Theory

WHEN IT COMES to the intricacies of the array of relationships between institutional functions and structures in complex societies, resilience is a case study of unparalleled relevance. First is the sheer importance of the function itself. To keep the social order together and functional and to ensure its perpetuation is by all accounts crucial. If there is a preeminent responsibility for any institutional system, this is it. Other functions, values, or performance criteria depend on it, and it is the necessary condition of any other form of institutional or systemic performance. In a society on its way to extinction, an assessment of the excellent manner in which its institutions fulfill other functions related to efficiency, justice, and growth is pointless. Then second, there is the complexity of this apparently simple-to-describe systemic task. The diversity of functions and structures mobilized for it, the pluralism of values and objectives, the trade-offs, the levels and meta-levels of institutional arrangements, make out of it an excellent illustration of the problems of the "second order" defined by Knight and Johnson (2011). In brief, the theme of resilience leads to a revealing nexus of institutional processes offering a unique window from the macro level into the inner dynamics of complex social or socioecological systems.

This chapter, by focusing on Elinor Ostrom's interest in the problem of institutional resilience, allows us to advance our discussion of the nature, potential, and future development of Bloomington institutionalism from a fresh and in some respects unorthodox angle. The examination of the most basic feature or function of an institutional system—its survival or resilience, one that also happened to be until recently the most neglected—puts us in the position to get an indirect look from a fresh viewpoint at institutional diversity and polycentrism. Resilience brings together in an unmatched way the themes of institutional diversity, pluralism, heterogeneity, second-order tasks, and polycentricity. This chapter takes advantage of that. At the same time, in presenting an overview of the issue, we tangentially note that Ostrom bridges the domains of environmental science, economics, and institutionalism, as well as some implications and potential directions of further development.

Indeed, the problem of the resilience of institutions and social-ecological systems (SES)—that is, their ability "to absorb change and variation without flipping into a different state where the variables and processes controlling structure and behavior suddenly change" (Holling 1996, 735)—cuts across domains and disciplinary boundaries. Resilience as a phenomenon and as a concept is strategically positioned in multiple ways between the natural and social orders. On the one hand, it is a feature of ecological, economic, and institutional systems. At the same time, it is a feature of the intricate compound systems that emerge as a result of the ecological, economic, and institutional orders working in conjunction. Environmental science, economics, and institutional theory are thus able to find a common ground and develop a common agenda around the theme.

Ostrom's preoccupation with the governance of natural resources and the robustness of institutional arrangements aimed at governing the commons put her in the position to contribute to the emerging bridge between natural sciences and social sciences via environmental studies. In a sense, resilience (a central but until recently neglected issue in institutional analysis and comparative economic systems) is one of the best illustrations of the new avenues that can be opened up for institutionalism by the Bloomington approach, with its focus on heterogeneity, diversity, and polycentricity.

The starting point is the observation that Ostrom's work on common-pool resources has led her inexorably toward an engagement with this emerging domain. This work invites us to consider two major issues: first, what institutionalism brings into resilience studies, and, second, what resilience studies bring to institutional theory. As regarding the first, Ostrom advances instruments for a better understanding of the role of the social, institutional, and human decision-making elements in the broader equation of resilience studies. Regarding the second, her investigations open the door to a broader framework that combines the ecological and economic relationships between nature and human-made social order. In other words, it highlights the fact that institutional processes are part and parcel of a wider natural system and that in many cases they should be conceptualized and modeled as such.

Exploring the theme of resilience, with the background of the Bloomington philosophy of polycentricity and its multiple-level institutional analysis, leads to an enhanced interpretation of the nature of the adaptability and viability of institutional systems. Ostrom and her associates explore the link between resilience and institutional diversity, arguing for a perspective in which the resilience of a system has something to do with its institutional diversity, while the resilience of an institution is a function of its position and role in the systemic institutional ecology. One can thus see at work the logic of the Ostromian project, as the focus in a discussion otherwise rooted mostly in environmental and natural sciences, shifts markedly in the social and cultural direction, pivoting on institutional diversity and the associated social and knowledge processes. At the same time, Ostrom's efforts need to be considered in the circumstances created by the fact that the theme of viability or resilience has been rather underdeveloped in the literatures on institutionalist and traditional comparative economic systems. Robustness, viability, and resilience have been low on the lists with systemic functions and performance criteria elaborated by researchers. By adopting the theme (as well as the ensuing theoretical apparatus) from the environmental economics literature for mainstream social theorizing, Ostrom creates the potential for a far-reaching research agenda.

Resilience and Performance Criteria

The research direction highlighted by Ostrom not only puts institutional theory in a position to contribute to the development of an enhanced tool applicable to social-ecological systems but also invites a reconsideration of the entire set of functional and performance criteria applicable in comparative institutional analysis and comparative economic systems. Although this chapter does not delve into this comparative economics, it is important to highlight it as a background of the entire discussion before we proceed with the overview of the Ostromian take on resilience. At stake is an alternative theoretical perspective. Each different function or criterion advanced in the literature (efficiency, growth, stability, resilience) offers a certain window onto institutions and social systems. Each forms a basis for analysis and evaluation. If we look through the theoretical lenses of the performance criterion of "static efficiency," some features of the institutional system will become salient, while others will fade away. If we look through the lenses of "dynamic efficiency" or "stability," the landscape will change. If we calibrate correctly the lenses of "institutional resilience," we have the potential to put things in a distinctive and novel light. In short, when Ostrom's and her associates' work pushes into the limelight the theme of resilience, they implicitly invite political economists to develop its theoretical implications, while reconsidering standard approaches to the comparative assessment of the performance of economic systems.

The significance of this position is hard to exaggerate. The study of the ways and degrees in which social and economic systems meet certain functions or performance criteria is a core component of institutional analysis. The conceptual tools used for such functional evaluations are usually at the same time analytical devices that contribute to a better understanding of the structural features of the systems. Given both the normative and positive importance of the issue, an entire literature dedicated to the articulation and application of such criteria of assessment has developed over the years. Probably the most comprehensive effort has taken place in the field of traditional comparative economic systems. Indeed, the comparison of economic systems goes beyond the effort to identify with accuracy various "systemic functions" and "performance criteria." It also develops, conceptualizes, and operationalizes tools meant to analyze and evaluate, allowing the comparison of different economic arrangements in regard to specific performance criteria. The various lists of such "performance areas" and "system performance criteria" produced in the field are a good reference point for this discussion.

In comparative economics, the most widely used indicator of systemic performance is economic growth (the increase in the volume of output that an economy generates over time or the increase in output per capita). Next to it is economic efficiency (the effectiveness with which a system makes use of its resources) at a particular time (static efficiency) or through time (dynamic efficiency). How "fairly" an economic system distributes income—the equitable or just distribution—is another major criterion for assessing its performance. Last but not least is economic stability, the absence of significant fluctuations (cycles of radical booms and busts), the maintenance of certain rates of unemployment, and the prevention of inflation (Gregory and Stuart 1999). The list may vary from author to author, but the core elements are pretty much the same. Pryor (2005, 32) presents a list of six performance indicators: economic growth, dynamic efficiency, economic stability, static efficiency of production, consumer sovereignty (or consumer efficiency), and an equitable distribution of income and wealth. But he adds that the list is not closed, and other indicators may be added: a high degree of economic security; a low level of unemployment or underemployment; a lack of exploitation; a low degree of concentration of economic power, and so on. Similarly, Bornstein (1994) advances criteria that include the following: the level of output; the rate of growth of output; the composition of output; single period ("static") efficiency; intertemporal ("dynamic") efficiency; stability of output, employment, and prices; economic security of the individual, including security of income and/ or of employment; equity, involving equality of opportunity; economic freedoms of occupational choice, consumption, and property. Other criteria may be derived from these, but for the purposes of this discussion the point is not what is on the list but what is neglected or missing.

In most discussions of comparative economic systems, one important criterion has been missing most of the time. As Gregory and Stuart (1999, 47) explain, "the ultimate test of an economic system is its long-term viability." Yet since the birth of comparative economic systems as a discipline, that is to say, since the launch of the Soviet experiment with planned socialism, there has been "little discussion of the long-term viability of the planned social-ist variant." The focus of discussion was instead on "the *relative* economic performance of planned socialism" because "most experts felt that planned socialism, though inefficient, would be able to muddle along—to survive at relatively low levels of efficiency and consumer welfare." That meant that the problem of resilience failed to become an object of active and intense interest for research.

Yet the crisis of communism and its collapse highlighted the issue of the long-term viability of economic and institutional systems. Now we are better able to recognize that "among the other basic performance criteria—economic growth, efficiency, income distribution, and stability—the long-term viability of the economic system stands out as the dominant test of performance. If an economic system cannot survive, it has clearly proved itself inferior to those systems that can" (Gregory and Stuart 1999, 47). So even if systems' vulner-ability and viability rarely have received more than passing recognition in the past, the problem looms large. The collapse of communism was, after all, a case study in "institutional vulnerability" and revealed with unmistakable clar-ity the importance of the neglected theme.

Paradoxically, the refocus of attention in the aftermath of the Cold War has slowly but steadily created a new environment in which the viability of institutions and systems becomes more and more salient. The last decade has brought a renewed attention to how communities and societies cope with natural catastrophes, social and political disruption, and economic shocks. For instance, the financial and economic crisis reopened debates about the viability of capitalism. This discussion has taken many forms, but one of the most significant research directions converges around resilience or "institu-tional robustness" and correlative concepts such as "institutional adaptability" or "institutional vulnerability," many of them originating in environmental studies. Yet, despite the increasing salience of the theme, its integration in mainstream social sciences is more a desideratum than a reality.

This is the point where Ostrom's interest in resilience becomes relevant. The simple fact that the 2009 economics Nobel Prize winner has put the issue on the table draws attention to it and the intellectual status it deserves.

Her efforts reinforce with her authority the idea that resilience is important and needs to be studied, even if we do it with the limited goal of updating our understanding with what we have learned in the last two decades or so. A minimal worthwhile objective may thus be simply to add it to the list of existing criteria and treat it as a full-status member.

However, Ostrom's interest in the topic not only signals that the time has come to take it seriously but also some possible clues about the ways to advance the agenda dedicated to it. As her work demonstrates, the theme of resilience comes with a theoretical baggage picked up in the process of its birth in the field of environmental research. What Ostrom does is to show how one can bolster (and in some cases to reconfigure) that luggage by an infusion of institutionalism on Bloomington lines. The result seems to be an enhanced version, and a step toward the maximalist objective of going beyond a mere addition of the notion on the list of performance criteria—that is to say, a step toward elaborating a resilience-centered perspective. Whether the outcomes would be able to change our perception of the entire list of criteria and perspectives remains to be seen. One may imagine in what ways and how far the relationship between various performance criteria or functional dimensions could be reconsidered through a resilience-centered framework. But it is too early to speculate on that. For now, the infusion of institutionalist ideas in the traditional environmentalist approach and the infusion of environmental science ideas in traditional institutionalism, all carried out around the theme of resilience, seem to be a promising agenda in itself, worthy of our interest. After all, to articulate and develop that agenda while drawing social scientists to its constructive program pivoting on resilience themes, seems to be one of the major challenges put forward by Ostrom's more recent work.

A Four-Step Approach

A look at resilience studies helps us understand the position and relevance of the institutional element and its diversity championed by Ostrom and her colleagues. With this end in view, we'll go through a four-step approach. The first three steps will successively and increasingly focalize on more precise analytical details. The first will simply situate the social-institutional dimension in the broad context of resilience studies and thus implicitly locate the main area of Ostrom's contribution. The second will take a closer look at some of the ways resilience has been conceptualized and place the Ostromian institutionalist perspective in relationship with each major approach. In other words, I will spell out how it operates in different conceptual systems defining resilience. The third step will take an even closer look, focalizing in more detail on the theoretically specified mechanisms and linkages as they connect various natural and institutional processes. The last step will return to the big picture. Having in the background the insights gained in the previous steps, we will revisit the place of the institutional dimension in the broad context of resilience studies, especially as seen from the perspective of notions such as "panarchy" and nested adaptive cycles.

The Dual Nature of Resilience Studies

Despite its apparent intuitive appeal and clarity, the notion of resilience brings with it notable theoretical, methodological, and philosophical questions. Currently, discussions about resilience are articulated in most cases as part of a larger interest in the relationship between human societies and communities and their natural environment. As such, they center around the concept of a social-ecological system (SES). We speak about the resilience of "social-ecological systems" (Adger 2000; 2006; Folke 2006; Folke et al. 2002; Jassen et al. 2004; 2007; Olsson et al. 2004; Pritchard et al. 1988; Walker et al. 2004) or of "coupled human and natural systems" (Liu et al. 2007a; 2007b). To be sure, human society involves a constant interaction between, on one hand, its cultural and institutional arrangements, and, on the other hand, its physical environment. The cultural and institutional arrangements are not just mediators of human interactions; they also determine the more or less efficient way in which the environment is utilized. Thus, it is understandable that for many authors dealing with resilience, society and nature are seen as intertwined, while the distinction between natural systems (biophysical processes) and social systems (rules, institutions, knowledge, and ethics) is considered arbitrary (Berkes and Folke 1998; Berkes et al. 2003; Carpenter et al. 2001; Folke 2006; E. Ostrom 2008).

But that assessment has significant analytical implications, as resilience has a dual dimension: natural and social. It is both a natural phenomenon and a socially constructed one. A temptation to reduce everything to a common logic that unifies the two facets methodologically and theoretically looms large. Consilience is a appealing philosophy (Wilson 1998). Yet one needs to keep in mind that institutions are special entities. The concept of institutional resilience, by its very nature, focuses explicitly on the human (or social) aspect of the human-environment relation (Janssen 2001; Adger 2000; 2006). Of necessity it includes, not just questions and concerns reducible to models of resource allocation or patterns of reaction and recovery from natural shocks, but political and cultural sources of instability and adaptation. The latter may, in fact, may play the preeminent role. Intentionality, foresight, and future-oriented strategic behavior also are factors. In other words, despite the relatively common rhetoric and conceptualization that frames the discussion in terms of abstract models of "systems" and "processes" in which society and nature intertwine at levels of abstraction at which dualism is lost, there are many reasons—including very important analytical ones—to uphold the distinction between natural systems and social systems. No doubt there are also reasons to avoid drawing a sharp distinction. But, even in the latter case, the socio-institutional aspect retains a clear salience. If a society fails to adapt to a particular environmental challenge, it is likely that its institutions did not respond appropriately, unable to elicit adaptive learning, coordination, and innovation from its members.

In brief: Resilience studies are intrinsically dualistic. An internal tension underlies them, between the natural sciences perspective and social sciences perspective. Institutions emerge at the boundary between the realm of the natural and the realm of the social to mediate and structure the relationship between humans and their environment. Once we look at things in this light, we start to see the reason that, among the vast array of social theories, institutionalism is best positioned to contribute to the development of resilience studies, and why Ostrom's research in institutional diversity in general (1990; 2005) is so relevant for this agenda. Resilience studies require the employment of a certain type of social theory able to operate at the boundary of the two domains, combining agency and structure, and being thus suited to capture the intricate dimensions of this interplay of ideas, rules, and natural constraints and opportunities in complex systems. This social theory is institutionalism, a middle-range theory that has in Ostrom one of its main promoters in the social sciences. Her work, through its focus on institutions' structural and functional diversity, gives analytic and operational substance to the observation that institutional arrangements occupy the central position in the study of resilience and an explanation why the relevant streams of literature come sooner or later to converge in the observation that socioecological resilience implies an institutional perspective incorporating human capacities of learning and discovery.

Varieties of Resilience and the Nature and Role of Institutions

A brief overview of various approaches to the problem of resilience of social-ecological systems (SES) substantiates the central role that the institutional perspective has both implicitly and explicitly. Such an exercise—which was introduced earlier as the second step of our approach—will also reveal two other things: first, the more concrete ways the institutional facet operates in these systems, and, second, the more precise ways the Ostromian approach is positioned in this context. The institutional dimension is emerging as crucial in all current approaches to the problem, irrespective of how one defines and operationalizes the issues. However, it is interesting to see more exactly how it happens in different circumstances.

As has already been noted, a large part of the literature on resilience is dedicated to interactions between human societies and their natural environment. One could say that this perspective is currently dominant; very few authors dedicate efforts to pure institutional resilience, independently of the social-ecological systems (SES) framework. However, within this broad perspective one can distinguish several different approaches. Let's take as a starting point the distinction between the "absorption capacity" perspective and the "speed of recovery" perspective. Some authors focus on the ability of a social system to absorb external environmental shocks. For instance, Walker and colleagues (2004, 2) point out that resilience can be understood as the "buffer capacity or the ability of a system to absorb perturbations, or the magnitude of disturbance that can be absorbed before a system changes its structure by changing the variables and processes that control behavior." This definition rests upon the notion of "absorption capacity" (Holling et al. 1995). An alternative approach to the same issue focuses instead on "the speed of recovery from a disturbance, highlighting the difference between resilience and resistance, where the latter is the extent to which disturbance is actually translated into impact" (Walker et al. 2004, 2). This difference in nuance may matter by shifting the focus of attention from a preventive stance (ability to absorb shocks) to a reactive stance (ability to return to normal functioning fast). Yet, despite these differences of focus, a large amount of agreement exists: for example, Liu et al. (2007a) define resilience as the capability of coupled human-nature systems to "retain similar structures and functioning after disturbances for continuous development," while Walker et al. (2004, 2) define it as "the capacity of a system to retain essentially the same function, structure, identity, and feedbacks."

In all of the above, an SES is understood as resilient if it is capable of successfully adapting to sudden, unexpected environmental changes. This concept of resilience, although relevant for social shocks too, has been applied and developed primarily with environmental shocks in mind (Berger and Spoerer 2001; Gray 1999; O'Rourke 1994). However, the story cannot be told without attention to institutional features that contribute to resilience. The concept incorporates this ability to cope with external shocks, but it cannot be limited solely to this ability. Conceptualizations in macro-level terms, such as general systemic flow charts, do not take us very far, as they do not unpack the institutional aspect and analyze it as one should.

A further step that transcends the distinction between "absorption capacity" and "speed of recovery" has been built around the notion of equilibrium (Gunderson 2000). Again there are two approaches. From some perspectives, resilience may be seen as the persistence of a system near or close to an equilibrium state. From other perspectives, resilience is about "behavior of dynamic systems far from equilibrium." A situation far from equilibrium is not necessarily chaotic, but may be a "steady state," that is, a state of constant change in which some structural features nonetheless remain invariant. The system theory perspective employed for the conceptual articulation of resilience is clear in both cases. Folke and colleagues (2002, 437–38) offer a synthetic perspective of the nonequilibrium paradigm. From their standpoint, resilience is defined in terms of (1) the magnitude of the shock that the system can absorb and remain within a given state; (2) the degree to which the system is capable of self-organization; and (3) the degree to which the system can build capacity for learning and adaptation. They point out that when some "massive transformation" is inevitable, "resilient systems contain the components needed for renewal and reorganization." In other words, "they can cope, adapt, or reorganize without sacrificing the provision of ecosystem services." And the only way in which they are endowed with such a coping ability involving adaptation and learning is to host "diversity—of species, of human opportunity, and of economic options." This is a good description at a certain level of generalization. Yet in order to make practical sense of it, one needs to further unpack it and get to a lower level of generalization. The intricacies of institutions and culture need be introduced into the picture.

This is when the operational relevance of the social and institutional perspective becomes even clearer. Ostrom's polycentricity-based approach (2005, chapter 9) elaborates the institutional diversity conditions of social learning and adaptation. As will be detailed later, an important part of her contribution is precisely an application of her work in polycentrism, self-governance, and self-organization. With Ostrom, what otherwise would be a rather vague or abstract discussion about adaptability and self-organization gets a solid grounding and a solid social science theoretical structure. For instance, Ostrom (2008) was a pioneer in investigations regarding the danger of "institutional monocropping," in which a single set of rules is imposed on a wide scale, replacing experimentation with expert idealizations, rendering institutional variation null, and thus hampering adaptability. To make a long story short, it looks like in order to become fully relevant, the Folke and colleagues (2002) approach (in many respects, typical for SES), needs operationalization precisely on the lines drawn by Ostrom. How are we to know whether an institutional system (and by extension an SES) truly has the capacity for self-organization, learning, and adaptation and thus the ability to absorb shocks of large magnitudes? To a large extent, Ostrom's and her collaborators' work on robustness and vulnerability from the polycentricity perspective may be seen as having been focused on this very problem of operationalizing the concept.

Second, Ostrom and her collaborators' approach has something to add in the nonequilibrium paradigm, too. They develop the notion of robustness, to a substantial degree by introducing innovation into the picture. This is far from being an entirely original idea. The originality comes again from the broader, general background—the polycentric, multiple-level institutional architecture facilitating or hampering innovation. Ostrom and colleagues point out that "a social system that rewards innovation can be robust to many external shocks, as long as it innovates quickly enough." This systemic feature is largely a function of institutional arrangements and incentives. However, this is far from the end of the story: "Unless a society can manage to organize around principles other than 'replacement technologies,' its eventual collapse is likely.... As time progresses and problems become more complex, the probability increases that the society will eventually fail to cope with a shock" (Janssen, Andereis, and Ostrom 2004, 1–2). One can thus note the contours of an approach to vulnerability and resilience that emphasizes not so much the reactive patterns of the re(equilibrating), absorptive side, as the dynamic and innovative side, which in turn is determined by the complexity of the institutional arrangement.

Let's continue our overview of several relevant themes of the literature and the way institutions, institutionalism and Ostrom's perspective fit in, by noting that the literature has pointed out that an SES is resilient not only if it has the ability to absorb shocks and/or adapt to them (or to recover quickly from them), but also if it manages to avoid slippery slopes toward catastrophic thresholds. A socioecological threshold is defined as a point in the relation between a society and its environment beyond which a very hard to stop, as accelerating degradation in the standard of living occurs, and beyond which the society cannot move without significant losses in its standard of living (Walker et al. 2004). Such thresholds exist because the relevant indicators cannot be expressed as simple, linear functions of environmental factors. This nonlinearity is part of what makes resilience so difficult to ascertain. It has been argued (Diamond 2005) that certain complex societies have collapsed by not noticing, or by lacking the institutional mechanisms to stop, their advancement on a slippery slope toward resource depletion.

Things are even more complicated because gradualism and continuity are so deceptive. Change is "episodic, with slow accumulations" that are "punctuated by sudden releases and reorganization...as the result of internal or external natural processes or of man-imposed disturbances" (Holling 1996, 774). To apply fixed rules for achieving constant results "leads to systems that gradually lose resilience, i.e., to ones that suddenly break down in the face of disturbances that previously could be absorbed" (Holling 1996). So we have to keep in mind that we are dealing with "moving targets, with multiple potential futures that are uncertain and unpredictable" and we need to flexible, adaptive, and experimental. The solution is to have in place mechanisms that detect and generate knowledge regarding these trends and the movement toward slippery slopes. Berkes and Turner (2006) review the ways existing knowledge relevant to conservation develops or evolves and how such new knowledge gets created. They organize the literature around two models: the depletion crisis model and the ecological understanding model. The first is that knowledge depends on learning the hard way, in the wake of a resource crisis, that resources are depletable. The second looks at the incremental elaboration of environmental knowledge. The second is crucial for a society that "can self-organize, learn and adapt." The self-organizing process, "facilitated by knowledge development and learning, has the potential to increase the resilience (capability to absorb disturbance and reorganize while undergoing change) of resource use systems" (Berkes and Turner 2006, 479–81). Threshold and slippery slope monitoring and the organization of reactions to them require such knowledge processes.

The bottom line is that these processes are in large part socially and institutionally determined. The flexibility and adaptability in SES are not purely mechanic or organic. They require (self-)monitoring, deliberation, choice, and learning. It is a "second-order task" on the lines defined by Knight and Johnson (2011) and discussed in chapter 2. Needless to say, this adaptability is strongly determined by the institutional arrangements within which these knowledge processes take place. In this respect, the Ostromian contribution is threefold. First, as discussed in chapter 2, the polycentric perspective helps identify some key issues and conditions of effective performance. Second, knowledge processes like those of interest here have been intensively explored by Vincent Ostrom in a broad social philosophy framework that details the polycentric perspective from a different, additional angle (see the next chapters of this book). His dynamic theory of social order as a knowledge process delineates a conceptual frame for the analysis of specific types of knowledge production, dissemination, and impact. Last but not least, Elinor Ostrom's work on common-pool resources offers a wealth of in-depth case studies of both the depletion crisis model and the ecological understanding model. In conjunction the Ostroms offer a solid basis and reference point for further explorations in this direction.

Related to the knowledge creation problem, the relationship between incentives and technological innovation offers another way of illustrating the operational importance of the institutional factor in resilience studies. More precisely, we can look at resources (a crucial variable for resilience studies) as a function of the endogenous nature of technological change (Lucas 1988; Romer 1990; 2007; Simon 1995; 1998; Kahn 2009). The idea is that technologies that impact a society's relation to nature are created as the result of incentives or opportunities for development inherent in that society. Nature's challenge is a perennial reality, a constant presence, but people tend to innovate more in times and areas where there are sufficient social and economic conditions and incentives for making the innovations. Once a relevant innovation is made, a new domain of nature becomes a resource. Whether something is a "resource" or not is thus technologically induced, and technology advances faster in certain social-institutional environments. It is in this sense that it is appropriate to say that, like any other product, the resources themselves are *created*, rather than being merely discovered and consumed (Kahn 2009; Simon 1995; 1998; Kling and Schulz 2009). To sum up, due to the law of diminishing returns in regard to nonsustainable resources, absent economic progress and systemic performance, the standard of living does not remain stationary but falls. Therefore, it appears that sustainability has to be achieved by constant innovation and adaptation (Simon 1995; 1998; Johnson 2000; Ruttan 2002; Rogner 1997). We reach again the conclusion that in order for a society to survive and prosper, to reduce its vulnerability, systematic adoption of institutional arrangements that favor adequate rates of innovation is needed.

Both the theme of innovation and the theme of slippery slope thresholds reveal the institutional aspect not as a static set of rules and incentives but as a dynamic process essential for the long-term resilience of a society. It is a process that not only pushes the system ahead but also provides the necessary feedback for corrections, adjustment, and adaptation. Modern societies do not have the option of stabilizing in a steady-state, static way of life, unchanged for centuries. Vincent Ostrom has explored at length the trade-offs of such an alternative in the context of a social order based on an ongoing growth of knowledge (see chapters 5 and 6 of this book). Because they lack the option of locking in a "safe" stable state, our ability to analyze the process of adaptation by which societies fit their institutions to new challenges (rather than focusing on mere steady-state sustainability) and our ability to evaluate the existence of slippery slopes become crucial. One can see how Ostromian themes regarding governance and social order as a knowledge process loom.

At this juncture, and before concluding this second step of our discussion, we have to note a relatively important problem emerging in a dynamic system in which innovation is pivotal. It is quite expected that when system-changing innovations take place, uncertainty and social vulnerability grow. Innovation solves problems but also creates problems. As Vincent Ostrom puts it, new knowledge increases the range of new possibilities, disrupting existing or established relationships and giving rise to new possibilities. New possibilities, "if acted upon, manifest themselves as new events, relationships, or occurrences which could not have been anticipated." In other words, new knowledge, and action based on an expanding body of knowledge, means two things: First, an ongoing creation of new social uncertainties about the future; second, an ongoing creation of trade-offs that need to be managed (V. Ostrom 1990a; 1991b; 1991c; V. Ostrom 1982a, 34). On a closer examination, the existence of trade-offs is a defining feature of the problem of resilience. The alternatives that present themselves create social dilemmas. This is something Elinor Ostrom and her colleagues are eager to highlight again and again. For instance, they note that

> Robust design often involves a trade-off between maximum system performance and robustness. A robust system will typically not perform as efficiently with respect to a chosen set of criteria as its non-robust counterpart. However, the robust systems performance will not drop off as rapidly as its non-robust counterpart when confronted with external disturbance or internal stresses. (Janssen, Andereis, and Ostrom 2004, 1–2)

The question is, what more precisely are the criteria defining it, from case to case and context to context; what is the nature of the disturbance and stresses and what are the trade-offs involved? Even more important: Are there social choice mechanisms in place to sort out and navigate the trade-offs, an informational and decisional support system of the ways the trade-offs are to be decided? Trade-offs, and the social dilemmas and uncertainties related to them, are hence a key issue, as demonstrated both by the broader, social philosophical standpoint of Vincent Ostrom and by the more applied one of Elinor Ostrom.

Last but not least, Elinor Ostrom's insights extend to the way these trade-offs and uncertainties are dealt with and navigated using rules as building blocks and organizing principles. When it comes to resilience, overly detailed systems of rules, attempting to provide a precise and "optimal" answer to every possible situation, are less robust. Things seem to be even worse when specification is done via centralization. As explained by Miller and Page (2007, 139) "the structures necessary for delicate behaviour require an underlying system that is rich in possibilities. In essence, we need a quivering system that will fall into the right state with only a gentle tap. In such a system, an improper tap can lead to very unpredictable results." We are thus getting closer to a core problem of social resilience. The more precisely one attempts to control everything by devising overly specific rules, the larger the number of variables becomes; the space of possibilities thus becomes larger. Hence the probability of error also becomes larger and the system's robustness to unpredictable shocks, that is, its ability to resist something more than just a "gentle tap" becomes smaller. Addressing the problem of social resilience from the perspective of complexity theory, Miller and Page (2007, 139) summarize the issue: "Adaptive systems have to deal with the tension between the benefits of achieving precise behavior and the cost of increased system fragility."

Authors like Miller and Page (2007, 139) hypothesize that self-organizing adaptive social systems naturally tend toward simple systems of rules that "are likely to be easier to find and maintain." Nonetheless, simple systems may gradually evolve toward more complicated ones, if one assumes the presence of an adaptive path from one to the other. Miller and Page hypothesize a limit to the complexity that can be achieved by bottom-up gradual adaptations, because adaptive systems tend to be risk adverse. The perspective offered by Miller and Page concurs with the one delineated by the Ostroms and focuses on an important aspect of the phenomenon: the intricacies of institutional arrangements as systems of rules and their evolution in time. The dynamics in time matter and the dehomogenization of time seems to be required—hence a renewed understanding of the relevance of case study methods promoted by the Bloomington scholars. Later in the chapter the problem of time and cycles of change will be addressed from an additional angle. For now it is important to note that any serious discussion of resilience in social systems needs to look at rules and how their complexity evolves in time. Again, trade-offs and tensions emerge as an intrinsic feature of the phenomena in question.

To sum up, irrespective of how one defines resilience, the dominant theme seems to be the problem of trade-offs between different functions, domains, and criteria in a broader dynamic process in which change, uncertainty, and heterogeneity are dominant. Institutional resilience is not about maximizing a certain performance variable (criterion) but about trying to manage a complex set of interrelated variables. In practical terms, this requires appropriate information and a knowledge base and an appropriate set of institutional arrangements able to reach the overall institutional system. Institutional resilience is thus an outstanding illustration of the problem of the "second-order task" as defined by Knight and Johnson. Moreover, it is important not to forget that SESs are not purely bottom-up, self-organizing social systems, but often also include various forms of reflexive, top-down elements. As discussed later in the chapter, they may be understood using a conceptual construct akin to the notion of polycentricity.

From "Highly Optimized Tolerance" to Institutional Diversity: Mechanisms, Linkages, Processes

The above overview has shown that the resilience of a social-ecological system can be understood from multiple perspectives, that these perspectives are convergent, and that ultimately the discussion comes to a problem of institutional arrangements and their rules-based configurations for a second-order task. In addition, it has been shown, at a general level, how the Ostrom perspective fits into this discussion. We have also seen how the multiple meanings of resilience are related to assumptions about the nature and specific features of the system, and about what is optimal (and what is considered to be normal and abnormal) for its functioning. At an even more fundamental level, there are tensions between efficiency and persistence, between equilibrium and disequilibrium, between constancy and change, and between predictability and unpredictability that are critical for the functioning and analysis of the system. In short, the notion of resilience, although apparently simple and intuitive, is a complex conceptual construct based on a series of assumptions as well as on more or less explicit normative judgments that all imply unavoidable trade-offs.

The magnitude of the challenge becomes even more evident when we realize that resilience is not only about things like stability, absorption of disturbances, and being persistent or robust. It is also "about the opportunities that disturbance opens up in terms of recombination of evolved structures and processes, renewal of the system and emergence of new trajectories" (Folke 2006, 253–54), or as the Ostroms put it, in more social-humanistic terms, about innovation, ingenuity, and "public entrepreneurship." Ultimately, resilience, be it socioecological or institutional, is about adaptive capacity as shaped, encouraged, or discouraged by institutional arrangements that fallible but capable human agents use to cooperate and coordinate in specific circumstances, by solving specific problems via knowledge processes leading to learning and innovation.

When it comes to the equation of resilience, the literature both in political economy and in environmentalism has reached a relative consensus that

flexible institutions, able to generate information and self-correction processes, are essential. Institutions, writes Holling (1996, 733–34), "are those
sets of relationships that connect people to people and to nature. Flexible
institutions are ones where signals of change are detected and reacted to
as a self-correcting process and where knowledge and understanding accumulate—in short, where learning is possible in a changing world." The real
problem is how to identify and generate such institutions. What are the properties (conditions) of institutional arrangements that will lead them to function along the lines conductive to resilience? That is to say, the big theoretical
challenge is how to properly operationalize our theory about adaptive capacity
in order to assess it in practice. We have seen how the Ostroms' institutionalism fits into the general picture. We need now to take a closer look at details
and the more precise theoretical and analytical logic of how things fit in. We
move now to a higher-resolution focus. Thus the claims made earlier about
the Ostromian perspective will be further substantiated and elaborated.

Elinor Ostrom's theorizing of resilience and vulnerability is intrinsically
connected with the development of the concept of "robustness" and is best
seen in connection to the notion of "highly optimized tolerance" (HOT). This is
well illustrated by the Anderies, Janssen, and Ostrom (2004) article that elaborates an approach inspired by and building on the Carlson and Doyle's (1999;
2002) analysis of robustness. The idea is that the logic behind what Carlson
and Doyle call "highly optimized tolerance" provides a rigorous grounding for
a firmer understanding of the institutions and institutional processes associated with robustness and resilience. Therefore, at this point, a detour through
HOT becomes indispensable.

The notion of HOT has been developed in relationship with a main theme
of complexity theory, namely the "power laws." As a matter of empirical observations, it has been noted that many complex phenomena (e.g., wealth distribution in modern societies, stock price variations over time, the size and
frequency of forest fires, the number of species extinguished, the size and
frequency of automotive traffic jams, air traffic delays, etc.) are governed by
power laws, instead of normal Gaussian distributions (Bak 1996; Mandelbrot
and Hudson 2004). The key difference is this: unlike Gaussian distributions,
power laws allow for differences (often very large) between statistical mean
and mode. The probability of large departures from the most probable event
can be much larger than in case of Gaussian probability distributions.

The applications to SESs are not difficult to imagine. To give an example,
let's take an ecological system—a forest—and an uncertain, potentially destruc-
tive event, a forest fire. Let's assume that there is no human-institutional
intervention, no resource design optimization, no form of reorganizing the

resource. Under this assumption, we have a pure ecological system model or benchmark. Analysis leads to the following conclusion: Yield increases as the resource density increases, but as the resource density increases, the probability of accidents also increases. There is thus a critical point in regard to resource density where yield is maximal. It turns out, however, that, due to the interconnectivity of various sites at which the resource is located, at this critical point in regard to overall resource density, the probability distribution of the size and frequency of resource destruction is a power law. That is to say, very large, even system-wide, accidents can happen with a much larger probability than one would expect from a Gaussian probability distribution. In other words, if the system naturally evolves toward maximizing yield, it also evolves, as a side effect, toward increased vulnerability.

Things change once we have a scenario in which the social-human element enters the picture. Social intervention creates the possibility of resource design optimization. The first outcome to be considered is, however, on the costs side. The cost of prevention (the cost of setting up the institutional-technological mechanisms in place and operating them) becomes an additional economic variable, apart from yield. One first result is that in this new scenario, resource design optimization allows for greater yields than the no-design, initial scenario. Setting up preventing devices that address the most probable causes of accidents changes the performance parameters of the system, now converted into an SES. There is now increased performance, but also a cost of intervention to bear. The bottom line is that now we have a system that is increasingly complex, as various preventing devices are set up, is more efficient (higher yield), and is calibrated or optimized to address very specific sources of uncertainty.

The notion of highly optimized tolerance tries to capture exactly this type of calibration of a system via institutional and technical interventions that are relative to specific sources of uncertainty. This is the point where the notion of trade-offs reenters the picture. Concentrating in one specific area creates vulnerabilities in regard to other, unforeseen sources of uncertainty: "[O]ptimizing yield will cause the design to concentrate protective resources where the risk of failures are high, and to allow for the possibility of large rare events elsewhere" (Carlson and Doyle 1999, 1416). The reference to "*large* rare events" is an echo of the presence of power laws.

In brief, the logic of calibrated institutional design and interventionism seen from the HOT perspective leads to the idea of a system that is "robust yet fragile." We now have a clearer theoretical basis for the already introduced idea that trade-offs and vulnerability are structurally unavoidable. Systems designed to tolerate better specific sources of uncertainty and whose complexity increases precisely by developing features that help it cope with those sources of uncertainty and danger, remain exposed precisely because of the remaining sources of uncertainty. Via the same process, the system develops weak points that open up the possibility of a "cascading spread of damage due to the seemingly innocuous breakdown of individual parts," thanks to its complex interconnectivities (Carlson and Doyle 2002, 2540). Moreover, as we have seen from Vincent Ostrom's work, uncertainty is a dynamic, protean variable, its very nature and sources changing over time. In brief, the important point reinforced by Elinor Ostrom and her collaborators, following Carlson and Doyle (1999; 2002), is that resilience is not a simple scalar variable (such as "absorption capacity" or "speed of recovery") but a mesh of variables between which trade-offs exist (Janssen et al. 2007) and which needs to be dealt with in most cases under conditions of Knightian uncertainty.

The terminology adopted by Ostrom and her collaborators is not entirely consistent across their papers, disclosing the exploratory nature of their work at this stage. However, the underlying theory and philosophy behind the terms used are clear and the message is consistent. In Janssen and colleagues (2006, 1–2) the authors reserve the word "robustness" for the non-equilibrium steady-state approach, while associating the word "resilience" with a more complex, adaptive approach. Unlike "robustness," which refers to the "structural and other properties of a system that allow it to withstand the influence of disturbances without changing the structure of its dynamics," that is, steady-state dynamics, "resilience" allows for larger changes: it is "the capacity of a system to absorb and utilize or even benefit from perturbations and changes that attain it, and so to persist without a qualitative change in the system's structure."

Furthermore, it is noteworthy that Carlson and Doyle define robustness as "the maintenance of some desired system characteristics despite fluctuations in the behavior of its component parts or its environment" and emphasize that "[a]lthough we can loosely speak of robustness without reference to particular systems characteristics, or particular component or environmental uncertainties, this can often be misleading" (2002, 2539). Thus, robustness is relative to a particular variable of interest and to particular sources of uncertainty. By contrast, resilience is understood as a more general and vague concept, roughly incorporating all variables. Following Carlson and Doyle, Ostrom and her collaborators note that

> systems subjected to a particular type and degree of variability may become highly optimized to tolerate this variability.... In so doing, however, the system may become more brittle and susceptible to

> changes that may occur in the type and degree of variability to which
> it has become highly adapted or to new types of disturbances. Put
> another way, systems cannot be robust to all types of variability and
> disturbances. Complex systems must trade off the capacity to cope with
> some types of variability to become robust to others. (Janssen et al.
> 2007, 309)

Following this line of argument, they also point out that this concept of robustness, which is relative to particular variables, is easier to use in a rigorous manner than other concepts such as adaptability, which seem very difficult to operationalize.

> How does one design for adaptive capacity? What is the cost of adaptive
> capacity? Robustness, on the other hand, emphasizes the cost-benefit
> trade-offs associated with systems designed to cope with uncertainty.
> As such, robustness is a more appropriate concept when trying to
> understand how SESs can deal with disruptions. (Janssen, Andereis,
> and Ostrom 2004)

This raises an intriguing question: is this concept of robustness a competitor with the notion of "adaptability" (Smit and Wandel 2006), or is it a conceptual tool that allows for a more analytical approach to adaptability? Ostrom embraces the second alternative and combines it with a sociocultural evolution view: "Rule systems can evolve.... As an evolutionary process, of course, there must be the generation of new alternatives, selection among new and old combinations of structural attributes, and retention of those combinations of attributes that are successful in a particular environment" (E. Ostrom 2008, 57). That being said, general societal changes are the consequence of a *superposition* of many cultural evolutionary processes in which institutional rules evolve to fit various competing goals, rather than just one. This is why robustness is not merely a single number, but is relative to various kinds of uncertainty encountered by a society and relative to various normative goals determining which yields should be maximized. Depending on their particular contexts, various societies deal with different forms of uncertainty, and, thus, they are robust relative to different forms of possible disturbances (Janssen, Andereis, and Ostrom 2004; Blomquist 2004, 1992; Janssen et al. 2007). This is also why it is dangerous to transpose without much thought a set of rules from one place to another—the originator may have evolved its rules in relation to its own set of uncertainties, while the recipient may have to deal with a different set of uncertainties and thus needs to develop a different kind of robustness.

As Anderies, Janssen, Andereis, and Ostrom 2004 ; 2007) demonstrate, adopting this perspective is an excellent way to connect the ecological, economic, and institutional domains of research. It provides a clear mechanism by which social-institutional complexity gradually increases. Employing the HOT perspective, one may conjecture that norms and rules are prevention devices designed to help society cope with various kinds of uncertainty. For example, Ostrom and her collaborators (1990; Ostrom, Schroeder, and Wynne 2003; Ostrom, Gardner, and Walker 1994; Gibson, McKeen, and Ostrom 2000) describe numerous cases of this type of institutional design in regard to common-pool resources where one of the main forms of uncertainty is due to the possibility of free riders. As the HOT perspective implies, the specifics differ from case to case. Institutional diversity comes both in form and in function. For example, one has to adopt certain kind of rules when free riding involves cutting wood from a forest as compared to the case when free riding involves overharvesting fish from the ocean. While the *function* of rules may be the same in both cases, their *content* necessarily differs. Thus, if, for instance, one finds a community that has successfully dealt with the free-riding problem in regard to its forest (e.g., by privatizing the forest into different individual parcels), it does not mean that one would be successful by simply transposing these successful rules to a fishermen community suffering from overharvesting (privatizing the ocean into parcels may not be workable because fish move from place to place). Fishermen would thus have to develop thier own rules for dealing with its specific form of uncertainty. This is a very simple example, but, once we have understood that social-institutional complexity comes about via the HOT process, we understand that the point holds to an even greater extent in the case of more complex issues.

The message is that this perspective leads to a more nuanced view on social-institutional diversity and complexity. Traditional structural-functionalist themes from sociology and anthropology are thus revived. For instance, we are alerted to the importance played by most rules and norms in maintaining the system, even when their specific role is not easily recognizable. The hidden nature of this complexity is due to the fact that each layer of organization in the system has specific details that are important for its robustness, but which are not immediately obvious to the untrained eye: at each layer, "we expect to encounter a new structure which is crucial to the robustness and predictability of the system." (Carlson and Doyle 1999, 1–2) The latent-manifest functions theorizing is thus brought to a new life under a new rendition. Ostrom and her collaborators (E. Ostrom 1990; Ostrom, Gardner, and Walker 1994) have indeed documented many interesting cases in which long-lasting institutional systems (e.g., the irrigation systems in Bali or traditional transhumance in

India) have been "reformed" with the best intentions in mind, only to tragi-cally discover later the importance played by various rules that were thought to be mere traditional relics with no real utility.

The strengths, limits, and nuances of this interdisciplinary perspective become clearer when it is used to pinpoint the nature and impact of insti-tutional systems on resilience by framing the issue as a costs-and-benefits problem. We learn from the HOT examples and thought experiments that introducing an institutional arrangement (set of rules), aimed at addressing a particular kind of uncertainty, comes with a certain cost-structure. The moni-toring and enforcement process requires resources (time, people, informa-tion processing, and capital), and it creates certain opportunity costs (prevents some productive activities that would happen in the absence of those rules). One might be tempted to say that an institutional device is good if these costs are lower than the societal benefits. But this is often debatable. It is not always the case that a consensus exists about what "societal benefits" should be con-sidered (Sagoff [1990] 2004, 2008). We are thus reminded of the need but also of the intricacies and limits of cost-benefit analyses in such circumstances.

Moreover, when one focuses on describing what happens, rather than pre-scribing what should happen, one has to adopt the public choice perspective and recognize that the benefits that matter may not actually be the overall social benefits (however we define them), but benefits obtained by the group of actors that has the upper hand in the institutional design process. In other words, one should never forget the relationship between a particular institu-tional arrangement and the interests of those who do the institutional design-ing. As we'll see, this type of public choice approach provides a very strong argument in favor of local self-governance and polycentricity as mechanisms for ensuring that the overall "societal benefits" have at least some chances to be factored in.

Last but not least, zooming in on the issue through theoretical lenses like those outlined in this section illuminates from another angle a key facet (or corollary) of the problem of institutional diversity. Considering the impor-tance played by details, one may ask in what measure the attempts to have a general theory are worthwhile. As Carlson and Doyle (1999, 1413) put it, "if we accept the fact that most real complex systems are highly structured, dominated by design, and sensitive to details, it is fair to ask whether there can be any meaningful theory of complex systems." That is to say, the ques-tion is, "are there common features, other than power laws, that the compli-cated systems...share that we might hope to capture using simple models and general principles?" When we adopt this perspective on robustness in the social-institutional sphere, this question translates into a quite familiar one to those exposed to the Ostroms' thought: To what extent can we have institutional recipes for success that can be transplanted from one region to another and replicate the desired performance? Or to put it differently, how can one use the success stories as valid sources of inspiration, without falling into the trap of "blueprint thinking"? To answer this question is the ongoing challenge posed by the Bloomington scholars' work.

The Ostrom team's research has produced an entire range of arguments for the thesis that there is no universal set of formalized rules that gives optimal results everywhere. Conditions can be so diverse that, depending on context, sets of rules that work best in one circumstance may fail in other (Ostrom 2005, 274–76). This particular danger is often compounded by external interventions, which, when guided by blueprint thinking, can "undermine local institutions" by distorting the existing incentive structures. Consequently, the focus has to be not, in technocratic fashion, on identifying an assumed ideal set of rules, a "blueprint," to be implemented everywhere, but on the meta-level and the sociopolitical process of rule design. Some sociopolitical processes are better than others at the task of identifying the best rules for their society's specific context in the shortest amount of time and with the least waste of resources. The theme of resilience illustrates, thus, not only the issue of the second-order tasks of institutional arrangements but also the problem of approaches that focus on process versus those that focus on end states.

To sum up, using the HOT angle, in conjunction with the standard logic of the Ostromian perspective, leads to a series of theoretically grounded insights into how the diverse institutional rules and norms that shape the complexity of modern societies come to have resilient functions preventing or reacting to specific sources of uncertainty. Different societies and communities have faced different types of challenges and uncertainties in their history and have created, as a result, different institutions. That diversity has benefits but also may have costs. Both costs and benefits are driven not only by the number and density but also by the structure and configurations of those institutional arrangements. Importantly, as Ostroms' work documents and analyzes (Ostrom and Ostrom 2004; Ostrom 2005), institutions exist at different levels of social interaction, ranging from the lowest operational level (involving rules about specific productive or distributive activities) to the middle-range public choice level (involving the rules by which communities cooperate in order to create their operational rules), to the highest constitutional level (involving rules regulating the proper workings of the public choice processes).

We have reached in this discussion an aspect that deserves special attention: the potential of the multiple-levels, polycentric perspective to shed light on linkages and transition mechanisms, as they operate between different levels of diverse institutional arrangements. In a sense, one may say that the resilience of social systems stems from (a) the ability of their low-level operational institutions to identify and signal problems and generate proper feedback responses to challenges when they arise, and (b) from the ability of the higher-level social choice and constitutional institutions to create the conditions for the society to adapt to new challenges. But engaging this topic is already leading us into the next objective of this chapter. The notions of polycentricity and multiple levels of analysis seem to match naturally with what has been called "panarchy," a framework of analysis developed in resilience studies. Authors such as Holling (2001, 392), advance such a frame as a way to explore processes taking place "in nested sets at scales ranging from a leaf to the biosphere over periods from days to geologic epochs, and from the scales of a family to a sociopolitical region over periods from years to centuries." With the discussion shifting toward notions like panarchy and polycentricity, we are moving again to a bigger perspective. Zooming out allows to get an ample view on what resilience studies bring to institutional theories, and how institutional theory looks when seen in the context of broader theoretical frameworks that incorporate both social and natural facets.

Panarchy, Polycentricity, and the Theory of Institutional Performance and Change

The previous chapter introduced and presented the nature and functions of the heuristic and analytic conceptual instrument (the IAD framework) developed for institutional analysis and design purposes by the Ostroms and their collaborators. Although a social science construct, the framework explicitly and systematically takes into account the relevant natural-environmental parameters. The conditions are thus created to further enlarge or link this conceptual instrument to a broader conceptual construct that incorporates the natural and institutional domains. Such a possibility becomes a necessity, as the study of resilience leads sooner or later to a point where the task of integrating and synthesizing the institutionalist perspective with the various attempts to conceptualize complex adaptive systems becomes inescapable.

As one may expect, there are multiple ways of approaching this task. The most interesting and potentially productive seems to be the one building on the idea of multilevel adaptive cycles and presented under the name of "panarchy," an integrative theory of natural and human systems advanced by some of the most insightful theorists of SESs. The concept of "panarchy" describes hierarchical natural, social, and hybrid structures, meshed as complex adaptive systems that are "interlinked in never-ending adaptive cycles of growth, accumulation, restructuring, and renewal. The functioning of those cycles and the communication between them determines the sustainability of a system" (Holling 2001, 390–91). A brief overview will show the affinities between the multiple-level, polycentric perspective and multiple-level panarchy, as well as the potential for cross-fertilization. At the same time, such an exercise will also explore the conjecture that the concept of panarchy has the carry capacity to lead to a further integration of Ostromian institutionalism with ecological and resilience studies and thus to inspire a constructive future research agenda.

The idea of panarchy combines two major elements: space (and time) hierarchies and adaptive cycles. It posits the existence of multiple, overlapping cycles operating at different scales and thus creates a basis for modeling a variety of dynamic, nested systems and subsystems. The researcher has to first identify, isolate, and analyze them separately, then to recombine and study their dynamics in conjunction. An important element in all this is indeed the time factor: the special focus on duration, speed, and rhythm allows a unique approach, especially when the elements of novelty or innovation are introduced into the picture. The emergence of newness, novelty, and innovation is revealed as being as much a time-related issue as it is a structural and substantive one. In many respects, this reconfigurations of new elements, in cyclical terms, is what makes the notion of panarchy different from other general-system type theories. In a "panarchy," explains Holling (2001, 390–91), "each level is allowed to operate at its own pace, protected from above by slower, larger levels but invigorated from below by faster, smaller cycles of innovation." As a whole, "panarchy is therefore both creative and conserving. The interactions between cycles in a panarchy combine learning with continuity." Similarly to polycentricity, attention focuses on the conditions that make a system "invent and experiment, benefiting from inventions that create opportunity while being kept safe from those that destabilize" (Holling 2001, 391–92). In brief, the language of its description sounds thus recognizable to all those familiar with the language of polycentricity, a continuation to an already established discussion.

A brief genealogy of the concept as presented by Holling (2001, 393), is instructive. Its origins are in Herbert Simon's (1973) discussion of the adaptive role of hierarchical structures. An important caveat is that the notion of hierarchy is not used in the more regular sense of a top-down chain of command and control. Instead, it is defined, following Simon, as a succession of semi-autonomous levels "communicating a small set of information or quantity of material to the next higher (slower and coarser) level." Each level has a certain pace and dynamics. The key in the overall picture is the transfer from one level to the other. These transfer points and the associated mechanisms and processes are as important as the various levels and cycles of the system. The main insight is that if the transfer is maintained, "the interactions within the levels themselves can be transformed, or the variables changed, without the whole system losing its integrity." Consequently, a system with such a structure "allows wide latitude for experimentation within levels, thereby greatly increasing the speed of evolution" (Holling 2001, 392–93). This means that such systems have a strong adaptive potential and are able to preserve continuity while various experiments take place, nested in each other, across different scales and different time cycles.

Ecologists found the notion intriguing and applied what Simon called "hierarchy" to ecological systems. That approach led to, among others, a change of perspectives, from the "small-scale view" to a "multi-scale and landscape view that recognized that biotic and abiotic processes could develop, mutually re-enforcing relationships over distinct ranges of scale" (Holling 2001, 392–93). Briefly, the idea seemed perfectly fit to be used as a conceptual framework for their work. Yet, given the fact that the word "hierarchy" implies in common usage the meaning of rigid and top-down, ecologists were not happy with the word. They wanted a different term that would "rationalize the interplay between change and persistence, between the predictable and the unpredictable." As it was impossible to find an existing word, they come to use the image of the Greek god Pan as "the epitome of unpredictable change" and combine it with "the notion of hierarchies across scales to invent a new term that could represent structures that sustain experiment, test its results, and allow adaptive evolution" (Holling 2001, 390).

Setting aside terminology and genealogy, the correspondence between this approach and the multiple-level approach of the Ostroms' polycentric institutionalism is easy to notice. For instance, the Ostroms and their collaborators think of the IAD framework in heuristics terms, a conceptual tool able to travel well across a variety of social situations. In turn, Gunderson and Holling (2002) and Holling (2001, 393) present the entire idea of panarchy as a "heuristic model, a fundamental unit that contributes to the understanding of the dynamics of complex systems from cells, to ecosystems, to societies, to cultures." The universality of the heuristic instrument becomes even clearer when the adaptive cycle is discussed in depth. According to the literature, panarchies have three properties that shape the adaptive cycle and consequently the state of a system. The first is resourcefulness or inherent potential (the "wealth" of a system); the second is internal controllability (which is a function of the connectedness between internal controlling variables); and the third is adaptive capacity (the resilience of the system). Authors advancing the argument claim that these three properties "are general ones, whether at the scale of the cell or the biosphere, the individual or the culture" (Gunderson and Holling 2004; Holling 2001, 393–94). In other words, if the IAD framework is supposed to travel well through various social circumstances and action arenas, panarchy is supposed to travel equally well through natural, social, and mixed systems, developing its approach as a function of a set of properties common to all these systems.

The consistent resemblance between the institutionalist and panarchy frameworks goes beyond such general and methodological features. For instance, the theory of panarchy is based on the observation that each level serves a double function: first, "to conserve and stabilize conditions for the faster and smaller levels," second "to generate and test innovations by experiments occurring within a level" (Holling 2001, 390). As one may note, this translates without any difficulty into the logic of the Ostroms' framework. The constitutional level in the Ostroms' approach has precisely the function of stabilizing conditions for the lower-echelon, public choice, and operational levels. In a similar way, the operational level is a hotbed of change, experiments, and innovations that may reach thresholds bubbling up and coming to alter the upper echelon, public choice, and constitutional levels.

In the same comparative vein, it is noteworthy that the same strong emphasis put on experiment, learning, innovation, and adaptability by the Ostroms in their discussions of polycentricity is to be found in discussions of panarchy. In the end, one of the key objectives in developing the concept of panarchy is to start for analytic reasons with the description and analysis of structural and functional features of specific building blocks but then to go beyond them to illuminate and analyze a set of processes. The prize is to capture the essential fact that social-ecological systems invent and experiment and to investigate what makes that creativity possible and what hinders it. The ensuing analytical narrative is about the conditions and sources of adaptation and change amid continuity in overlapping hierarchies and adaptive cycles across scales. We have already seen that as in the multiple-level, polycentric perspective, each level operates at its own pace in a dynamic balance that combines change with continuity (Gunderson and Holling 2002, 76). Given the fact that panarchy and Bloomington polycentrism seem to share an underlying logic, it is no surprise that sooner or later the problem of human agents and of individuals with their ideas, preferences, and creativity becomes an unavoidable part of the panarchy framework.

We have been introduced to how Ostrom and her associates integrate the problem of rules and institutions in the analyses of socioecological systems. A closer look reveals that a two-tier, rather sophisticated approach is at work. The effort to integrate the institutional perspective (rules as an interface between human societies and nature) is strongly tied to an effort to integrate in the institutionalist perspective the human element, human decision-making with imperfect information, errors, learning, and creativity, as it operates as a driving force behind institutions and social systems. Tentative and perfectible as this effort is, it is sufficient to learn from it that institutionalism and, by implication, panarchy, without microfoundations based in human action, without a human-centered approach, are incomplete, not fully functional epistemic instruments.

This fact has not been missed by the authors developing the notion of panarchy. Human systems, as opposed to purely natural systems, write Gunderson and Holling (2002, 100), exhibit "unique features that change the character and location of variability within the panarchy and that can dramatically enhance the potential of the panarchies themselves." These features are foresight, communication, and technology. Technology is about the scale of the influence. In a conceptual framework in which scale matters, it is important to note that humans have a unique reach and impact because of technology. Technology "amplifies the actions of humans so that they affect an astonishing range of scales from the submicroscopic to global and—however modestly at the moment—even extend beyond Earth itself." Communication brings, in a similar way, a radical jump when it comes to humans. Organisms "transfer, test, and store experience in a changing world genetically." Ecosystems "transfer, test, and store experience by forming self-organized patterns that…function over specific scale ranges and form a mutually reinforcing core of relationships." But when it comes to human systems, although the self-organized patterns emerge with similar strengths, an additional feature emerges, too: the capacity to communicate, more specifically to communicate ideas and the experience that led to them. Ideas and the associated cognitive processes come to make a difference, changing profoundly the nature of the game as communication becomes part of a complex growth-of-knowledge process. Institutional order is in large part affected by ideas that "can become incorporated into slower parts of the panarchy, such as cultural myths, legal constitutions, and laws" and that in turn become meta-levels stabilizing conditions for the lover, faster, levels (Gunderson and Holling 2002, 100).

The inclusion of foresight on the list is more than significant. The next chapter of this book will elaborate the theme of ideas and foresight while taking a closer look at the critical role the neglected problems of prediction and predictability have in institutional theory. For now, it is important to emphasize the difference made by human foresight, predictions, and forward-looking behaviors in panarchies. As the authors dealing with the theme note, they are truly game-changers—factors that act as drivers in themselves. Foresight generates strategic behavior that transcends levels and cycles. It factors in anticipated events into current incentives and alters cycles because it inspires actions that cut through time horizons and scales, thus changing the entire dynamics of the system. With the problem of foresight, we are at the center not only of the problem of knowledge and communication processes but also of the problem of technology (and especially of social technology and institutional design). As noted, the next chapter will deal extensively with these issues, in the context of a discussion of institutional design. At this point, it is important simply to note that only when the problem of foresight is addressed are the real dimensions of the difference made by the human element fully appreciated.

To sum up, even a brief overview like the one above gives a sense of the affinities between panarchy and Ostromian institutionalism. Several aspects stand out in this respect. First is the idea of levels, scales, hierarchy, complex configurations that have different structures and dynamics and operate at different speeds and rhythms. Second is the idea of process (cycles): A system or a level is not to be described and analyzed statically but dynamically. In other words, one should not confuse a snapshot at one moment of a cycle in the life of phenomena with phenomena seen from the comprehensive perspective of the various stages of the cycle. Third is the idea of learning, testing, inventing: Although there are natural cycles, these cycles do not mean endless repetition of the same because even without deliberated human-induced interventions, novelty and adaptive learning are possible in SES. However, humans raise all this to a new level. Learning and invention become dominant features in SESs. Last but not least, looming behind all this, is the idea of self-organization: The principles and dynamics of organizations vary across scales, levels, and stages of the cycle. The organization of the system as a whole allows (in fact depends on) the quasi-autonomous organization of the subsystems.

Probably the most important difference is the relatively strong emphasis on the time factor and time scales in the panarchy approach, as opposed to the relatively minor emphasis in polycentric IAD. This shouldn't be a surprise, as such aspects are indeed more salient when one looks at them from the broader, ecological perspective as opposed to the smaller-scale, institutional one focused on human action and human community. The relevant differences of scales are not just spatial, structural, and functional but also temporal. That is to say, the time-related dynamics (with their continuities and discontinuities) vary with level and scale. This is a major insight and a significant contribution coming from the panarchy literature. Institutional theory has yet to catch up with it and its implications. But, that being said, the evidence is sufficient to support the conjecture that panarchy and polycentrism are part of the same theoretical family, possible facets of the same theoretical construct to be developed in the future. Ways to integrate the two, and the value added created by their integration, as well as the ensuing theoretical synthesis, are all part of a promising emerging research agenda.

Integrating Economics, Ecology, Institutionalism

Following the theme of resilience, this chapter has offered a sample of the integrative capability of the Bloomington approach. Ostrom's and her collaborators' have developed an interdisciplinary, multiple-level approach to the integration of the issue of rules and institutions in the analyses of socioecological systems, their vulnerability and their resilience. In doing that, they bolster the integration of the concept of resilience in social sciences and at the same time further develop resilience studies by strengthening their social sciences component. Institutional theory informed by a look at the forces and the factors endogenous to social systems gains an enhanced understanding of the nature of SES and their vulnerabilities.

The ultimate assessment of their efforts needs to keep in mind that the Ostroms' framework may be seen as a part of a broader theory of socioinstitutional evolution, a theory that incorporates both the bottom-up, emergent process of rule creation (self-governing) and the top-down, rational process of institutional design. The insights resulting from these efforts are, as one may note, fully consistent with other themes of the Ostroms' work. In practical terms, the message is simple: resist the monocentric, static, top-down approach. That doesn't mean that institutional design, top-down, is excluded. It means that our approach should not concentrate on unachievable standards of centralization and sturdiness but on innovation and a society's ability to adapt to challenges. For that, one has to concentrate on social self-organization and emergent phenomena, rather than on a top-down perspective that assumes that all relevant information is more or less known to a central authority that also happens to have all the relevant means of social design and control at its disposal. Moreover, in order to understand the possibilities and limits of this approach, as the example of panarchy demonstrate, one needs to continually transcend and reconsider disciplinary boundaries, to combine economics, institutional theory, and environmental sciences in new and unorthodox ways.

When all is said and done, the emerging unifying theme is one of an evolving order, of a complex phenomenon in which self-organization based on knowledge processes is the main force at work and the focus of investigation.

We are in a sense back to the discussion about the comparative merits of various institutional arrangements. More precisely, we are revisiting the theme of two major principles in tension: decentralization versus centralization. And in this case, this discussion, whether one likes it or not, has to go back to the example or reference point offered by the theory of the market. The pioneers of the study of spontaneous orders, of agent-based self-organization, have been economists who identified and studied such processes, especially as they manifest themselves in more or less "free markets." Whether one likes it or not, in the social sciences literature the classic bottom-up self-organizing social system is the market, and thus market theory provides the main model and benchmark. The insight that a market is an information-processing "machine," having the price system at its core, is a crucial inspiration for the study of other self-organizing social phenomena (Hayek 1945; 1952).

But if for one reason or another, one insists on avoiding the model and lessons of market theory, or its refinement in Public Choice and Austrian theory (Brennan and Lomasky 1989; O'Driscoll and Rizzo 1985, Boettke 1994; 2012; Storr 2010, 2012; Klein 2012; Pennington 2011), one may simply look at a variety of authors who either have described the related logics of evolutionary theory and microeconomics (Shermer 2007) or have simply translated the insight from economics to complexity theory and social theory. One such argument is that the market is a form of "social computer" that solves the giant coordination problem of allocating scarce resources to their "optimal" uses (Axtell 2003; O'Driscoll 1977). One could simply restate the discussion in these terms. For instance, authors such as Miller and Page (2007, 137) develop a "social computer" perspective in the very general terms of complexity theory and point out that a social system's ability to solve social problems, and thus function productively, depends on its "ability to compute answers," which in turn depends on "its ability to transmit and process information." Moreover, "Because computations must give useful answers, intuitively we would suspect that the rules that can undertake computation must lie in a regime that is neither too chaotic (since no consistent answers will be forthcoming) nor too ordered (since insufficient computation can take place)." In other words, this restates from a different angle the Hayekian emphasis on a functioning system of "rule of law," providing actors with a reasonable amount of predictability ("consistent answers"), but avoiding a stifling, overly bureaucratic system that would eliminate all innovative variations ("insufficient computation").

The Ostroms' perspective recognizes the power of the market model and, in general, of the "social computer" family of models but also recognizes some of their limits. Using the theoretical lenses of an idealized market or social computer model is one thing, but determining the extent to which the theoretical equivalence between profit maximization (or optimal informa-tion flows) and optimal institutional systems' self-calibration takes place in real-life cases is something different. The departure from idealized conditions for social computers' optimal operation involves significant social choice and public choice issues (Ostrom and Ostrom 2004; Tullock et al. 2002; Winston 2006). As authors such as Sagoff ([1990] 2004) have amply argued, there are social decisions that cannot be carried out via markets, due to the fact that the market does not always capture the relevant values and preferences, or it does not aggregate all the relevant information, or due to the fact that for various reasons, a price system cannot be established as a guide for all social matters. People may care about other issues than economic efficiency, such as fairness, or different versions of "social justice," and may have different views about how to implement them socially. Resilience as a composite systemic feature is an example. As Elinor Ostrom's studies have shown, a price system can be difficult to establish for common-pool resources; hence problems of efficient use get transmuted into problems of viability and resilience—not to speak of cases in which people may be reluctant to approach some matters by means of markets and their rules, because of a tension or clash with other norms and rules defining other institutional arenas.

Consequently, alternative systems of rules and institutional arrangements are needed in order to fulfill the two tasks that the price system fulfills in the areas where markets are functional: aggregating preferences and guiding entrepreneurial activities toward "optimal" uses of resources. These alterna-tive systems of rules, informal and formal, can be seen as market-like phe-nomena, but they don't fit the classical distinction between market and state (Ostrom 1994; Aligica and Boettke 2009). Thus we return again to the prob-lem of institutional diversity. Simple market exchanges are replaced by actions under a given set of rules and norms, and preference aggregation via the price system is replaced by various collective choice arrangements that determine, among others, the specific content and nature of the rules and norms. Seen from a broader perspective, the market itself is only a special case of complex institutional arrangements of this sort, and it is often one among the many components of the social system to be analyzed. Moreover, as has already been repeatedly noted, "efficiency" is not the only normative criterion to be consid-ered; others, such as fairness, participation rate, or resilience can be equally important to various communities. But, overall, above and beyond the variety of combinations, layers, rules, and institutions, the system has to be able to aggregate information, provide feedback, give the right incentives for innova-tion, and, generally speaking, use social rules effectively for both first-order and second-order problem-solving.

Thinking of resilience is, in the end, thinking of rule and institutional design processes that are likely to ensure the conditions of high levels of adaptability, because they are likely to allow the system to incorporate new pieces of information quickly when conditions change. The polycentric perspective and the panarchy perspective lead, via related logics, to related conclusions: a built-in flexibility of the system, a flexibility based not on command and control, that is, on rigid structures, but on rules, incentives. and knowledge processes. At the same time, that being said, our enthusiasm for these conclusions should be tempered by the Ostromian caveat that irrespective of domain, function, or performance criteria, there is no universal set of formalized rules that gives optimal results everywhere.

5

Institutional Design, Ideas, and Predictability

INSTITUTIONAL DESIGN—THE practice of analyzing and devising the "rules of the game" that the "agents" will play in specific "action situations"—has been a tacit but constant presence in the previous chapters: first, because the entire work of the Ostroms is predicated on the assumption that institutional design is the ultimate testing ground of the viability and relevance of institutional theory; second, institutional design occupies a special position in any discussion in which the dichotomies monocentrism-polycentrism, centralization-decentralization, spontaneous order–social engineering are so salient. The notion and the practice behind it have to function as mediator in more than one way. This strategic position allows an exceptional insight into the inner nature and workings of institutions, including significant aspects of their emergence and change. The previous chapter identified and used the issue of resilience as such a window, able to open an inside view from the macro level. In a parallel way, institutional design will be used in this chapter for an inside view, this time from the micro level. As in the previous chapter, this exercise will allow us to outline promising directions of possible further development of a research agenda inspired by an Ostromian perspective.

A discussion about institutional design is a discussion about the role of ideas, and a discussion about the role of ideas is a discussion about the ways the human mind deals with uncertainty and the future, about "reflexivity" (i.e., the self-fulfilling and self-denying properties of human public conjectures and predictions) and about the institutional consequences of all of the above. The chapter explores the thematic and conceptual landscape illuminated following the logic of the triad of institutional design, role of ideas, and shadow of the future, as it emerges from an interpretation and elaboration of some of the less explored but potentially productive insights gained from the Ostroms' writings. More precisely, the chapter looks at how the focus on the role of ideas introduces into the picture the problem of the future and its uncertainties as a challenge to social coordination processes, and with it, the problem of predictability. It discusses the crucial role that prediction and predictability have both in the architecture of social order and in our theorizing about it, and identifies reflexivity as a major theme of interest for institutional theory. An approach in which the dilemmas of social prediction and reflexivity are central opens the way for a research agenda replicating the strategy Elinor Ostrom perfected in her treatment of the problem of the commons. Some of the ramifications of the effort exploring the ways individuals and social groups find solutions to predictability problems and generate in the process a variety of institutional forms are profound and lead to serious challenges to the way we think about the relationship between institutional theory (ideas), institutional theorists and social reality. In brief, the chapter is a renewed demonstration of the enduring capacity of the Ostroms' vision to inspire unconventional research ideas and profound intellectual challenges, pressing—in the Bloomington scholars' long-established manner—against the theoretical limits and the philosophical foundations of the conventional wisdom.

Institutional Design and the Role of Ideas

By its very nature, institutional design, as an applied expression of institutional theory, is an attempt to change a specific social system in predetermined directions, based on a conceptual understanding of the system (Ostrom 1993; Goodin 1996; Weimer 1995; Koremenos et al. 2001). That understanding may be correct or incorrect, viable or nonviable, but the bottom line is that institutional design assumes the existence of a minimal control powered and shaped by a conceptualization that takes both descriptive and prescriptive forms. The process of institutional design, based as it is in social knowledge and social prediction, is one of the purest and most outstanding forms of ideas-driven social processes, of institutional order based not on accident but on "deliberation and choice." Therefore, like it or not, institutional theory has to deal with what has been called the problem of "the role of ideas" in institutional order and change. Even in the most decentralized and spontaneous social order in which planning and design are reduced to a minimum, ideas matter. Institutional design is just an extreme case in which this role is so salient and obviously irreducible to other factors, that its relevance as a case study becomes incontestable.

If "institutional theory" is a departure from standard neoclassical economics, then "institutional design" is a departure from the standard model of economic policy theory. To be more precise, institutional theory represents a departure from the model of economic policy growing out of the postwar neoclassical synthesis. As explained by Eggertsson (1997, 63), that model was built around the relation between "targets" and "instruments" within given "systemic parameters." A policy had targets (desired values of endogenous variables derived from the preferences of policymakers), and the targets were reached by applying instruments (exogenous variables controlled by policy-makers). The policy model prescribed what target values were attainable and how they can be attained. Policy targets may have been conceptualized as absolute, or may have been weighted together in a target preference function. Thus the notion was that policy instruments were to be employed either to attain absolute targets or to maximize the target preference function (Hansen, 1963, 7; Tinbergen 1967; Eggertsson 1997, 63).

A theory of economic policy defined in these terms leads ultimately to the view that there are two types of policies: On the one hand is the approach described above—the standard, the so-called quantitative economic policy that takes as given the structure of the economic system and manipulates existing economic relationships toward a specific target. On the other hand, there is a different type of policy, one that seeks to change the structure of the system, the so-called structural policy. If in the case of the first the (immediate) goal is to achieve a new value for a target variable in its model, in the case of the other the objective is to add new variables and to create a new relationship between (new) instruments and targets (Eggertsson 1997, 64). In quantitative policy, the economic system or the structural parameters are exogenous. The rules of the game are given. However, in structural policy the targets are the very parameters. That introduces institutions into the picture. By their very nature, institutions are about the formal and informal "rules of the game"; they are about parameters. This means that structural policy can not be employed effectively without a minimal theory of institutions and institutional change (North 1997, 14–16; Eggertsson, 1997, 63). Structural policy is ultimately insti-tutional policy. We thus have entered the territory of "institutional design," an approach of a nature and magnitude that transcend standard policy designs and theories.

As in the case of any other type of "design," the basic logic of institutional design is constructed by the interplay between ideas about reality (both posi-tive and normative) and reality itself. Understanding the diversity of ways through which ideas shape institutional order is a step further in understand-ing the specific link between institutional theory, institutional design, and institutional change. Ideas shape social order in many ways: as norms and val-ues, as mindsets, as images, as beliefs and background assumptions, as con-ceptual frameworks, as design principles, and so on (Beland and Cox 2010).

When acting through institutional design arrangements, institutional theory ideas are materialized in constitutions, organizational structures, reward systems, strategic plans, practice codes, selection processes, and so forth. Hence in most cases these arrangements reflect the ideas of their designers not only as assumptions, intentions, or values but also as explicit models of causal relationships between rules and consequences. Institutional design starts with the "institutional theorist" (who may well be a layman) who, based on empirical knowledge about the social arena in question (and individual and collective preferences), develops (folk) theories and models about preferable institutional arrangements. The theories are the basis of a potential plan containing ideas for social change. Adopted in various ways by social actors considered guides for action and its evaluation, they end up affecting and changing institutional reality. However, "institutional theory" broadly defined may have an influence at an even deeper level by offering a language for comprehending the world. Language is the ultimate framework shaping the interpretation of reality. "The way people talk about the world has everything to do with the way the world is ultimately understood and acted in" (Eccles and Nohria 1992, 29; Sabetti 2010). Theories become a factor of institutional structure and change as they infuse language and assumptions individuals use to see, understand, and act in the social reality (V. Ostrom 1997).

As a parenthesis it is worth mentioning that all the dimensions of ideas' influence outlined above were, at one point or another, the object of the Bloomington scholars' attention. However, the problem of language itself was a recurring theme in Vincent Ostrom's work. In fact, his work is outstanding within the institutionalism and public choice literature of his generation because of the attention given to the problem of language, a theme otherwise marginal for the mainstream most of the time. This feature did not make his work very popular with his generation of public choice scholars, but may be one of its strengths in the eyes of future generations.

The numerous ways through which ideas and theories can shape reality are not mutually exclusive and, actually, reinforce each other. Yet, for analytical reasons, we have to distinguish between "institutional design" *sensu stricto* and the conceptual framing and the linguistic avenues of institutional construction and change. By its very definition, *institutional design* points toward ideas-driven dynamics in their most unadulterated and rational (conscious) form. The process of institutional design is deliberated, intentional, unequivocally goal-directed, and rooted in strategic rationality. As such, it instantiates one of the most salient roles ideas have in social change, and does so in an explicit and neat mode. Because institutional design *sensu stricto* is one of the clearest forms of ideas-driven social change, it can be seen for analytical purposes as an "extreme" or "crucial" case. In this respect, its study may well exemplify one of Elinor Ostrom's famed research strategies aimed at identifying and studying the "extreme" case, that is, those "social organisms in which the process in case occurs in a clarified, even exaggerated form" (Ostrom 1990, 26). That is to say, students of the role of ideas in institutional order and change have in the problem of institutional design an example of precisely such a case. Symmetrically, students of institutional design have in the problem of ideas a remarkable source of insights and a privileged avenue toward their phenomenon of interest.

The Ostroms' Institutionalism and the Role of Ideas

The outline provided above offers the background against which we can get a preliminary sense of the underlying presence of the theme of ideas in the Ostroms' works. Nonetheless, to identify the specific ways in which this presence and role are theorized, we need an additional effort. As a starting point, one may note that for the Ostroms, political action and institution building can be seen as a continuous series of experiments based on ideas articulated as institutional design principles. For example, when devising rules for grazing rights, people act on ideas and experiment with the consequences of those ideas implemented through rules and institutions. Also, when organizing the access to water rights, people experiment with ideas about the relation between rules and allocation. Or, finally, when implementing a social policy, people experiment with ideas about the causal connection between rules and behavior. And the list continues on.

The Bloomington scholars were not the first to discuss the issue in terms of the links between ideas, action, and social experiments. In this respect, they followed the steps of authors like John Dewey, who in his *Logic* (1938, 508–9) noted that "every measure of policy put into operation is *logically*, and *should* be actually, of the nature of an experiment" (V. Ostrom 1991b, 3–4). An experiment, writes Vincent Ostrom (1993, 19) is an "artifactual creation" that tests a conjecture about hypothetical relationships. In other words, the experiment is informed by a conception (idea, conjecture) about what would be expected to occur. Once designed and implemented, these creations become natural experiments. Consequently, to study institution building is, in many cases, to study something akin to natural experiments in which people try to isolate and engage a set of conjectures about social relationships.

The Ostroms' arguments about the role of ideas could be further presented from an additional angle (Aligica and Boettke 2009; 2011). In order to increase the chances of a society or a community to adapt, grow, and prosper through successful social experiments, one type of knowledge needs to be encouraged as much as possible: the knowledge of social rules and their consequences. Other things being equal, the better the members of a community understand the relationship between rules and behavior, as structured by institutions, the better the society will be organized. This pool of ideas is a crucial communal resource. In fact, writes Vincent Ostrom (1991b, 20), one could even conjecture that the success or failure of modern societies increasingly depends on the knowledge of how these rule-structures transform human conduct at different institutional levels. In this respect, modern societies have created the conditions for the emergence of a science of "knowable regularities, skilled practices, and conjectures about how problematic situations might be conceptualized, structured, and transformed," a more or less systematic effort that explores how "rule-structures may transform individual behavior either in a perverse or benign way" (V. Ostrom [1980] in McGinnis 1999a, 390). This observation offers an undeniably interesting view on institutional theory and institutionalism and their social and evolutionary function.

Taking a closer look at the knowledge of "rule-structures" mentioned above offers an additional angle on the issue. Following the Institutional Analysis and Development framework, such ideas can be classified into three categories, corresponding to the three institutional levels theorized by the Bloomington scholars: (1) the operational level ideas: ideas about the day-to-day decisions made by the social actors, ideas about social and technological processes, and about the most common rules and institutional arrangements of production and exchange; (2) the collective choice level ideas: ideas about the immediate institutions and rules encapsulating the operational activities, the nature of specific organizational arrangements, the procedures and acceptable parameters of institutional change and, in general, about the social technology governing the operational level; (3) the constitutional-choice or constitutive level ideas: ideas that define the meta-level creating a broad conceptual and normative framework within which interactions and institutions are to develop. They are crucial in determining the legitimacy of actors and the rules to be used in crafting the set of collective-choice rules that, in turn, affect the set of operational rules. Constitutive or constitutional ideas are the ultimate framework, the code of operation as well as the source of the institutional meaning of a social system (V. Ostrom [1980] in McGinnis 1999a, 391–92; Aligica and Boettke 2009; 2011). Rule-structure ideas thus function at multiple levels, not only stabilizing the operational environment of individuals' actions but also giving it meaning. Individuals come to operate on the same page, under common knowledge assumptions, in a multiple-level arena. All in all, the emerging grand picture is one in which societies are constituted by the simultaneous operation of several institutional levels, shaped by actions and experiments inspired by various types of ideas that carry with them meanings, operational codes, and values.

In the light of all of the above, we are now in the position to introduce and better understand the relevance of the concept of epistemic choice, as advanced by Vincent Ostrom ([1980] in McGinnis 1999a, 390). In many respects, his argument is a challenge to what he considered to be the increasingly formulaic nature of the second and third generation of public choice scholarship. The concept illuminates the various choice dimensions—operational, public, and constitutional—but at the same time emphasizes that choice in institutional matters is eventually a choice of ideas, and moreover, something intrinsically linked to learning and knowledge. Furthermore, seen from a broader historical and intellectual perspective, social scientists and policy analysts are contributors to a knowledge base (consisting of ideas, theories, and models) for better choices in institutional affairs. We'll get back to that. For now, we should just note, together with Ostrom, that "an emphasis on the intellectual, epistemic element ensures continuity with older traditions" and that Thomas Hobbes, David Hume, and Adam Smith were all preoccupied with "the contingencies of language and their relationships to knowledge, choice, and action." Not only they did "give us foundations for dealing with language, learning, knowledge, communication, artisanship, and moral judgment in the exercise of choice" but they also help us understand why "problems of Epistemic Choice—the choice of conceptualizations, assertions, and information to be used and acted on in problem-solving modes—must necessarily loom large" (V. Ostrom 1997a, 91).

Ideas and Institutional Change

The previous remarks outline the context in which the concept of institutional design is placed in the Ostroms' work. They are an encapsulation of what may be called the "level 1" view of the role of ideas and institutional design (Ostrom 1993; see also Goodwin 1996; Weimer 1995; Koremenos et al. 2004). Such a perspective, relatively static and not very complex, is always the first and easiest theoretical snapshot of the problem. It is in many respects the standard and better-known one. (For an overview of the literature, see Beland and Cox 2011.) Indeed, such a mode of conceptualizing ideas and their role is handy and hence most common among social scientists. Most of them touch it in tangential ways when they discuss the practical implications of their theories; some explore it, but very few go beyond it. In policy terms, its logic invites, more often than not, a plain, clear-cut social engineering interpretation. In the end, by its very definition, institutional design points out toward ideas-driven institutional change in its most unadulterated and rational (constructivist, deliberated) form. In fact, one of the easiest ways to emphasize the role of ideas is to point to the process of rule making and rational design when dealing with social change and to use an input-output policy process model: ideas as inputs, frames, building blocks in the social construction of reality or policy process. It should be no surprise that this invites a reading that sounds close to social engineering.

Even so, mere looking at things in this light, however easy, raises some thought-provoking questions. In what measure is institutional design a form of social constructivism on the lines discussed by F. A. Hayek? In what measure is institutional design vulnerable to the standard criticism of constructivism? What are the limits of the social technology, social construction model? Is the social technology metaphor good enough to understand the phenomenon in question? What is the relationship between institutional design and social engineering? Are they different? And if they are, how are we to characterize the difference? In other words, interesting questions and theoretical insights may be open up once we start to press further.

The fact is that any step beyond the simple and linear "ideas have consequences," "level 1," will confront us with a conceptual jump out of the comfort zone. Few are prepared (for a variety of reasons including methodological stance, metaphysical belief, or mere scientific prejudice) to step further. And indeed, in social sciences a deliberated strategy of radical simplification may be in many cases justified. Nevertheless, in this chapter we'll make the step and take the jump. After all, we try to follow some of the less explored but intriguing and potentially productive insights gained from the Ostroms' writings. And in this respect, there is no doubt that they contain the seeds of a profound and intricate perspective that leads to some intriguing implications, including a more nuanced understanding of institutional design in relationship to, or as opposed to, social engineering. This is a "level 2" view that looks at a more complex and dynamic picture. It is an approach in which time matters, and that shifts the focus toward the problem of the future, toward its structural uncertainty and toward humans' search for predictability and certainty. With it comes a focus on how ideas and institutions operate under the shadow of the future, around the issue of predictability, as instruments of social coordination. The rest of the chapter will look at predictability, at its significance, and even more important, at its implications.

Institutional change theory gives us the context needed to introduce the more dynamic and complex perspective that characterizes the "level 2" approach. Institutional change is approached in a large part of the institutionalist literature from the perspective of long-run equilibria. However, the possibility of multiple equilibria and the fact that these multiple equilibria are a norm rather than the exception makes the limits of this abstract notion obvious. When there are multiple equilibrium paths, the question becomes: which equilibrium is going to be actualized? Two types of possible solutions seem to emerge (Krugman 1991). On one side, one could say that the choice among multiple equilibria is a result of past events, processes, and forces that push toward one institutional configuration or another. "Path dependency" is one extreme member of this family of arguments consisting of a wide variety of styles of reasoning. Ranging from historical accident to historical determinism, the institutional dynamics by which "history matters" is extremely diverse. Arthur (1986), Pierson (2000), Mahoney (2000), David (1994), and Hayek (1973), all offer examples in which the role of past events or processes in determining the long-run equilibria path is very powerful, and one would expect "history" to play some role in most cases.

However, there is another possible approach that circumvents (or at least dampens) the determinism of the past and initial conditions. In this view, the crucial factor affecting the choice of equilibrium is individual beliefs or ideas, via expectations. The mechanism is simple: decisions are a function of the expectations actors have about the future. When expectations feed other expectations, one may even have cases in which pure expectations-based mechanisms are activated. The so-called self-fulfilling prophecies (predictions that evoke new behavior so that the prediction becomes true) are the best-known members of the family. Indeed, one can imagine many cases with multiple equilibria, each of which could be a self-fulfilling prophecy. If everyone thinks that institutional equilibrium A will be the one in which most interests will be satisfied and expects that most will chose it, that may be sufficient to bring to life that equilibrium despite some initial inimical conditions. However, if they believe in B, that may be sufficient to bring to life that alternative equilibrium. In both cases, the equilibrium could happen even in the absence of any *ex ante* coordination plan. From that result one may conjecture that there are many situations in which expectation rather than history is the crucial factor in determining equilibrium and institutional change.

When discussing this issue, the institutionalism literature, with its ever-shifting focus on a variety of factors and variables—number, heterogeneity, scale, trust, reciprocity, social capital, path dependency—has constantly been distracted from it. These essentially ideas-based processes are assumed but rarely, if ever, explicitly investigated. Yet the fact is that in the emergence of institutions, such mechanisms of self-reinforcing circles of beliefs and expectations are essential. One can thus further conjecture that at least some cases of emergence and maintenance of institutional order are best understood through the study of such ideas and future-driven mechanisms (Engel 2005; North 2005; Arthur 1997; Denzau and North 1994; Yee 1996; Sikkink 1991).

In brief, the distinction between past-driven and expectations-driven processes is a useful heuristic device to isolate an important but neglected phenomenon: It is obvious that in most cases a mixture of history and future-oriented ideas and expectations matters and that simple fact should be reflected in our methodologies (Goldstone 1998; 2004; 2008; Tilly 2006; Abbot 2001). Some "common-pool resources" solution mechanisms investigated by Ostrom (1992) offer a good illustration in this respect. Yet for a series of analytical reasons, it is important to start by separating the two. Identifying two ideal types, one in which history matters and one in which future-oriented ideas (sometimes in the pure form of self-fulfilling expectations) matter, puts us in the position to isolate and focus on an issue that although not much discussed in the relevant literature, is crucial: predictability as an inherent functional feature of institutional order. Intrinsic to it is another ancillary theme, as important: the reflexivity of ideas (and by extension, of social systems). We are alerted to the fact that the basic nature of the phenomenon that institutional theory and design are dealing with (i.e., human action) is special in the sense that it has a reflexive feature—the ability to intelligently and strategically react and adjust to past, present, and anticipated changes in rules, environment, or functioning (Buck 1963; 1969, Hands 1998; Boudon 1977; Henshel 1976; 1982; 1993).

To sum up, what we call the "level 2" perspective reorients our attention from the past or from the modeling of (quasi-mechanical) linkages between atemporal ideas and social phenomena, toward a dynamic future. Once we start to recognize how the shadow of the future is casting its influence, we can start to explore the many ways in which the picture changes. Real-time and, more precisely, future-oriented thought and action introduce a new dimension. Images of the future, planning, and expectations bring in dynamism and reflexivity. In the end, "reflexivity" does not just give a clue regarding the purest forms of ideas-driven institutional change but also is a defining feature of the phenomena relevant and associated with institutional design. Its investigation is an investigation of the very essence of institutional design. Taking it into account when operating with phenomena that display it is what makes the difference between social engineering and institutional design. And although as Elkin and Soltan (1999) put it, "the analogy between institutional design and the design of other objects, making rulers into a professional class of social engineers," has been very influential, once the human nature and the nature of social institutions are considered in the light of their reflexivity attribute, the analogy breaks down. To conclude, the important role of expectations and beliefs about the future carried by the social actors in the process of dealing with and constructing the future illuminates the role of ideas. Conversely, the role of ideas and—when it comes to institutional design—their necessary predictive content illuminate the future-oriented dimension, what we called the omnipresent "shadow of the future." In conjunction, the two problems, the reflexivity of ideas and the future dimension intrinsic to ideas in action and design, shift the discussion to a different level.

Predictability Reflexivity and Institutions: Ostrom and Beyond

In Vincent Ostrom's work we find one of the clearest expressions of the "level 1" view of ideas and institutional design. However, the same work also introduces the elements of reflexivity and the future orientation that illustrate the "level 2" perspective. To further substantiate and elaborate this claim, we need to revisit one facet of the social philosophy of institutional order and change advanced by Ostrom. This is a social philosophy that has at its core the problem of knowledge, ideas, and learning, and in which the theory of institutions is part and parcel of a theory of the dynamic and reflexive nature of knowledge processes (Aligica and Boettke 2011b).

Discussing the "threat of uncertainty" as a major problem humans have to confront in their attempts to create social order and looking at the dynamic relationship between ideas and institutions intrinsic to these attempts, Ostrom notes that learning and generating new knowledge "necessarily imply that human beings cannot anticipate the future course of human development" (V. Ostrom 1990; 1991b; 1991c; Popper 1964). Because one cannot predict future knowledge, one cannot anticipate and control the directions of change created by it. But Ostrom (1982a, 34) goes beyond the recognizable Popperian argument. He notes a paradoxical phenomenon: as human capabilities for learning and communication increase, the growth of new knowledge increases the range of imaginable possibilities. That is an inherent source of uncertainty, in addition to the better-known, long-established sources. The growth of knowledge has positive consequences but also undermines existing relationships and disrupts the expectations about the future that are based on them. New possibilities, "if acted upon, manifest themselves as new events, relationships, or occurrences which could not have been anticipated by those who failed to take account of those new possibilities in anticipating the future course of events." Knowledge reacts to knowledge, changing and adjusting itself. An expanding (or even just structurally changing) body of knowledge is nothing less than an ongoing source of new uncertainties and unpredictability.

V. Ostrom makes a complex and sophisticated argument, but its central point is simple. Humans have to deal with the unknowns of the future on an ongoing basis in ways that cannot be standardized. Uncertainty is not a residual when it comes to institutional theory and design: it is a structural problem. Social interaction, even more than nature, has a predictability deficit. Humans need to do their best to predict or control, and for that, they use knowledge and knowledge processes to carve islands of predictability in the ocean of uncertainty. But knowledge cuts both ways. While new knowledge may reduce uncertainty in some areas, it may increase it in many others (V. Ostrom 1982a, 27). Setting aside for a moment the brilliant observation that more knowledge may in fact not reduce uncertainty and unpredictability but increase them, the deepest and most important point is drawing attention to the very problem of predictability itself, as a fundamental task and function of institutional order. Ostrom was not alone in identifying the problem of predictability and management of uncertainty as central to institutional theory. The theme is present in the works of other contemporary authors. Yet,it is easy to miss because it is strongly intertwined with better-known and better-studied problems. Studies of coordination, cooperation, trust, reputation, and so on, all pivot around predictability. That is the reason predictability is always in the picture, most of the time assumed, but rarely dealt with explicitly and on its own terms. Ostrom is among those authors who help us to discern and isolate predictability as paramount for institutionalism and to focus our attention on it.

Given its importance, the relatively low interest that predictability generated until recently is intriguing. After all, the division of labor itself is structurally dependent on it. Simultaneous exchange is, after all very, rare. Most exchange is sequential. Time lags and expectations-based interactions are the norm. In brief, the foundations of comparative advantage and the advantages of a social order based on exchange are a function of it. But the importance of predictability goes beyond exchange. The reciprocal predictability of humans' behavior is essential in almost all types of social interactions. As Christoph Engel (2005), the scholar who has done most in recent years to focus our attention on the issue, notes, we manage to predict reasonably well and interact successfully despite "the almost unlimited plasticity of human behavioural dispositions." Engel claims that, to a substantial degree, it is because of institutions. As he explains it, one can surmise that "in an institution-free environment, the problem of generating predictability would be overwhelming." The human mental apparatus with all its plasticity is a necessary but not sufficient condition to deal with the challenge of the uncertainly in the shadow of the future. The sufficient condition is of an institutional nature. Various degrees of predictability are created by various institutional arrangements, but these areas of stability, in which the plasticity of human behavior is restrained, are sufficient to generate the foundations for social cooperation, coordination, trust, and so on.

This is precisely the direction Vincent Ostrom's argument goes. Containing the threat of uncertainty and chaos requires institutional solutions. Institutions stabilize the range of behavior in predictable patterns. This line of investigation, championed by Engel and anticipated by Ostrom, can be associated with the tradition of research on the rationalizing effect of institutions, that is, a (micro) functionalist tradition of looking at the supportive effect of institutions (O'Driscoll and Rizzo 1985; 39–40). Arnold Gehlen, quoted by Engel (2005, 12), encapsulates the thrust of this line of research: "Institutions protect the individual from the need to take too many decisions. They give him orientation when tossed around by impressions and stimuli... knowing the institutional framework suffices to predict behaviour." Likewise, Ronald Heiner (1989, 1–3) links institutions to predictability. Social institutions should be analyzed as a function of the problem of uncertainty, devices that allow social coordination and cooperation "enabling each agent in the society to know less and less about the behaviour of other agents." Another related line of research identified by Engel is the one opened by authors such as Peter Berger and Thomas Luckmann (1967, 70–85) for whom institutions are building blocks of social construction that help the actor overcome "a double problem of predictability," about the evolution of the context and about other social actors' behavior. Through institutions, the actor "not only gives the context meaning" but also "does so in the same way as all others under the spell of this institution." Similarly, for Jon Elster (1989) there are two fundamental social problems. The first is the cooperation problem, which has been the object of extensive interest on behalf of economists. The second, the predictability problem, was relatively neglected. In brief, institutions may be analyzed both within and outside a standard functionalist model, in the light of their contribution at stabilizing expectations and thus helping to overcome social dilemmas.

Ostrom further develops such ideas in a sophisticated direction. Containing uncertainty need not and cannot amount to generating static predictability. One has to be prepared to deal incessantly with the ongoing "threat" created by relatively dynamic and open social systems in which learning and knowledge production take place continuously, in which ideas, by their very social existence, change social order (Aligica and Boettke 2009; 2011). Hence, the need of rules and institutional arrangements that leave open to choice an entire range of actions and learning processes and at the same time try to channel them in the most beneficial direction. Learning becomes the key. The domain of learning should be understood in broad terms. For instance, learning takes place in markets through prices—profit and loss. Learning also takes place through organizational experiments, failure and success. These are ways to administer knowledge and implicitly manage uncertainty. They all give the possibility to correct errors, to adjust and adapt. This means that, in conditions of uncertainty and reflexivity, the key problem is the error adjustment process, that is, predictability and coordination adjustment. The solution is not a stabilization through rigidity but a process harnessing the learning and reflexivity properties of the system in order to generate a dynamic predictability (Aligica and Boettke 2009; 2011). In other words, as we have already learned from the previous chapters in the discussion on polycentricism and resilience, the focus is not on perfect social mechanisms engineered under the assumption of quasi-total control and full predictability, but on the necessity to try reduce error proneness by building "error-correcting procedures in the organization of decision-making processes" (V. Ostrom 1982a, 32; [1973] 2008; 1990b; Aligica and Boettke 2009).

Such insights emerging from a complex social philosophy of institutionalism and knowledge processes are characteristic of what has been called a "level 2" approach. They are the logical result of a perspective in which the problem of the future (expectations, predictions, and predictability) is central. From such a perspective, institutional arrangements may be seen as mechanisms of coping with the threat of uncertainty by creating spheres of predictability and a process of ordered dynamic social change. That implies a complex mix of institutional and knowledge processes.

In the years since Vincent Ostrom articulated this perspective, an entire research agenda has gained ground at the boundary between institutional theory and behavioral sciences. But that hasn't been easy. We have already noted Engel's work, the scholar who has done most in recent years to focus our attention on the theme of institutions and predictability. Engel remarks that the study of the relationship between institutions and predictability "has never been a fashionable topic" and "has attracted fairly little academic interest so far," despite the underlying consensus in social sciences "that predictability is crucial for social interaction" and despite the endeavors of authors like Elster or Heiner. Engel (2005, 3) explains the long delay through the fact that until recently institutional analysts "have fallen prey to their own role as actors within environments shaped by institutions. They have thus implicitly confounded the roles of observers and actors. In real-life environments, the predictability problem is indeed often not grave." In real life, the most basic problems of predictability have already been solved at the juncture where the analyst starts the investigation. Analysts are simply taking for granted an entire system of coordination that is so deeply embedded and smoothly functioning that is almost imperceptible.

> When they designed their research questions institutional analysts wrongly started from their own real-life experiences. But the neatness of this situation is not natural. It is generated by heavy institutional intervention. Put differently, most context is not simply out there. It has been generated by institutions. This neglected institutional task becomes visible if the analysis starts from the broad concept of predictability. (Engel 2005, 3–4)

It goes without saying that if Engel is right, a fresh look at institutions from this particular angle would reveal that "many of them serve a purpose that is typically neglected by institutional analysis: the generation of predictability" (Engel 2005, 6) and that an entire new domain of social theory is to be built on this insight. In this respect Engel's argument evolves on lines that bolster Ostrom's analytical narrative and advances a three-step approach. First, a behavioral sciences approach shows how "the human mental endowment is a source of dramatic unpredictability." Then a game theoretic approach shows "the limited ability of interaction partners to solve the predictability problem from scratch." And third, an institutionalism approach shows that the solution to the predictability problem is institutional—that is, that "many existing institutions can be interpreted as tools for easing the predictability problem" (Engel 2005, 6).

To sum up, the study of the social and institutional solutions to the problems of uncertainty and predictability emerges as a domain in itself that has its own distinctiveness. Yet this distinctiveness is easy to miss because the central phenomenon defining the domain is strongly intertwined with better-known and better-studied phenomena (studies of coordination, cooperation, trust, reputation etc., all pivot around the problem of predictability) and taken for granted even by some of the most astute institutionalism scholars. In these circumstances, probably the best way to outline the contours of the research domain is simply to delineate it by contrast. First, the social scientific problem of predictability is different from the problem of cooperation or coordination. They may be related, but they are different. In a similar way, rational choice modeling of intertemporal coordination is important and revealing but is far from fully defining it or capturing the essence of the problem of predictability. Methodologically speaking, the important thing is to avoid the trap of analyzing the predictability problem exclusively within the rational choice framework. Also, one needs to separate the rational choice incentives-based approach from an approach in which cognition factors are preeminent. That means avoiding the trap of motivational models in which the cognitive problem is assumed away. Incentives-based analysis could be related to cognition based-analysis, but it operates on essentially different parameters. Last but not least, in studies of predictability, the psychological approach and the institutional approach complement each other and need to be seen in conjunction. In other words, problems of predictability should be considered as part of a broader social process in which cognitive processes and institutional processes intertwine. In light of the clarifications introduced above, the "level 2" perspective gains consistence and contour. Using its logic, old puzzles can be addressed from a fresh angle, while an entirely new set of insights may be developed.

The thrust of the emerging research agenda is thus rather clear: The study of the crucial position prediction and predictability have in the architecture of social order as well as in our theorizing about this order. How do people deal with the problem of uncertainty and predictability? In what ways is that relevant when it comes to institution building and institutional design? How do people deal with the problem of reflexivity? What is the role of institutions? In this respect, it looks possible to rewrite and rethink a large part of social and institutional analysis and theory in the new light offered by the future-oriented, reflexivity-aware perspective. The knowledge process perspective outlined in Vincent Ostrom's social philosophy, seen in conjunction with other convergent lines of research, opens the door to a promising research program. An entire agenda focused on the empirical, theoretical, and phenomenological study of predictability and reflexivity seems to be possible once we decide to look at familiar problems from a new angle. This is not about theories of abstract sequential games or logical paradoxes, including the time factor. It is about the real challenge of predictability in real time and a variety of real-life circumstances and their interdisciplinary analysis. It is about social context, institutional arrangements, and concrete predictability and reflexivity situations or patterns. It is about knowledge-institutional processes and their systematic study.

Based on all of the above, the rest of the chapter will illustrate the intricate insights brought by the link between institutional design, prediction/predictability, and reflexivity, underlying the "level 2" perspective. The first case takes a theoretical puzzle typical for the agenda and demonstrates how the research logic pioneered by Elinor Ostrom's approach to the problem of the "tragedy of the commons" can be replicated in a research topic defining the core of the reflexivity-ideas-design agenda: "the paradox of prediction." The idea is that in this domain, as in those already charted by Ostrom, theoretical models of decision-making and their predictions are just the beginning of a genuine social scientific investigation. The real insights come from the studies of real-life people dealing with the dilemmas and paradoxes postulated in theory and defying in many cases what the abstract logic of models would dictate. The second case uses another future-oriented, reflexivity-related phenomenon (the "prestige loop") to develop some intriguing and challenging insights regarding the complex social processes of which institutional theory and institutional theorists are part and parcel.

Paradoxes of Prediction: Avenues to the Study of Predictability and Reflexivity

Most institutionalist authors, irrespective of the variety of institutionalism they endorse or the mother discipline inspiring them, seem to agree that the object of institutional theory as "a science of rules and their consequences" (Ostrom 1993) is precisely the production of propositions, generalizations, and conjectures about the anticipated dynamics of choices, decisions, and behavior under specific rules of the game. While institutional theory is an epistemic basis of institutional design, institutional design can be seen as an extension in the practical realm of institutional theory. All these features imply a strong predictive element. As an applied theory, its goal is to inspire and guide social change, with the help of those very laws or theoretical generalizations it produces and supports. But in the light of our renewed awareness of the reflexivity problem, the natural question that comes next is this: Do these generalization and predictions really apply as planned when used as design principles? Once things are framed in the context of the "level 2" viewpoint, this question gains new relevance and new dimensions. Following it, we are led to several important insights not only about institutional design but also about the entire research domain we have delineated so far.

Speaking about social theory or social science, Robert Merton (1936, 895) was among the first social scientists to conclude that the "other things being equal" condition used so often in social theory and economics is never true "because the scientist has introduced a new 'other thing': The [scientific] prediction." This is a very interesting observation supported by other scholars. As Nagel (1961: 468–73) pointed out "even when generalizations about social phenomena and predictions of future social events are the conclusions of indisputably competent inquiries," these conclusions "can literally be made invalid if they become matters of public knowledge and if, in the light of this knowledge, men alter the patterns of their behavior upon whose study the conclusions are based" (Nagel 1961, 468). Therefore one can see "social movements developing in utterly unanticipated directions" not only despite but also because of scientific theories and their predictions. This phenomenon indubitably means that the phenomenon "assumes considerable importance for social planning" (Merton 1936, 894; 904). This is a long-established theme that has manifold roots in sociology, decision theory, philosophy, and economics. Its overdue examination in the context of institutional theory may thus benefit from the insights gained in multiple attempts to deal with it in multiple disciplines.

As many scholars have pointed out, the social sciences' predictions would "certainly cause actions which would upset the predictions" (Merton 1936, 895–6; Popper 1964; 1948; Grunberg 1985). Why should institutional theory based on prediction be different? Any regularity observed or detected can be introduced as an institutional design principle in an attempt to change and stabilize the institutional reality around it. But once introduced, it can be "reflected" by social actors through an adjustment of expectations, and therefore "the outcomes of reflection may transcend the earlier observed regularity" (Veld 1991, 4; Henshel 1976; Vetterling 1976; Buck 1969; Kemp 1962; Krishna 1971). As a consequence, in the institutionalist case, too, "the regularity may potentially lose its validity, because the underlying assumptions concerning human behavior have undergone change" (Veld 1991, 4). According to this line of reasoning, any regularity or law concerning institutional systems, once formulated and made public in the system where it is aimed to be a design principle, is in danger of becoming ineffective (Aligica 2008).

In brief, the propositions produced by institutional theory that are institutional design relevant are potentially vulnerable to reflexivity. Hence, a problem: On the one hand, due to reflexivity, social systems may react (in unanticipated ways) to applied propositions. On the other hand, attempts to reach levels of abstraction and generalization that may increase the propositions' immunity lead to propositions that are useless for applied purposes. The bottom line is that reflexivity manifested as an "altering prediction" weakens the effectiveness of prediction. Scientific predictions in institutional affairs can easily become altering predictions. If that is the case, not only has one identified a difficulty in theory building and prediction making about institutional affairs, but one has also identified a fundamental difficulty for institutional design.

Despite the marked relevance of the phenomenon, the institutionalist literature seems to forget it much too often. Institutional design principles emerging out of institutional research sound too often like lists of propositions about natural systems impervious to reflexivity, contingency, and strategic rationality. Even if they recognize the importance of ideas, they embrace only what we have called the "level 1" perspective and assume a illusory linearity in the ideas-design-practical applications sequence (Coram in Goodin 1996, 94). That has very important repercussions for the relevance and usefulness of the institutional theory as a policy-relevant discipline. One can thus pinpoint the predicament of the institutional theorist: On the one side is the double temptation to think of institutionalism as a standard scientific technology and forget that the phenomena of its interest are defined by reflexivity, as well as the temptation to make everything too abstract and too general and thus contextually irrelevant for practical purposes. On the other side is the danger of reflexivity and the ambiguity that it introduces. Generalization and simple rules recede into the background. Contextual and conjunctural strategic rationales take the front stage. The "level 2" dimension in thinking about institutional design and the role of ideas brings with it a universe of profound complexities and uncertainty.

Let us push the discussion further and make a move that echoes the unconventional spirit of the Ostromian approach as well as the very notion of reflexivity. What happens when we apply the insights we gained in the study of institutions to the very institution that produces institutional knowledge (i.e., knowledge, ideas about institutions)? We have already seen that if we take seriously the relationship between public predictions, social action, and institutional change, then the problem of institutional design and public predictions emerges as a pivotal problem of applied institutional theory. Announcing the identification or implementation of a new regularity, institutional theory can alter the system it is making predictions about. Following this logical line, one can infer from the impossibility of predicting the dynamics of institutional systems not only the limits of institutional theory but also the impracticality of institutional design. This argument profoundly preoccupied the pioneers of the study of predictions (Stack 1978; Henshel 1971; 1982). How can the infinite regress—prediction, self-alteration, revised prediction, self-alteration—be stopped? The question seemed to be more than a mere theoretical game—such regress invalidates the very notion of regularity-based public policy design. The theoretical possibility of regress and the prediction "impossibility" paradox were identified from the beginning as a key problem in social sciences and generated a literature that branched into rational expectation theory (Grunberg and Modigliani 1954; Simon 1954; Lucas 1976) and sociology of knowledge (Merton 1948; Henshel and Kennedy 1973; Bloor 1976). It looks like the attempt to solve this paradox of the ever elusive match between ideas and reality (or expressed in institutionalist terms, between the theory of institutions and the reality of institutional processes) was crucial as a step in the legitimization of the public policy relevance of their work. How is institutional design possible despite the paradoxes of prediction? Or, assuming the existence of such predictions, how is it possible to have a consistent theoretical account of the possibility of institutional design?

Once we have reached this point, we can easily detect a familiar pattern, from research done recently in social sciences. The pattern is this: A theoretical claim is made regarding a certain class of phenomena or a certain type of situation, based on a model (usually a rational choice one). For instance, rationality dictates that in normal circumstances a common-pool resource will be overused because collective action won't happen. The prediction comes with the full legitimacy and weight of a powerful and highly regarded analytical engine. But once the theoretical prediction starts to be seriously examined through case studies, it collapses under the pressure of empirical evidence and more nuanced theorizing. This is a something well illustrated by Elinor Ostrom's work on the tragedy of the commons and theories of collective action. The question is in what measure that approach may be extended. The "paradoxes of prediction" theorizing seem to be a member of the same family. If that is the case, one can simply look at the aforementioned studies and use them as an outline of some plausible research directions of a "level 2" research agenda. In this respect, one can even say that we are talking about an agenda that is inspired both by Vincent Ostrom's social philosophy of knowledge processes and institutions and incorporates the basic logic of Elinor Ostrom's most well-known research strategy. But the most important thing in the context of the current discussion is that, mirroring approaches that have a similar logic and using them as models, we can even anticipate and sketch the various directions the work may take.

First one may expect some theorists to revisit the line of literature originating in Grunberg and Modigliani (1954) and Herbert Simon (1954), who tried to show that under specific conditions it can be formally demonstrated that a "coordinated prediction" exists for certain self-altering situations such that the infinite regress of prediction/self-alteration/revised prediction/ self-alteration/... "comes to a halt in a finite number of steps" (Henshel 1976, 14; Grunberg and Modigliani 1963; 1965; Galatin 1976; Devletoglou 1961). The problem of infinite regress is thus removed. These theorems do not identify the specific solution but demonstrate that a solution is conceptually possible. Or, as Henshel (1976, 14) put it, "such possibility theorems merely show that

the door is not barred; they do not furnish the precise tools for opening it."
And thus one may expect a series of theorists to further elaborate and speculate on these lines.

A second line of response may be to simply say that although theoretically
possible, the predictive regress is not a significant problem in real life. The
domain and magnitude of such phenomena are limited. An entire set of quali-
fying factors creates strong limits: unpublicized predictions, highly esoteric
predictions, predictions incorporating magnitudes that individuals cannot
measure unaided, predictions requiring technical skills, predictions released
solely to a selected audience, predictions invoking opposition from "gatekeep-
ers," predictions about persons with limited comprehension or about social
isolates, predictions regarded as unimportant or unbelievable, predictions
about unalterable events, and so on (Henshel 1976). Other factors and variables may enter the picture and change the parameters of the process. This
is both a theoretical and an empirical point. However, its ultimate relevance
for institutional design rests on empirical grounds. Because the problem is
not "present across all of the topics of social science" by itself, "it does not
demonstrate the inherent unpredictability of all events and processes of the
entire domain" (Henshel 1976, 14; Henshel and Kennedy 1973). It requires a
situational analysis. Some situations and predictions are immune, while others are more vulnerable. By implication, this statement applies to institutional
design situations. All of the above make the task of institutional design less
vulnerable. One may anticipate a lot of work on these lines, exploring concrete
cases and their specific configurations of variables.

These types of arguments can lead (separated or in conjunction) to further elaborations using the paradox of prediction as a vehicle to a better
understanding of the conditions of institutional design and predictability.
For instance one can make the case that institutional design is still possible
despite the regress paradox because of the uncertainty, knowledge asymmetries, and other structural information imperfections present in social systems. Thus institutional design prediction becomes operational due to the
"arational" dimension of the social system. The introduction of that dimension gives a more realistic representation of the nature of the system than the
full information, full rationality implied in the abstract assumptions that lead
to the theoretical possibility of an infinite regress, with no accurate public
prediction possible. That means that the models and discussions of institutional design assuming full rationality are bound to exaggerate both the
incidence and the magnitude of the phenomenon. Also, they distort the reality of institutional design, and do not capture realistically the situations when
design predictions accomplish their task. One may go as far as the claim that

the entire discussion reveals the problems created by uncritical reliance on rational choice theory, following up to the extremes of the logic of abstract rational choice models. An alternative approach integrating ignorance, uncertainty, asymmetric information, and learning in social contexts opens thus the door for further elaborations that look at the problem from a more realistic and nuanced angle.

A telling example of how this alternative could be developed is to follow Veld (1991, 3–19), who outlines a process in which institutional design is not a matter of total success (i.e., the design is 100% implemented and effective) or total failure. Instead, attention shifts to the more realistic situation where one has a mixture of design effectiveness combined with a structural diminishing effectiveness of design and control due to a process of learning and adaptation. In it, the institutions, or more precisely the individuals affected by the institutional design, gradually change and adapt as they react in a reflexive manner, illustrating exactly the features Vincent Ostrom described in his discussion of learning, error, and adaptability in social systems. Initially they will take the new rule as an incentive to change their behavior in a direction that corresponds more or less to the intentions of the designer. But "that change at the same time, in many instances, contains deviation from their own most preferred alternative, and therefore is experienced as a disagreeable event." It is just natural that "in due course the reflecting actors will utilize their learning capacity to avoid the disagreeable effects of the policy concerned." Actors do not predict from the beginning and then get trapped or paralyzed in a prediction regression cycle instantly set into motion. Instead, they learn and adjust their behavior as time goes by. The learning lags and the time factor are crucial. At the same time, the processes affecting the application of design principles, while still reflexive, are different from the pure logic of reflexive alteration. In general they will gradually succeed better and better as time goes by. "Avoidance, sabotage, disobedience, resistance, and any other kind of creative activity to restore the original level of satisfaction can be observed. Thus the objectives of the regulating will go through a gradual decrease of effectiveness" (Veld 1991, 5). Cycles can appear in this case too, although they are of a different nature: "we might expect that after a correcting accumulative policy measure a new period of diminishing effectiveness will start. A seemingly infinite series of interactive actions could take place." And thus, "Gradually the corrective adaptations will decrease in impact, [and] as a consequence effectiveness will decrease more and more until eventually crisis will emerge" (Veld 1991, 4–6).

The bottom line is that once a layer of complexity and realism is added over the initial model, the dynamics of the reflexive phenomena look quite different. A "gradual decrease of effectiveness" of the institutional change, as prompted by the institutional design principle, is different from the total and instant annulment of the design concept from the very beginning, through the regress of prediction, alteration, revised prediction, and so on. The diversity of mechanisms by which ideas, knowledge, and learning affect institutional design and institutional change can be thus larger. And the reflexive predictions' domain, although sizable, is less extended than the pure rational choice-based theory may lead us to believe. The self-fulfilling prophecies at work in reality are less clear-cut and more intricate than the theoretical models imply. Yet, when all is said and done and the feasibility domain has been delineated with a modicum of clarity, the bottom line remains the same: Reflexivity remains a key challenge for institutional design and institutional theory. The fact that the challenge is more empirical and situation-dependent and difficult to generalize makes it even more noteworthy.

To sum up, an approach that recognizes the primacy of the situation-dependent elements shifts our attention from the abstract theoretical formulas to the concrete ways in which the problems are solved in social reality. One can see here a pattern similar to the manner in which Elinor Ostrom has dealt with the tragedy of the commons, as theorized by Garrett Hardin (and incidentally with the game-theoretical predictions regarding collective action). Ostrom took as a starting point the theoretical predictions and the speculations based on them that claimed irrefutable tragedies and failures of collective action but went beyond that. She demonstrated that although in some cases those predictions were valid, people cooperate in many other cases, avoiding the predicted consequences. She refuted the abstract scenarios and made an effort to show how people deal in real life, in real circumstances, with the social dilemmas created by commons. Her work was focused on the phenomenon, not on the various formal renditions of it. It was a genuine social research agenda, concentrating mainly on social and institutional realities, not on abstract models of reality. In a similar way, the paradox of prediction challenges us to think seriously about how people manage to overcome in real life such problems of reflexivity. In brief, it suggests the beginning of a research agenda. Instead of commons and their tragedies, one looks at predictability and reflexivity and their dilemmas and paradoxes. We take the conceptual puzzle as a starting point, but we go from there to a grounded research effort. After all, the truly interesting thing when dealing with the problem of reflexivity is not the logical and formal nature of such paradoxes but the real-life social, psychological, and institutional processes people use to deal with the problems of uncertainty, expectations, and predictability.

Prestige Loop, Predictive Power, and Institutional Design

We complete this exploratory discussion prompted by insights from the Ostroms' work and that started with a rather unconventional focus on institutional design and the role of ideas, returning to the theme of institutional design and its relationship with institutional theory. As the recent literature on "performativity" (particularly performativity in economics) demonstrates, the relationship between the dynamics of ideas and social reality is a fascinating ground for understanding the role of social and economic theories in social change and the social construction of social reality (MacKenzie 2006; MacKenzie, Muniesa, and Siu 2007). Indeed, in an ironic way, the best illustration of the institutional design and social change relevance of reflexivity and predictions is precisely in the area of schools of thought or scientific disciplines. More precisely, the concept of self-fulfilling predictions may put us in the position to identify avenues through which the phenomenon they designate works in establishing and sustaining the salience, impact, prestige, and influence of disciplines (or schools of thought) in the social sciences. Reflexivity comes full circle in an ironic twist when we use institutional theory to study institutional theory itself. To outline the argument, we'll follow Richard Henshel's work, the scholar who introduced the key concept for this discussion: "prestige loops" (Henshel 1976, 43; Aligica 2009, on which the rest of the section is based).

The origins of the concept of the prestige loop can be identified not only in the abstract theory of self-fulfilling prophecies but also in the plain observation that the practical performance of a social theory or discipline is a condition of its prestige. Once a social theory is employed in practice, the results, predictions, and applications matter. The more successful they are, the more prestige the theory and discipline will get. The more prestige they get, the more they will be employed, used, referred to, and so on. This standard feedback mechanism is straightforward and uncontroversial. This is a virtuous circle that any discipline or theory wishes to set into motion (or a vicious one if its functioning the other way round, and then the disciplines try to avoid it). Yet in discussing this essential feedback loop, one important possibility is usually forgotten: that disciplinary prestige can influence predictive power. What if the very prestige of a predictor sets into motion the self-fulfilling mechanisms leading to the confirmation of the prediction? This is indeed a very intriguing phenomenon. Scenarios in which the prestige of predictions generates self-fulfillment via a feedback loop are not difficult to imagine:

> The "prestige loop" begins with a prediction from a source identified with a particular discipline. The prestige of the discipline, via one of

> several paths, affects the accuracy of the prediction, and this degree of accuracy, in turn, acts upon the prestige of the predictor and his discipline. (Henshel 1976, 4)

As Henshel explains, the real nature of the process is further illuminated when one shifts the attention from single predictions to a sequence of predictions and then to their long-run consequences. In both cases, the reliability of the prediction will be strongly influenced by the credibility and prestige of its source. But in the case of reiterated predictions, the initial prediction alters the context of the following predictions (Simon 1954). The credibility of the next forecast will be affected by the previous predictions. Each new round builds on the previous rounds. Thus the reiteration process generates an increase or decrease of prestige. Election poll predictions constitute an excellent example in this respect. Polls affect contributions. A poll predicting a winner results in an increase of enthusiasm and contributions. Funding affects logistics, strategy, advertising, and staffing. The election results reflect these factors. That increases the prestige of polling. Next electoral cycle, polling predictions get attention, prestige, and even more influence.

> Each individual increment of influence extended on predictive power by changes in disciplinary prestige may be small, but once a threshold is passed, "deviation amplification" can occur...and make small incremental changes cumulatively important. One could speak of a prestige loop for individual prophecies with a built-in multiplier effect. (Henshel 1976, 43)

The phenomenon, if properly understood, can offer indeed a unique understanding of the relationship between social sciences and social reality and, more precisely in our case, between institutional theory, institutional design, and institutional change.

The pioneering work of Richard Henshel on the influence of prestige on predictive power (1975; 1976; 1990; 1993) shows that prestige loops "represent radical departures from accepted views about the nature of prediction" but are more than a theoretical curiosity. They are a challenge to the way we understand the relationship between theory and design, between ideas and reality. The circularity defining them "is no mere game of the intellect but a severe practical problem" because it is not just a matter of academic, technical prediction but also a matter of social construction and control. Henshel presses the discussion to deal explicitly with the issue of design: The more a discipline is involved in creating/designing systems, the more chances it has to stabilize the range of the social reality of disciplinary interest under a set of regularities. The more that happens, the more its predictive power will be manifest, and the confidence in it will consequentially grow. In fact, one can classify various types of natural and social systems as points on a continuum as a function of the different mechanisms and processes by which degrees of organization and "stabilization" are introduced. And that, in his view, is related to how "regularities," once introduced, influence prediction capabilities through prestige loops. As we have seen, at one extreme are "engineered systems"—artificial systems that give almost full control over their functioning to their draftsmen. At the other extreme of the continuum are the "unaltered systems." In between are the "designed systems" (Henshel 1976, 4, 43).

Engineering systems are usually seen as a reference point and a yardstick for the assessment of the relationship between theory, prediction, and design. Once the test is applied to social sciences disciplines, two facets of the same reality are revealed: First, the fact that there are few engineered systems in society has definitely something to do with the limited predictive capacity of social sciences. Second, the fact that successful social prediction is very rare may have something to do with the fact that there are few engineered systems in society. However, notes Henshel, "rather than an 'either/or' choice this can be viewed as a vicious circular process." As long as a discipline "is low in prestige it lacks the *power* and *legitimacy* to create engineered systems." But "so long as engineered systems are absent, disciplinary prestige remains low because social phenomena in an unaltered state do not lend themselves readily to prediction." Leaving aside for a while the issue of social engineering and its moral and political implications, the emphasis should be put on the "dilemmas of social research" given by "a peculiar circularity." As Henshel synthesizes the issue:

> So long as engineered social systems are lacking, prediction will remain impoverished, although progress in limited regions may be detectable. Yet without the assurance provided by predictive successes, the confidence to think in terms of system creation and the conviction required to overcome resistance to such creation is lacking. This failure to create scientifically based designed systems in society results in predictive mediocrity, so that the circle remains unbroken. (Henshel 1976, 41–42)

Or, as Dewey explained in "Social Science and Social Control," putting the discussion on pragmatist terms:

> It is a complete error to suppose that efforts at social control depend upon the prior existence of a social science. The reverse is the case. The

building up of social science, that is, of a body of knowledge in which facts are ascertained in their significant relations, is dependent upon putting social planning into effect.... Physical science did not develop because inquirers piled up a mass of facts about observed phenomena. It came into being when men intentionally experimented, on the basis of ideas and hypotheses, with observed phenomena to modify them and disclose new observations. This process is self-corrective and self-developing. Imperfect and even wrong hypotheses, when acted upon, brought to light significant phenomena which made improved ideas and improved experimentation possible. The change from a passive and accumulative attitude into an active and productive one is the secret revealed by the progress of physical inquiry. (Dewey [1931] 1998, 277)

Economics is indeed considered by many the sole social sciences discipline that comes close to inspiring something comparable to engineered systems, via the materialization of its theories through institutional arrangements. Because of its many applications, both at the macro and micro level (the Federal Reserve System, production and distribution optimization systems in business, etc.), economics has a considerable impact on "the way in which major contemporary social institutions are organized and carry on their business" (Biderman 1969, 129; Wible 1998; Coats 1993). And when institutional arrangements "take forms that accord with the postulates and conceptual apparatus of the science [of economics]," that definitely facilitates the prestige and influence economics has. In other words, economics is a paradigmatic case study of how a discipline "with sufficient prestige" can eventually "shape the institutional forms of its subject matter" within certain limits imposed by the social reality and "pervade the thinking on the subject [such] that many of its postulates appear obvious a priori science" (Biderman 1969, 130).

The ramifications of the process, once set into motion, go even further. For instance, once a theoretical framework is institutionalized, data start to be created or collected on the predefined conceptual lines of the theory that inspires the institutional design. This has, to be sure, consequences for the mother discipline. With more data (and also data that happen to be prefitted to a theoretical framework) the status and the potential of "scientific analysis" of the discipline increase. In the case of economics, it looks as if "the life of the society produces data that accord directly with the models of economics with regard to units, processes, and relationships, precisely because these models are the ones used to guide and rationalize so much of social activity" (Biderman 1969, 129). Not only are more data available but also the standards and criteria through which policy evaluations are made "become, unconsciously, quite close to the mode of thinking of the scientist, so that the predictive validity of his instruments becomes increasingly easy to demonstrate" (Henshel 1976, 45; Biderman 1969; Coats 1993). Thus, in the end, the very existence of available data may work as a reconfirmation mechanism for the disciplinary paradigm inspiring the data collection in that specific frame.

The feedback loops may also explain the financial and public support for a discipline. As many have pointed out, the growth of a discipline depends to a considerable degree upon the financial support it receives. The number and quality of researchers of a school of thought depend in a significant measure on the available resources (Wible 1998; Coats 1993). But financial support can be also seen as part of a feedback loop. "Support enhances predictive power, predictive power enhances prestige, and prestige in turn unlocks the coffers. Where and how does this cycle begin? The concept of the prestige loop may provide a conceptual tool for this question in the sociology of science" (Henshel 1976, 41–42).

To sum up, prestige loops are far from a mere theoretical construct. Economics offers an outstanding example of this phenomenon at work. Once locked in a prestige loop, social science predictions may get increasing self-fulfilling attributes and set into motion a dynamics that in the case of economics has pushed it as a discipline to visibility and social influence. In fact, a two-way street between effectiveness in applications and disciplinary reputation is being opened.

A Change of Perspectives

The logic of what we called the Ostromian "level 2" approach to the problem of ideas and institutional design has taken us slowly but steadily into a less known and less understood domain of institutional theory. We saw how the theme of reflexivity and feedback loops invites us to raise a series of important questions regarding the way we understand not only the link between social theory and social reality but also the nature of what counts as disciplinary success and the means to achieve it.

Thus the discussion lays bare the complex and captivating role of the applications aimed at designing institutional systems and arrangements that, once institutionalized, create the conditions for the emergence of robust prestige loops. A key lesson one can learn from these studies is that prestige is a rare and domain- and issue-specific powerful resource. One may speculate that prestige loops suggest that, within certain given limits, a social theory can conceivably alter its own accuracy and prestige by a judicious selection, or withholding, of predictions. There are grounds to think that applied institutional theory can influence the accuracy of its own performance (predictive or design) through an intelligent administration of the combined effect of institutional theory predictions and the institutional designs associated with them. This discussion sheds a totally new light on the paths of advancement of the interface between theory and social reality. And although the practical and operational consequences of that relationship are far from clear or certain, the conceptual and theoretical implications are rather consequential. We have reached a very interesting conjecture: institutional design really matters for the prospect of institutionalism as a research school or program, because to be effective, ideas and theories are packaged and presented to the public not so much as a corpus of knowledge but as institutional designs or institutional design solutions.

Recognizing the relevance and legitimacy of the problem of prestige loops and self-fulfilling prophecies has theoretical implications for the applied institutional theory agenda and, in general, for any social science discipline aiming at a significant applied dimension. The most fundamental is a reconsideration of the relationship between the pure epistemic element of a discipline (theoretical and empirical generalizations) and the nature and objectives of its applied agenda. Although the literature speaks of a confrontation of theories, hypothesis testing, and so on, it may be the case that the place where the institutional theory gets its final validation and is confirmed as a worthy pursuit is the public debate arena and institutional change practice (Wible 1998; North 2005; Ostrom 1993). Because institutional theory is at its core a science of rules and behavior within rules, institutional theory (perhaps more than any social sciences program) lives or dies through its social applications.

That doesn't mean that epistemological and methodological accuracy defined by the standard criteria are not important. Yet their role is instrumental in the sense that it is probably best defined from a pragmatist philosophy perspective: a view in which the social practice is an important factor and criterion. If the processes identified as "prestige loops" are a good predictor of disciplinary success, then the academic disciplinary arena cannot be seen in isolation from the larger arena that includes the domain of applications. As one may have noticed by now, the argument of this chapter leads inexorably toward an already familiar theme: a challenge to the conventional wisdom and especially complacency in accepting uncritically a certain set of epistemological and philosophical stances. One may see again how the sociology of the "growth of knowledge" becomes as important as its epistemological legitimization. Both seem to be inviting, again, a more or less philosophically pragmatist outlook. If the agenda advances not only by cumulating small bits and pieces of knowledge gathered by researchers but also through a much larger social process, of which design and applications are a critical element, the processes of institutional change, institutional design, and the intellectual agenda of the discipline are related in profounder and more intricate ways than we may have thought under the conventional assumptions.

The corollary of the previous point is that the applied agenda of a research program (such as the "new institutionalism") means more than applying (more or less pretested or empirically established) propositions to specific situations. Like it or not, it also has something to do with the creation of institutional and reputation bases with a view to practice; and in fact this is precisely what happens in the real life of the field, although none of this is described or prescribed by the epistemology and philosophy claimed to be its source of inspiration. Accordingly, institutionalists may have something interesting to learn from investigations into the institutional basis of institutional theory itself.

Taking seriously the applied-level ambitions of institutionalism, what has been dubbed the "level 2" perspective that leads us to the problem of predictions, predictability, reflexivity, and prestige loops, invites thus a radical change of perspective in which institutional theory ideas and the agents and organizations promoting these ideas are not mere neutral observers but elements of a dynamic and reflexive social system. With that comes indeed a more nuanced understanding of the role of the "institutional theorist" in a social change process in which institutional theory ideas are a factor of institutional change, institutionalism as a discipline is a vehicle of change, and institutional design (via expert knowledge or citizens' competence) is a tool of social change. That is indeed a bold claim as it challenges profoundly the way we think about the role of institutional theorists and their ideas, as well as the role their epistemic communities play in the process. The institutional analysis of the institutionalization of institutional theory seems to be a fascinating topic.

To make a long story short, the ramifications of this perspective that privileges "practice" in relationship to "theory" for the way institutionalism and the progress of its agenda are considered, are substantial. There is a sharp contrast between, on the one hand, the standard views that emphasize the predictive and explanatory power of independent propositions or hypothesis and, on the other hand, the more holistic and socioinstitutional approach involving practical applications, prestige loops, and the growth of the institutional infrastructure of the discipline itself. In the second view, the production and refutation in academic settings of the standard scientific conjectures and propositions continues to be a vital part of the process. Yet that activity is recognized as being not more nor less than exactly what it is: an important input into a larger process. That means a shift from a perspective focused almost exclusively on the purely epistemic and technical aspects of the internal debates in the epistemic community (i.e., discussing and testing ideas in closed communities of like-minded scientists) to an enlarged perspective that balances the pure academic view with a concern for what happens outside of the discipline when the ideas produced by academic institutionalists are implemented or evoked and used in practice.

That being said, it is important to also recognize the concerns many institutionalist scholars may have with the ethical repercussion of such an approach. Many may fear that the preoccupation with the design of social systems entails what may count as forms of manipulation or of altering (up to annihilation) established institutions by a dictatorship of optimization social engineers. Regarding these claims, it is interesting to note institutionalists' widespread ambivalence toward the applied dimension of their work. On the one hand are the emphatic claims of policy relevance that they make in favor of their field. Yet, on the other hand, they do not seem to be prepared to think thoroughly what that relevance may mean in practical and ethical terms. Hence, one observers a lingering vagueness regarding the practical and ethical dimensions of their claims. But the fact is that to be an "institutionalist" means that the knowledge you produce, if worthy, may be used in practice for good or evil. Even more important, institutional design happens in all societies all the time, whether one admits that or not. The question is how informed those designs are by the accumulated scientific knowledge on institutions and their impact. Designed social systems may sometimes be a threat to human freedom or well-being, especially when they are fueled by a social engineering and constructivist attitude (Hayek 1973/1974). However, to conclude from that that all attempts to design institutions would be dangerous and immoral is a fallacy that should be avoided (Henshel 1976, 58; Simon 1969; Ostrom 1992).

In this respect, the way Elinor Ostrom (interview in Aligica and Boettke 2009, 159) defines the ultimate questions and objectives of te Bloomington institutionalism is telling because it shows that besides the negative and gloomy side, things may also be seen from a more pragmatic and hopefully angle:

> How can fallible human beings achieve and sustain self-governing entities and self-governing ways of life? How can individuals influence the rules that structure their lives?...[O]ne of our greatest priorities...has been to ensure that our research contributes to the education of future citizens, entrepreneurs in the public and private spheres, and officials at all levels of government. We have a distinct obligation to participate in this educational process as well as to engage in the research

enterprise so that we build a cumulative knowledge base that may be used to sustain democratic life. Self-governing, democratic systems are always fragile enterprises. Future citizens need to understand that they participate in the constitution and reconstitution of rule governed polities and to learn the "art and science of association." If we fail in this respect, all our investigations and theoretical efforts are useless.

The Ostroms thus join the company of those who reject the notion that institutional design should be the exclusive object of a profession, a specialization, and expertise; on the contrary, they consider it a core element of citizens' competence and as such a basic ingredient of self-governance and democracy (Elkin and Soltan 1999; Boettke 2010; Boyte 2011; Levine 2011; Soltan 2011). In so assessing it, they suggest that social manipulation and control may not be the inescapable outcome of the growth and refinement of our institutional knowledge. No doubt it is something to be concerned about. But at the same time, there is no alternative way to deal with this concern other than to better understand the nature of institutional order and change given the diversity of human beliefs, preferences, and institutions and to spread that knowledge among citizens as much as possible. Diversity—human and institutional—plus a widespread understanding of the basic ideas of the "science and art of association" by the social actors interacting within a polycentric system may lead (with a little bit of luck) to a self-governing, free, and resilient social order. We are again, as in the case of each of the other intellectual itineraries outlined by the previous chapters, returning to an underlying theme of the Ostromian theoretical universe. This is the point where, before drawing a final line, we need to note another recurring theme. As we have repeatedly seen in the previous chapters, the new or refurbished conceptual lenses needed to approach and describe this type of order come with a challenge. They seem to require a reassessment of the epistemological and social philosophical foundations of our approach to institutionalism and political economy in general. The next chapter will concentrate on a possible response to that challenge.

6

Institutionalism and Pragmatism

OUR OVERVIEW OF Ostromian institutionalism in the light of a number of concepts that have a central position in its architecture and that are still a work in progress, inviting further elaborations, has revealed how the research directions intrinsic to their development are opening the way for a new phase in theorizing about collective action, governance, and institutional arrangements. At the same time, we have seen again and again how, followed to their logical implications, they invite us to rethink assumptions, methods, and entire foundational perspectives. The idea that the Ostroms' work challenges us in more than one way to reassess the interface between philosophy and social sciences needs no further illustration. The question is: Is there an underlying theme, a certain philosophical profile emerging out of all this?

To answer the question, one has to look not only at the textual references but also at the clues offered by the underlying logic of this work. The most elementary clue is that the focus on social dilemmas, governance, coordination problems, and their solution in real-life settings sets up from the very beginning a particular tenor that gives a place of preeminence to social practice and problem-oriented perspectives. This "primacy of practice" brings into the picture particular philosophical assumptions and implications. We have already seen this at work in several instances in the previous chapters. In a sense, these chapters can be read as a series of case studies that share a converging logic. If we consider them in conjunction, we discern between the lines a philosophical contour that is unmistakably associable with the pragmatist intellectual tradition. A nonpositivist, fallibilist, and realist epistemology, a social philosophy of knowledge processes and social coordination, a penchant for normative pluralism and experientialism—this is a cluster typically associated with the pragmatist tradition, broadly defined. In brief, it is plausible that the Ostroms' work entails a broader pragmatist philosophical stance and that, as such, it resonates with an incipient scholarly movement that is repositioning the foundations of institutional theory and political economy in that direction.

This chapter will elaborate this argument. Before moving further, let's make clear what this chapter does not do or claim. First, it does not explore the indirect link between the classical pragmatist agenda and Ostroms' work as revealed by the "old institutionalism" whose influence on Elinor Ostrom's theory of social rules, via John R. Commons ([1924] 1968) has been both acknowledged and discussed in the literature (Groenewengen 2011). Second, it does not claim that the Ostroms have deliberately and systematically built up a social philosophy perspective that they called "pragmatist." The chapter does not even claim that they have been fully aware of the entire range of consequences emerging from the fact that their work has such a strong affinity with philosophical pragmatism. What it is claimed instead is that their views and attitudes have a natural propensity toward assumptions and modes of theorizing, toward approaches, ways of asking questions and of finding solutions, that we normally associate with a broad intellectual tradition that we call pragmatism. They have been dissatisfied with the mainstream approaches in terms of both methods and philosophical foundations, and they have searched for an alternative. Hence the chapter argues that pragmatist elements have been a constant tacit presence in their work and that the task of fully developing the philosophical dimension of institutionalism on those lines emerges naturally, once we start to recognize the underlying logic of their endeavors.

Common Themes, Converging Logics

The presence and influence of pragmatist themes and ideas in the Ostroms' work is documentable, and the textual evidence is uncontroversial. In a similar way, their discomfort with the epistemological position embraced by the mainstream, more precisely with its positivism, is documentable and unmistakable. One of the clearest expressions of that dissatisfaction may be found in a book edited by Elinor Ostrom and dedicated to strategies of inquiry (Ostrom 1982). In the preface, she discusses (under the telling title "Beyond Positivism") what she considers the predicament of political sciences in the second half of the 20th century. This discussion is more that illuminating, and it is worth delving into it while taking a closer look at her choice of words.

Her argument starts with a double observation. While a general theory of political life would be more than desirable, no such theory has emerged despite the programmatic efforts of contemporary political scientists (Ostrom 1982, 16). To explain why that is the case, she looks at the way political science as an academic discipline (and the training in it) evolved in the second half of the 20th century. The novel and fashionable, more sophisticated methods taking social sciences by storm required substantial methodological and quantitative training. And thus, many graduate students who did not have a philosophical, logical, or quantitative schooling as undergraduates came to "take heavy courseloads in statistics and methods and fewer courses where they might be exposed to the development of systematic substantive theories." That was not without certain costs:

> The combined effect of this recruitment process interacting with this type of socialization may have produced a "know nothing" era in the discipline. Many scholars who presumed they were building our new empirical foundation did indeed know very little about substance and about the relationship of the statistical languages they used to the absence of theoretical models to which the language of data analysis should have been related. The criteria for what would be accepted as "facts" became a significant correlation coefficient or a high R^2, even when it meant the acceptance of nonsense or the rejection of long-established knowledge. (Ostrom 1982, 16–17)

Hence the rise of new generations of young political scientists who "considered themselves to be in the vanguard of the discipline" and who rejected the work done by their forerunners while thinking that they were "creating the empirical foundation for the final development of a science." For them, noted Ostrom, "political science itself began in the 1950s," and one could find articles in which "repeated references were made to the *classical* work in the field" while "all of the works cited were written after 1960!" However, that in itself wasn't a problem. The problem was that they came to largely dominate the major journals.

> With the "rock bottom" approach, as Popper calls it, scientific theories could not be constructed until political science had undertaken substantial hard-nosed empirical work to find the empirical laws to become the bedrock of the discipline. With missionary zeal, several generations of young colleagues went forth to collect data so that a political science could be constructed using their empirical findings as *the* foundation. (Ostrom 1982, 17)

The problem, hence was twofold. First, many of these revolutionaries had negligible real training for such statistical endeavors. Second, and more important, the entire philosophy of their approach was flawed. After all, "the way a process is conceptualized should affect the analytical techniques to be used for estimating statistical parameters in empirical models of that process" (Ostrom

1982, 17). Or as Vincent Ostrom (quoted in E. Ostrom 1983, 18) quipped, any serious scholar would "doubt that one could find many statements in Hobbes, *The Federalist*, or Tocqueville that conceptualized the effect of institutions in a manner similar to that of fertilizer added to labor and land to produce corn." In short, the mainstream was guilty of allowing the language of data analysis and method to dominate the language of theory construction. Even more, once certain methods declared to be more scientific have become the driver of the entire enterprise, not only theory and understanding suffer but also problem identification. Not only are many problems approached in a distorted way but an entire set of problems and phenomena simply disappear from the radar.

In the light of all of the above, it is no shocker that Elinor Ostrom argues for the reversal of the trend. Steps should be taken, she writes, "to reestablish the priority of theory over data collection and analysis" so that "the development of theory precedes the choice of appropriate methods to test a theory." But more important for our discussion, she gets straight to the core and points toward the deeper, foundational issue: the philosophical assumptions involved in all this. The idea is simple: the dominant philosophy (and more exactly philosophy of science) shapes in certain ways how we understand and assess our theory-building and theory-testing practices. The dominant views of theory and method are in large part framed and legitimized by the prevailing philosophy embraced more or less tacitly by scholars. In a word, these philosophical views have a major responsibility for the developments in question. The solution is to seriously reconsider and replace them. And in this respect it is noteworthy that Ostrom explicitly looks beyond the mainstream at a variety of traditions and perspectives. The alternatives she looks at are revealing, as Toulmin, Kuhn, Lakatos, and Habermas are all names that indicate efforts to depart from the positivist and the more or less Popperian mainstream.

> The covering-law perspective has not been replaced with another dominant philosophy of science. Among the important alternative views are those of Kuhn (1970), Lakatos (1971), and Habermas (1973). Among the authors who have provided useful overviews of the different traditions and important attempts at synthesis are Moon (1975), Toulmin (1977), and Shapiro (1981). (Ostrom 1982, 17)

Later in the chapter we'll return to these epistemological and methodological themes with a closer look. For now, it is important just to note them and then to add that the discomfort with the mainstream is even more visible in Vincent Ostrom's writings. In the same writings however, we could also identify the unequivocal traces of the influence coming from one of these alternatives, pragmatism. This influence is multifaceted and we'll turn now to it.

Ostrom's argument that ideas, language, and learning processes are critical elements for any serious theoretical attempt to explain and understand institutional order was in the 1960s, when he started to articulate it, both outdated and premature. To the behavioral and positivist revolutionaries, it sounded as an echo of a previous stage in the evolution of social sciences. At the same time it was premature because it preceded by decades the new interest in cognition and belief systems that became a mark of many social science research programs in the 1990s (Aligica and Boettke 2009). In any case, Ostrom was passionately against the new "operational mode of social scientists" according to which interests dominated and ideas were "pictures which concealed the reality of politics":

> Awareness that the pursuit of interests in human societies turns both upon an architecture of authority relationships and the place of ideas (the use of theory) in the constitution of complex configurations of rule-ordered relationships in societies was increasingly lost. It was as though the play of the game of who gets what, when, and how in relation to whom so preoccupied attention that the conception, design, and conduct of great political experiments were lost.... That the facts of human activity might, in part, have been artifactual creations of the theory used to design a political system was neglected. (V. Ostrom 1991b, 11)

In this respect, he identified the philosophical roots of the situation in the mimetic application of approaches copied from natural sciences under the influence of positivism and the associated behavioral revolution of the 1950s and 1960s. He repeatedly insisted on the importance of the basic ideas about the nature and structure of reality that both social actors and researchers hold. For instance, it is a simple and uncontroversial observation that people "create their own social realities by reference to some shared community of understanding (pictures in their minds) and live their lives within those realities as artifactual creations" (V. Ostrom 1991b, 11). If that was the case, then one of the most serious mistakes in the social sciences was to follow the philosophical dogmas and taboos of the day and to ignore the ontology of the social order, that is, the role of "ideas, conjectures about regularities, and the careful use of informed practices that are constitutive of that reality" (V. Ostrom 1991b, 11). The departure from positivism would bring a return to a more realistic understanding of the nature of institutional order.

It is not an accident that the discussion of the role of ideas opens an explicit link to the pragmatist perspective. The link ideas-action-experiments is central to the Ostroms' institutionalism. In this they follow explicitly in the steps of John Dewey (1938, 508) and his observation that "every measure of policy put into operation is *logically*, and *should be* actually, of the nature of an experiment," a quote repeatedly invoked by Vincent Ostrom. Thus the Bloomington scholars concurred in Dewey's notion that the ideas inspiring policies (and the expectations about practical consequences based on them) "can be treated as hypotheses and acting on the basis of an hypothesis can serve as an experimental test if accompanied by discriminating observation of the consequences that follow from its adoption" (Dewey 1938; V. Ostrom 1991b, 3–4).

A closer look at the textual evidence supports the conjecture that Dewey was a significant influence on Ostrom and through him on the Bloomington school. Quoted repeatedly at critical junctures in his work, Dewey was important enough that an entire section in *The Meaning of Democracy and the Vulnerability of Democracies* (Ostrom's last book) was dedicated to him (in the chapter "Conceptions of Democracy and the Language of Political Inquiry," a section is titled simply "John Dewey"). Dewey, wrote Ostrom appreciatively, was preoccupied with the place of ideas in human experience as well as with the conditions of life in a democratic society. Both themes, we know, are central to Ostrom's own investigations.

Dewey's effort to frame and analyze democracy "as a system of governance" in his *The Public and Its Problems* (1927) seems to have found a strong echo in Ostrom's thinking. The Bloomington scholar repeatedly writes approvingly of the way Dewey criticizes the uses of "the concept of the state," more precisely its consequences for our thinking and practice: "Like most concepts which are introduced by "The," is both too rigid and too tied up with controversies to be of ready use" (Dewey 1927, 8). Ostrom may have not agreed with the solution offered by Dewey to the problem thus diagnosed. However, he was in enthusiastic agreement with the diagnosis: the mere utterance of the words "The State" hinders more than helps our understanding and analytical capacities. Too much confusing baggage comes with it. The notion draws us away from facts of human activity toward abstractions and logical constructs, and even worse, it does that imperceptibly. Dewey is right that it is preferable to start from concrete "facts of human activity" before shifting toward generalizations and abstractions. We need to understand the phenomenon of "the state" in the light of human problem-solving actions and the endeavors related to them, not the other way round (Ostrom 1997).

The mode in which Dewey approaches the conceptualization of the notion of the public, a conceptualization that anticipates the public goods-collective action perspective of modern political economy, also meets with approval. Dewey defines the public as "those affected by the indirect consequences of human actions that are of sufficient importance to be controlled in ways to secure some consequences and avoid others" (1927, 12). The distinction between private and public turns, then, on the significance of consequences for those not directly involved in transactions: "The line between private and public is to be drawn on the basis of the extent and scope of the consequences of facts which are so important as to need control whether by inhibition or by promotion" (1927, 15). That concept, notes Ostrom (in McGinnis 1999b, 32–33), is closely related to the concept of externalities, although the exclusion principle of economics is superior because it overtly takes into account the practical aspect of the process of denying benefits. However, he is aware that the philosophical rendering of the problem opens up perspectives that simply do not exist from the political economy standpoint.

From there the philosophical and the political economy interpretations take separate ways but not before some elaborations of consequence are made. Not all public goods are of the same scale in their function and structure. Geographic domain, functional domain, and intensity of the externality all matter. Therefore, there are public goods and public goods, each public good having its own corresponding "public." That is to say, "the public" is not a homogenous, national-level entity. In Dewey's definition, "the public consists of all those who are affected by the indirect consequences of transactions to such an extent that it is deemed necessary to have those consequences sys-tematically provided for" (Dewey 1927, 15–16). Even if Dewey may not have fully realized this, the deep pluralism and dehomogenization of "the public" is intrinsic in the very definition he uses. A quote approvingly used by Ostrom confirms that Dewey had a solid intuition about the role of local, personal, tacit experience and knowledge: "The man who wears the shoe knows best that it pinches and where it pinches, even if the expert shoemakers is the best judge of how the trouble is to be remedied" (Dewey 1927, 207). At which Ostrom was eager to comment: "He might have added that the man who wears the shoe is also the best judge of the appropriateness of the shoemaker's remedy" (Ostrom 1997, 32), Dewey's logic coming thus full circle.

Ostrom recognizes in Dewey's take on democracy a vision that goes beyond the mere procedural and formal, a vision that seems to have influ-enced his own work. For Dewey, democratic participation was more than simply voting and petitioning; it was for all intents and purposes communi-cative; citizens are in an ongoing process to "convince and be convinced by reason" in a common effort to achieve common objectives (Dewey in Talisse and Aikin 2008, 134). This communicative process is the essence of any form of social organization. Ostrom's preoccupation with the role of language in the constitution of social order echoes and develops this very insight. Dewey's emphasis on communicative processes warns us that democracy is not something exclusively related to the state or the national government but is a way of life, a mode of social organization, a formula that "must affect all modes of human association, the family, the school, industry, religion" (Dewey in Talisse and Aikin 2008, 134). This means nothing less than "making our own politics, industry, education, our culture generally, a servant and an evolving manifestation of democratic ideals" as well as that "the struggle for democracy has to be maintained on as many fronts as culture has aspects: political, economic, international, educational, scientific and artistic, and religious" (Dewey in Talisse and Aikin 2008, 134). In a comparable way Ostrom's own vision of democracy goes far beyond the procedural and formal, dwelling also in culture, education, and language.

That being said, as one may expect, Ostrom is not always on the same page with Dewey. In *The Meaning of Democracy and the Vulnerability of Democracies*, and more precisely, in the chapter on conceptions of democracy (1997, 59), Dewey is criticized next to Woodrow Wilson on methodological grounds for theorizing the flawed doctrine that one may be able to look straight to the "facts" of human behavior to discover "reality," forgetting that "words" that "govern men" from ideas are also part of those facts and reality. Whether Dewey fully deserves this criticism is a discussion in itself. In a similar vein, Ostrom expressed doubts that Dewey fully understood that "how an *inchoate public* is brought to the *consciousness* of a *shared community of understanding*" depends much on "the existence of *decision-making arrangements* in an *open public realm* and on a willingness to explore how to pool, rearrange, and compromise existing interests" (Ostrom 1997, 290). But the most important divergence with Dewey was the grand and abstract statism the latter exposed, contrary to the logic of his own pragmatist assumptions and principles. When you see the notion of "The State," complains Ostrom, described as "an effort to articulate the Great Community" (as Dewey does) you start to wonder how it can "evoke a conscious understanding of the specific and practical problems that define the real governance of common public endeavors." Floods and droughts, for instance, require the real public, collective effort of a genuine, concrete community:

> working through the stocks and flows of knowledge, information, and shared understandings that are constitutive of such a public enterprise is a vastly different task than discovery of the State. If Dewey had been a careful student of *The Federalist* and *Democracy in America*, ... [s]uch a

conception would have been more closely related to his philosophy of pragmatism and education, concerned with learning by doing. Great Societies are not organized by some single center of Supreme Authority exercising tutelage over Society. (Ostrom 1997, 291)

But when all is said and done, Ostrom had a healthy respect of Dewey, and it is safe to conclude that Dewey had a significant influence on him, and through Ostrom, on basic positions of the Bloomington school. That respect is demonstrated by the fact that Ostrom considers Dewey's perspective compatible with Tocqueville's "new science of politics," the science and art of association so dear to him: "I presume that such a science of association is consistent with Dewey's concern for the creation of coherent communities of relationships among inchoate publics in their search for becoming self-conscious, articulate identities" (Ostrom 1997, 295). Given the importance this Toquevillian theme has for Ostrom (Aligica and Boettke 2009, 2011b; Ostrom 1997), this is more than a small sign of approval.

To sum up, Ostrom shared Dewey's pragmatist vision of political order in which a broad process of knowledge communication and discovery, involving citizens in an ongoing self-governance activity, is both a principle and an open-ended experiment in governance. The notion of "science and art of association" could be easily conceived as a natural corollary of that vision. Democracy, one possible name for all this, conceived as a social process, not as a mere institutional and procedural arrangement, is both a goal and a means. It is a grand experiment that is always a work in progress. But the association goes deeper than that. Using Ormerod's (2006, 902) succinct but penetrating insight and concentrating on the epistemological level, one can imagine the following parallel between what seems to be the most fundamental thrust of their intellectual attitudes. Dewey criticized "spectator" theories of knowledge, the self-aggrandizing view of philosophy and philosophers posing as a priesthood, and emphasized the concrete task at hand, practical problem-solving. Ostrom criticized "seeing like a state," monocentric theories of politics, and the self-aggrandizing view of political scientists and economists posing as philosopher-kings, and emphasized the concrete task at hand, practical problem-solving. Dewey did his best to keep away from "big 'wholesale' questions of metaphysics and epistemology" and refocused instead on the empirically specific "retail" problems of specific individuals and groups. Ostrom did his best to keep away from speculations about "The State" as an articulation of abstract principles or "grand communities" and refocused instead on empirically specific "retail" problems of specific individuals and groups. Both pursued a bottom-up, problem- and practice-first reconstruction of their field.

This correspondence of attitude reveals, like it or not, a pragmatist stance for the Bloomington scholar and his school. It appears that Ostrom followed in political economy and took to its ultimate social philosophy consequences the general logic advocated by Dewey. The result has become a distinctive feature, a trademark of Bloomington school institutionalism.

Visions of Social Philosophy

We have seen so far some significant commonalities between Vincent Ostrom and a key author of the pragmatist tradition, John Dewey. These affinities may be made clearer if we look at what seems to be the centerpiece of both the Ostroms' and pragmatists' social philosophies: a conceptualization of institutional order as a knowledge process. Let's take as a starting point Posner's (2003) brief outline of pragmatism, especially because its avowed simplicity and programmatic lack of philosophical sophistication allows us to identify in simple forms the basic elements of interest. For pragmatists, he explains, "intelligence is environmentally adaptive rather than a means by which we can reason our way to ultimate truths"; hence they "believe that the *experimental* method of inquiry is best."

> That means trying one thing and then another in an effort to discover ways of better predicting and controlling our environment, both physical and social. The model is natural selection, a process essentially of trial and error, of experimentalism writ large.... Experimentalism implies the desirability of a diversity of inquirers, just as natural selection depends on genetic diversity to bring about adaptive change.... People of different background, experience, aptitudes, and temperament will be attuned to different facets of the environment and will have different ideas about how best to proceed in trying to predict and control it. Only by trying different things—not only different ideas but different ways of life—and comparing the consequences do we learn which approaches are best for achieving our goals, whatever they are. (Posner 2003, 9)

Posner suggests a two-step move in our understanding of even the most simplistic definition of pragmatist social theory: first, experimentalism (ideas-driven experiments with the environment in attempting to achieve certain goals) and, second, the implications of experimentalism. The important thing here is that both bring with them the problem of knowledge, ideas, and learning via experience. From this context emerges a philosophy of institutional order, conceptualized as a knowledge and information process, in which ideas, experiment, and learning are pivotal. Seen from this angle, Ostrom's perspective is nothing less than one of the possible systematic elaborations of this basic conceptualization. To make this point clear, we need a brief detour through his philosophy of social order and change.

Ostrom's theory builds on a form of methodological individualism preoccupied by the issue of how the human condition makes human beings depend on social organization and hence on institutions (V. Ostrom 1982a; 1984; Aligica and Boettke 2011b; Boettke and Coyne 2005; Herzberg 2005). Ostrom is an individualist in both the methodological and the normative sense. The defining feature of the human condition is that individual human beings can make decisions. Social organization is in large measure a function of individual and collective choices, some of them direct, some of them indirect. In evolutionary theory terms, choice is a particular form of selection. The better founded the choice, the better the adaptation. Because choice is a basic form of adaptive behavior, social organization can be considered the expression of choice as a form of adaptive behavior. A pivotal element in this analytical narrative is that language radically amplifies human capabilities to shape ideas, to accumulate and transmit knowledge. With language, choice itself gains new dimensions and powers, unprecedented and unique in evolutionary history (V. Ostrom 1982a, 7–11). But while language makes possible an increase in options (imagined or real), by that very fact it also increases uncertainty, a situation that makes the act of choice more complex and more difficult. Thus, rules and their institutionalization become increasingly necessary as ways to stabilize expectations, coordinate and work through the looming chaos of subjective and structural uncertainty. Reason-based choice becomes more and more dependent on institutionalized heuristics that reduce the diversity of possibilities, economize, and focus cognitive effort. Reason, institutions, and decisions are socially intertwined. The institutional and cultural ecology of choice is inseparable from decision theory, and decision theory is inseparable from institutional and cultural context.

This is the background against which one can see the problem of social organization, be it in metropolitan governance, the governance of the commons, or international regimes: part of a broader process, of a cycle of adaptation in which organizations solve problems but also, at the same time, create new problems. People are able to explore solutions in the given ecology of choice. Adjustment and adaptation through learning and new choices ensue. The very solutions create, at their turn, new problems, generating a cycle, a dialectic from problem to solution to new problem. Social organizations get increasingly complex, the outcome of choice engendering new choices. Social order is always a work in progress, fluid and vulnerable to ongoing challenges. Yet it is a mistake to think that the most important challenge is external, that is, the natural, social, and cultural ecology of choice; the most important is human nature itself:

> Any creature that has unique capabilities for learning and generating new knowledge inevitably faces an uncertain future. Learning and the generation of new knowledge are themselves marks of fallibility. Infallible creatures would have no need to learn and generate new knowledge. Fallible creatures need to accommodate their plans to changing levels of information and knowledge. (V. Ostrom [1980] in McGinnis 1999a, 382)

The more complex the institutional order, the deeper the division of labor, the more complex coordination and cooperation processes become, and the less one single person can "see" or "know" the "whole picture." Hence there is a strong relationship between accepting the limits of individual and human knowledge in such circumstances and accepting the necessity of a pluralist and polycentric institutional system functioning on the basis of heterogeneous and dispersed knowledge. Alternatively, argues Ostrom, there is a relationship between the position that assumes the perspective of an "omniscient leader" and the belief in the viability of centralism, monocentrism, and comprehensive social planning.

> Those who have recourse to the perspectives of "omniscient" observers in assessing contemporary problems, also rely on political solutions which have recourse to some single center of authority where officials can exercise omnipotent decision-making capabilities and dealing with the aggregate problems of a society.... Somebody who takes the perspective of an omniscient observer will assume that he can "see" the "whole picture, "know" what is "good" for people, and plan or predetermine the future course of events. Such a presumption is likely to increase proneness to error. Fallible men require reference to decision-making processes where diverse forms of analysis can be mobilized and where each form, of analysis can be subject to critical scrutiny of other analysts and decision-makers. (V. Ostrom [1973] 2008, 1–23)

In brief, fallibility, uncertainty, ignorance, experiment, learning, and adaptability become key concepts in this stylized narrative of the emergence and nature of social order. In the end, the cause of vulnerability of humans' social arrangements can be found in the same forces that produce their dynamic resilience. This is indeed a profound paradox and an inexhaustible source of social dilemmas, and Ostrom discusses extensively how these paradoxes and vulnerabilities are dealt with through institutional arrangements that try to capture and mobilize the knowledge and resources of human communities engaged in concrete problem-solving (V. Ostrom (1982a, 3; [1973] 2008; [1971] 20081982c; 1986; 1999a,b; Aligica and Boettke 2011a, 2011b, 2009).

At the most basic level, Bloomington social philosophy connects a theory of choice to a theory of rules and institutions via a theory of learning, knowledge, and ideas. The theory of democracy it advances is obviously an extension (or a subdomain) of this conceptual and theoretical architecture. The argument leads to a broader governance theory as a knowledge process, a theory of the knowledge (both practical and theoretical—the "science and art") to devise various rules and metarules and to support their operation by a mix of force, incentives, deliberation, and reason. Knowledge and learning are both the stabilizers of institutional order and the drivers of social change. Ultimately, an account of social order is about the social avatars of ideas and knowledge, manifested through choices, essentially about a huge knowledge process.

The fact that this Ostromian social philosophy converges with the typical pragmatist social philosophy can be amply demonstrated by any overview of the relevant pragmatist literature, beyond Dewey's work. In fact, such an overview leads rapidly to the observation that one is dealing with a perspective that is common to all authors who in the 20th century have ever tried to articulate a social philosophy from a pragmatist position. Let's take, for instance, C. I. Lewis's foray from epistemology and logic to social philosophy. In *Our Social Inheritance* (1957) he develops a description of the good social order on older pragmatist lines, attempting to be fully consistent with the principles inspiring the rest of his work. As Colella (1992, 3) summarizes the result, Lewis comes to describe "a dynamic and progressive social order which makes advances by means of the constant renewal and modification of the beliefs and ideals upon which its members act." Thus, "the social order itself becomes the mechanism through which these beliefs and ideals are transmitted from one generation to the next." Moreover, "it is through the critical activity of individual human beings that such modification, in the interest of the more effective meeting of human need, is carried out" (Colella 1992, 12–14).

Lewis's description echoes Dewey's with its general emphasis on the evolutionary and experimental. Lewis goes further, elaborating the idea of the social order seen as a "storehouse and transmitter of beliefs and ideals," but the two perspectives betray their common conceptual origins. At the same time, Lewis departs from Dewey in several respects, and, interestingly enough, that happens exactly in issue-areas where we can see Vincent Ostrom departing too. It is important to keep in mind this apparently minor point. As we'll discuss in this chapter, there are two major schools of pragmatist philosophy. Dewey is on one side of the intellectual divide and Lewis on the other. As one may expect, the Ostroms are closer to a form of pragmatism exposed by Lewis.

A major point of divergence between Lewis and Dewey is their stance on individualism. Individualism is crucial for Lewis, not for Dewey, or at least not in Lewis's radical way. For Lewis the good social order is built precisely on it. The same goes for the distinction between the individual and society and the way it is supposed to be conceptualized. In his lectures at Indiana University in 1956, published in 1957 as *Our Social Inheritance*, Lewis deals extensively with the role played by the autonomous individual in the interplay between the social inheritance of ideas and the progressive evolution of human society. It is true, he writes, that the preservation of ideas and knowledge and the practices they inspire (avoiding an inefficient and volatile process by which each generation would start from zero) are the basis of progress. Social memory, the social inheritance of ideas, knowledge passed on to next generations are vital. Nonetheless, the social inheritance of ideas is insufficient without the actions of self-critical, autonomous, and self-governing human beings. These individuals amend and improve the social inheritance. They are able to do it because they are the bearers of several traits (most of them culturally induced): autonomy, experimental and fallibilist views, and the ability to challenge, adjust, or reject socially held beliefs.

A similar outlook emerges from another major representative of the pragmatist tradition in the 20th century, Hilary Putnam. Putnam's foray from epistemology and mathematical logic to social philosophy is materialized in an epistemological argument for democracy, avowedly inspired by Dewey. Putnam takes as a starting point what he considers Dewey's success in providing a "philosophical backup" for democracy and sees a strong relationship between, on the one hand, pragmatism as a theory of knowledge and, on the other hand, (radical) democracy. Such a position is built on the typical pragmatist belief that democracy is ultimately a "cognitive" process, an extension of the very principle of experimental inquiry. Putnam takes the theme to the extreme. He elaborates Dewey, arguing that "the need for fundamental democratic institutions as freedom of thought and speech follows...from requirements of scientific procedure in general: the unimpeded flow of information and the freedom to offer and to criticize hypotheses" (Putnam 1992, 180–82). Therefore "democracy is not just one form of social life among other workable forms of social life." It is more basic than that: "it is the precondition for the full application of intelligence to the solution of social problems." The conclusion is unavoidable: "To reject democracy is to reject the idea of being experimental" (Putnam 1992 in Westbrook 1998, 129).

The centrality of the analogy between democratic community and scientific communities of inquiry guided by instrumental logic for pragmatist social and political theory is reconfirmed by the intellectual historian of pragmatism Kloppenberg (2000, 90). In this respect, pragmatism operates on the basis of an analogy that is viable precisely "because the democratic community replicates the community of broadly conceived scientific enquiry that serves as the prototype of instrumental reasoning." Democracy is a knowledge process. "Free and creative individuals, in democratic as in scientific communities," writes Kloppenberg (1994 in Westbrook 1998, 90), "collectively test hypotheses to find out what works best. These communities set their own goals, determine their own tests, and evaluate their results in a spirit of constructive cooperation."

Westbrook (1998, 131), another major student of the pragmatist tradition, elaborates the significance of this approach. Pragmatists believe that politics should be a mode of organized intelligence. If that is the case, then there are ways of conducting politics functionally and effectively and ways of failing to do so: "The intelligence of political communities, like that of all communities of inquiry, should be organized democratically" (Westbrook 1998, 131). A community defined in terms of inquiry, knowledge, and learning should be democratic not on ethical or social grounds, but on cognitive grounds. Its inclusiveness and openness is based on pragmatic reasons of effectiveness. The participation of the public in shaping public policy is the best way to capture the needs, preferences, and interests of the community in case. Only citizens can identify these needs and interests, and democratic consultation and discussion is the quintessence of the process of identification. Moreover, this process engenders a virtuous circle of progressive improvement because democracy is a system that "develops the capacities of all its men and women to think for themselves, to participate in the design and testing of social policies, and to judge results" (Putnam in Westbrook 1998, 137).

To sum up, pragmatist social philosophy (and by extension its view of social organization and institutional order) is built around the theme of knowledge processes. Its theory of democracy is salient in this respect and as such is the best illustration of this point. Pragmatism holds a "cognitive" view of politics and democracy, a good matching with other "cognitive" theories of political or economic institutions, such as Hayek's views of market and law as a knowledge process. The Ostroms' views are of similar nature, part and parcel of the same broad, extended family of social philosophy. The Ostromian perspective on democracy is broad, flexible, and sometimes made to look coextensive with a broader governance process that includes the standard institutional arrangements typically associated with democracy but that goes beyond them. Hence, democracy in relation to governance is a source of ambiguity and an area in which further work in clarification and elaboration is needed. What is the relationship between, on the one hand, democracy in the typical understanding and, on the other, a broader governance process of an inevitable polycentric nature? The fact that this is not a mere semantic problem is now clear thanks to the Knight and Johnson (2011) attempt to raise the typical institutional form of democracy to systemic institutional primacy. As discussed in chapter 2, despite the semantic ambiguities in its discussion of democracy and polycentricism, the Ostromian approach seems to be able to offer an alternative way of understanding the structures and processes associated with second-order tasks. The effort to disentangle democracy and polycentricity and to elucidate their functional relationships is a work in progress that lies ahead for the next generation of Bloomington scholars.

Before concluding, let's mention that this discussion pivoting on knowledge processes and their institutionalization helps us to better capture and understand the ramifications of the concept of epistemic choice, the intriguing notion advanced by Ostrom toward the end of his career (1997a; 1997b; 1993a). His dissenting argument is that the most important potential of the current work in the public choice tradition is not to apply "economic reasoning" to "nonmarket decision-making" (the standard view of the mainstream public choice scholars about their core research program). Instead, it is to look at emerging concepts that depart from the hard core. One of them is epistemic choice, a notion that combines two key ideas, choice and knowledge (both essential for this theory of institutional order and change). The merit of the concept is that it goes beyond the mechanics of rational choice, opening up from another angle the idea of knowledge process, a social and institutional phenomenon whose full relevance, both positive and normative, can be clearly grasped in the context of a pragmatist social philosophy on the lines outlined above. The notion illuminates the various choice dimensions—operational, public, and constitutional—while emphasizing that choice in institutional design is ultimately a choice of ideas and is intrinsically linked to learning and knowledge. At the same time, it reminds us that there is something special about the choice of ideas, principles, and beliefs and that, in general, there is something special about "choice" as a function of the specific domain of choice. This, in itself, is an interesting challenge to any approach based on decision theory models, and it is worthwhile mentioning it before returning to the epistemological themes in the next section, even if the intriguing directions suggested will not be pursued here. The principles of choice "applicable to the warrantability of knowledge," writes Ostrom (1997a, 90), "are different than the principles of choice applicable to a choice of goods in market and public economies." In turn, "these are different than the principles of choice applicable to the constitution of rule-ordered relationships in accordance with standards of fairness." These are different domains, with different principles and different structures and rules of motion. It is true that similar principles can apply to each, but the criteria, as well the overall processes, "vary among different types of choice."

Pragmatism: Methodology and Epistemology

Once engaged in a conceptual reconstruction of the philosophical assumptions and implications of the Ostroms' work, we soon realize that it coalesces almost naturally around pragmatist ideas, more so than around any other competing perspective. This is true not only when it comes to matters of social philosophy or views about the nature and significance of governance processes. It seems to be true also when it comes to methodology and epistemology. Putting together the pieces helps us to better place the Ostroms' work in theoretical perspective and to recognize the sources of their structural uneasiness with the mainstream.

At its origin, pragmatism is about a specific theory of truth and its implications. As C. I. Lewis (1957) explained, the pragmatist position is built on the notion "that knowledge is an interpretation instigated by need or interest and tested by its consequences in action." To see knowledge not so much as representational, but as something intrinsically linked to action, even as a form of action, is to see in a new light an entire range of basic and familiar philosophical and scientific themes. A view of cognitive processes as actions leads naturally to the notion that knowledge is practical. The meaning of beliefs emerges in the interaction between goal-oriented human beings and their environment. It is, after all, commonsensical that beliefs (theories, concepts) are an intrinsic part of purposeful instrumental behavior. They have instrumental natures and values in relationship to specific goals. Success and failure in action is a test for knowledge and beliefs. In brief, pragmatism forces us to rethink our approach to knowledge and social action and in doing so has significant repercussions for the social sciences (Baert 2005, 36; Holmwood 2011; Gross 2009; Joas 1993).

The task of exploring pragmatism's relevance for institutionalism is facilitated by the fact that several recent works have addressed the link between pragmatism and institutional theory (Bromley 2006; Knight and Johnson 2011; Ansel 2011). Bromley's book on "volitional institutionalism" is the most ambitious effort to reconstruct from a pragmatist perspective the epistemological basis of institutionalism. As such, it helps us understand what is involved in such an effort, and it further illuminates the affinity between the Ostroms' work and the pragmatist perspective.

Bromley starts with a criticism of the mainstream, using as a vehicle the problem of its excessive reliance on the hypothetico-deductive method, considered the alpha and omega of epistemology and methodology in social sciences (for a nuanced discussion of the theme see Rescher 1980; Lawson 2003; Goldstone 2004; Johnson 2006; Clarke and Primo 2012). It is well documented that mainstream economics has embraced this philosophical idea up to the point that it has thoroughly identified itself with it. The postulates of rationality, self-interest, and utility maximization are used in an interplay of axiomatic and covering laws to build hypotheses that are then to be tested (verified/falsified) with empirical data. The view seems commonsensical and beyond any suspicion. But such an approach is not without problems and limits.

Bromley points out, for instance, that as in any deductive approach, the axioms (covering laws) and assumptions dictate the cognitive value of the conclusions. The "explanation" of a phenomenon is always bound to the limits set up by axioms and assumptions. Excessive reliance on one and only one analytical engine leads toward validationism. This means that "we do not explain events—we justify them" (Bromley 2006, 166). The problems are obvious: Should we be concerned about an explanatory strategy that has always and everywhere the same limits set up by the same axioms and assumptions? Is it possible to successfully study a phenomenon, a diversity of situations and cases, using one and only one analytical engine, based on the same set of covering laws, axioms, and deductive inferences?

Bromley (2006, 104, 115), as all authors influenced by pragmatist ideas do, argues that irrespective of what mainstream economics thinks, scientific method is something more complex and definitely not so narrow. The problem is not so much that the hypothetico-deductive method has limits and problems. Any tool has its own functions and limits, and that truism applies to cognitive instruments as well (Clarke and Primo 2012). The problem is that the mainstream seems to be missing the existence of the rest of the epistemological and methodological toolbox, fixated on one single item. Pragmatism has from its very beginning argued that, broadly speaking, there are in fact three classes of methods scientists employ: deduction, abduction, and induction. Explanations (including those in economics) rely on all of them.

Deduction and induction are familiar. However, the third member of the triad, abduction, is the less known but in many respects the most important and interesting. Exploring it illuminates why the pragmatist view is so relevant for contemporary developments in social sciences epistemology. Peirce, the founder of pragmatism, distinguished abduction, induction, and deduction, but warned that it is important to see the three working in conjunction. Abduction connects deduction and induction. For Peirce abduction is undeniably linked with "the operation of adopting an explanatory hypothesis" (Mullins 2002, 200). We develop a hypothesis assuming that it will be able to elucidate some facts. The form of inference is, accordingly, "(1) The surprising fact, C, is observed; (2) But if A were true, C would be a matter of course. (3) Hence, there is reason to suspect that A is true" (Peirce 1998, 5.189). Suspecting that something is true leads to deducing consequences and inductive testing. "The end of abduction is that the deductive consequences of it may be tested by induction" its adaptation "being of such a character that its deductive consequences may be experimentally tested." In other words, "when Peirce brings together his pragmatism and his discussions of the logic of abduction, the intimate connection between abduction, deduction, and induction quickly surfaces" (Mullins 2002, 200–201).

The widespread error of conflating abduction and induction was noted by Pierce from the very beginning as he discussed the relationship between the members of the triad (Mullins 2002, 200; Peirce 1998, 7.218). Accordingly, he gave special attention to the neglected problem of the generation of hypotheses and the discrimination among hypotheses, but in the end the major point of interest for us to note is what he thought about the relationship between pragmatism and the logic of abduction:

> If you carefully consider the question of pragmatism you will see that it is nothing else than the question of the logic of abduction. That is, pragmatism proposes a certain maxim which, if sound, must render needless any further rule as to the admissibility of hypotheses to rank as hypotheses, that is to say, as explanations of phenomena held as hopeful suggestions.... For the maxim of pragmatism is that a conception can have no logical effect or import differing from that of a second conception except so far as, taken in connection with other conceptions and intentions, it might conceivably modify our practical conduct differently from that second conception. (Peirce 1998, 5.196)

It looks like the pragmatist approach is far from a departure from the idea that hypotheses should be capable and subject of experimental verification (Peirce 1998, 5.197). On the contrary, it reinforces the epistemic position of "experimental verification," while making the case that it is something rather complex and multifaceted, requiring an approach that goes beyond the formulaic (Mullins 2002, 200–201). Explaining and understanding reality requires a more diverse, robust, and sophisticated analytical engine. Again, the main point is not that the hypothetical-deductive method is structurally questionable (although that should be a matter of concern) but that reducing the entire spectrum of the philosophy and methodology of science to it is unwarranted.

The concrete relevance of these observations can be exemplified following Bromley (2007, 102) while keeping in mind the Ostroms' focus on concrete social dilemmas and problems of social cooperation. The abductivist, he writes, "cannot merely offer universal theories that would be true in each particular case *if only* the data were a little better." Rather, "the abductivist must produce plausible reasons for—explanations of—the results." Abduction is devoted to observed phenomena. To paraphrase Bromley, when dealing with a research case, for instance, a practical puzzle related to a common-pool resource social dilemma, general theoretical propositions about collective action are only of so much relevance. This social dilemma, at this time, in this place, puzzles us. One can imagine many deductive explanations for social dilemmas. But we are in search for the one reason for the case in point. This is the place where abduction enters the picture in search of identifying, explaining, and understanding that reason.

Bromley goes on to emphasize that because institutional, economic, social facts are the result of human decisions and options in institutional theory and economics in general, explanation has to identify and deal with "reasons." The question is whether the axiomatic, maximization postulates and the covering laws of the mainstream are able to capture correctly or at least realistically the various ways reasons operate as causes of social order and change. The abductivist perspective would explore the range of "plausible reasons" for the phenomena in question and investigate them in an attempt to reach real explanations and not produce mere self-referential arguments. We'll get back to this later in this chapter. For now all we need to note is that the attempt to go beyond the narrow view concentrated on the hypothetical-deductive method, using as a route of escape a pragmatism-inspired approach that regards induction, deduction, and abduction in a unified way, has implications of considerable theoretical and operational significance.

Indeed, all of the above places our discussion at the core of philosophy of knowledge. The relevance is hard to exaggerate. As the influential logician and philosopher of science Jaakko Hintikka (1998) put it:

> Peirce's idea of abductive inference as the source of all new hypoth-
> eses stands in a stark contrast to any hypothetico-deductive theory of
> science. Here you can begin to see what I have in mind by calling the
> problem of abduction the basic question of contemporary epistemol-
> ogy. The most general problem to which both the hypothetico-deductive
> approach and the idea of abduction are attempted solutions is: What is
> ampliative reasoning like?

In a remarkable paragraph Hintikka concisely and penetratingly elaborates the point clarifying why the strategy of making the hypothetico-deductive method the pillar of our theory and philosophy of science is so problematic. This is one of those paragraphs that should be on the required reading list of any aspiring social scientist:

> Purely logical (in the sense of deductive) reasoning is not ampliative.
> It does not give me any really new information. Yet all our science and
> indeed our whole life depends on ampliative reasoning. But what is that
> reasoning really like? When we speak of the reasonings of the likes of
> Sherlock Holmes...as "deductions" accomplished by means of "logic,"
> we do not mean philosophers' deductive logic which is not ampliative.
> But what are they, then? The hypothetic-deductive approach tries to
> brush them all under the carpet of "contexts of discovery" which can-
> not be dealt with by means of logical, epistemological or other rational
> means. Such a way of thinking might be congenial to the cultists of the
> irrational, but it is deeply dissatisfying in that it leaves unexamined an
> important part of the cognitive lives of all of us. (Hintikka 1998, 506)

To sum up, Bromley's effort to systematically reconsider the epistemological foundations of institutionalism has the merit of identifying the key problem for such a reconstruction (i.e., the fascination with a limited and limiting model of scientific investigation) and the directions to be taken for its solu-tion: the pragmatist reconstruction of the theory of scientific methodology around the issue of abduction as a pivotal element of an analytical engine that does not discriminate in the appropriate use of induction, deduction, and abduction. One already notices that the multi-method, multidisciplinary approach advocated by the Ostroms, their IAD framework, and their interest in case study research gain a new and enhanced dimension and significance in the context of this discussion probing and reorienting the epistemological bases of social sciences. To get the full picture, we need to make a further step.

Reasoning, Induction, Tentative Knowledge, and Epistemic Pluralism

An excessive focus on the "context of verification" and the neglect of the "context of discovery" leads to a distorted and incomplete view of the nature of the research process. This is more than a matter of philosophical view. As Hintikka suggests, the lack of interest in problems associated with the context of discovery leads to a disregard of the empirical facts of the cognitive and psycho-social processes associated with the growth of knowledge and knowledge acquisition, despite the dramatic advances made in the last decades in understanding the intricacies of these processes. The preoccupation with the formal, even formulaic logical processes of the "scientific method," reduced to a technical procedure of applying recipes and rules, an "N-step procedure," a "mechanics of inference," has a cost. It leads, among other results, to a disinterest in how people, including scientists, acquire, develop, validate, and act on knowledge in reality, that is, the real-life cognitive procedures employed in knowledge creation and inference.

Adopting a reductionist model of scientific process may be acceptable for specific purposes and specific research contexts, as long as one is not trying to make of it the normative model for all research endeavors. But there is no reason that we should limit ourselves to such model, a fact confirmed by even the briefest look at the recent studies of methods of reasoning done in artificial intelligence, cognitive psychology, and logic and at the new perspectives on induction and inductive reasoning as truth estimation developed in epistemology. These studies substantiate and illustrate the criticisms against the mainstream and give a better sense why alternative approaches like those advanced by the Ostroms may have a more robust epistemic backing in the relevant literature. Models of reasoning, concept formation, and conceptual change, of generalization and various forms of abstraction, are now better understood. So are mental models and the relationship between idealization and generalization.

For instance, the study of methods of reasoning done at the crossroads of philosophy and cognitive science during the last couple of decades has shown that there are many ways of performing intelligent and creative reasoning that are simply missed and not covered by the theories considered definitive and foundational by the mainstream. These results put in a new light the cognitive and epistemic bases of scientific endeavors. For more than two decades we have seen emerging above the standard models of inference and induction a new and deeper understanding of abduction, connecting it to "the central epistemological question of hypothesis withdrawal in science" and "model-based reasoning, where abductive interferences exhibit their most appealing cognitive virtues" (Vosniadou and Ortony 1989, 2). Likewise, the research done during the ending decades of the last century on similarity and analogical reasoning in scientific discovery and creativity has noteworthy implications for the way we understand the nature of scientific process. As Vosniadou and Ortony (1989, 2–3) explain, interest has been generated by "the realization that human reasoning does not always operate on the basis of content-free general inference rules and Aristotelian principles but, rather, is often tied to particular bodies of knowledge and is greatly influenced by the context in which it occurs." This means that "learning does not get accomplished by merely adding new facts and applying the same inference rules to them [but] depends on the ability to identify the most relevant bodies of knowledge that already exist in memory so that this knowledge can be used as the starting point for learning something new." The relevance for the ways we understand the hypothetico-deductive method and the role of abduction is evident.

But probably the developments that best put us in a position to reassert the status of mainstream epistemic assumptions are those described by Gigerenzer's (1989; 2000; 2008) criticism of the impact of positivism and the "probabilistic revolution" on ideas of science and scientific reasoning. Gigerenzer studied how statistical ideas have influenced not just methodology but also theory construction, for instance, how statistical theory generated a new model of the mind: the mind as an "intuitive statistician." He documents how cognitive processes were modeled on scientists' own tools as statistical inference and hypotheses testing and how explanatory metaphors came to be treated as a scientific fact. That, needless to say, rested well with the formal theories of scientific research advanced by positivists at the same time. The metaphor of the mind as an intuitive statistician, explains Gigerenzer, transformed our understanding of cognitive processes but also imported some rather far-reaching confusions. The blind spots and illusions of statistics theory were often carried over into the theories it inspired. Among others, the exaggerated emphasis on statistical analysis "eliminated the processes of information search" and the notion that "informed judgment, flexible and sensitive to particular circumstances" plays any role "in either psychological research or everyday reasoning" (Gigerenzer 1989; 1987, 22–23).

Thus, Gigerenzer focuses on the study of man as an intuitive statistician as an opportunity to test not only the applicability of the metaphor/analogy but also an opportunity to expand the research, leading to the identification and exploration of a variety of approaches and practices of inferential reasoning. From there to the questioning of the universality and normative legitimacy of the standard statistical inference paradigm is just a small step.

In brief, an entire array of research programs and their findings have questioned the conventional wisdom about methods and scientific practice, about explanations, analysis, and theory building in social sciences. The deductivist-falsificationist orientation was seriously challenged, forcing the revaluation of the way we understand and define the nature, goals, and limits of the research process. Recalling Elinor Ostrom's 1982 book on strategies of inquiry and her discussion of the state of the discipline, we are now in the position to pick up from where that discussion was left and ask how long one can continue to neglect the implications of these developments for mainstream theories and methods. How long would it take for the attitudes and practices of the political economy epistemic community to align itself with the new findings, information, and interpretations already available?

Such an update is even more necessary as the aforementioned developments have been reinforced by parallel developments in epistemology. For instance, induction itself has been reassessed and reformulated in ways that make the mainstream views look like a footnote to a broader theory of epistemic cognitive methods. Nicholas Rescher's work (1980; 1999) is exemplary in this respect. The new ways of understanding induction in a pragmatist framework as well as the implications for the way scientific processes are construed find one of the best illustrations in his philosophy of "methodological pragmatism." No epistemological formula and no methodological prescription, writes Rescher (1980, 21), irrespective of its logical perfection, can help us to do more than is possible with the means at our disposal. Induction irrespective of its forms or the technical sophistication with which it is executed does not *guarantee* the final truth of its result. "Indeed, if the history of science has taught us any one thing, it is that the best estimate of the truth that we can make at any stage of the cognitive game is generally to be seen, with the wisdom of hindsight, as being far off the mark." Nevertheless, induction helps us to settle for the *best available estimate* of what is going on in this world, which has a structure, a complexity, and a law of motion that overwhelmingly escape our control.

In Rescher's pragmatist view (1980, 7–8), induction is naturalized: a mundane and realistic human resource for doing the best we can in the typical conditions of imperfect information in which we actually find ourselves most of the time. This comes as a corrective to the attitude induced by the hypothetical-deductive mindset and the projection of methods on pure logical and abstract grounds.

From a methodological pragmatist perspective, induction is seen as practice- and context-driven truth-estimation, "a methodology for obtaining answers to our factual questions through optimal exploitation of the information at our disposal." That sheds some light on the epistemological basis of the intuitive claims that problem- and question-driven research is structurally different from method driven research. Induction, explains Rescher (1980, 8), "is at bottom an *erotetic* (question-answering) rather than an *inferential* (conclusion-deriving) procedure." The question and its context matter. Shifting the focus on the process of truth approximation and on the idea of question-driven imperfect knowledge leading to contestable and imperfect knowledge, invites a different attitude to methods and methodology. In this respect the Bloomington school's work, always trying to keep close to the social puzzle and its circumstances, resonates again with the pragmatist worldview, in which it may well find its most solid epistemological basis.

To sum up, induction in any of its methodological forms (techniques of scientific method, statistical theory, the design of experiments, mechanics of inductive argumentation) is not something idealized; it is a matter of doing the best, given the epistemic circumstances. If we consider induction's role in scientific method, the implications are not negligible. Rescher's theory reminds us that the real circumstances (as opposed to hypothetical perfect, methodology textbook scenarios) in which we develop our investigations and apply our methods and techniques, matter. The difference between the real and ideal circumstances matters. And even more importantly, we are reminded that any technique of scientific method is not a fail-proof instrument for generating certified correct answers. The pluralism of methods and perspectives is thus vindicated by the very logic of the theory of induction. In the absence of any one superior alternative, we need to rely on a combination of methods, each doing the job as well as permitted by its limits and the epistemic circumstances of the case. As Baert (2005), notes, methodological diversity characterizes science, and pragmatism is simply a reflection of this reality. Social sciences are based in and require methodological pluralism. Any "tendency to put the social sciences in a methodological straitjacket" is doomed to fail. And as Goldstone (2004) demonstrates, multimethod research is simply the natural and logical conclusion of a scientific attitude in social research, above and beyond any philosophical preconceived notions. The Ostroms realized as much very soon, and over the years their work never lost track of that basic insight.

From all of the above, one can see how taking a fresh view at the cognitive-epistemic problem in social sciences (including deduction, induction, abduction, and the associated cognitive and psychological processes as well as their interplay) leads to a broader, more complex way of understanding the nature of the research process. It becomes clear that there is no reason to shape our criteria and methods from one and only one perspective (be it a variant of positivism or Popperian deductivism) and to enthusiastically build epistemologically unwarranted expectations evoking them. A methodological pragmatism approach to science as a process of truth approximation—an endeavor that uses tentative knowledge to generate tentative knowledge—leads to a reformulation of our expectations and methodological criteria. The unavoidable diversity and complexity of the toolbox of the institutional theorist emerges as a natural corollary.

This is precisely the point repeatedly made by the Ostroms. For them the academic revolutionaries of social sciences who took it on themselves to reconstruct from the bottom up a field defined by Aristotle, Hobbes, Adam Smith and Tocqueville, using a unique methodological recipe in which the permutation of statistical data was the alpha and omega of their endeavor, were heading toward a dead end in more than one respect. A pluralism of conceptualizations is natural, writes Vincent Ostrom. Restraining it cannot be other than detrimental to any inquiry. This is even more so in social sciences, where one has to move back and forth across frameworks, theories, and models, "so as to appropriately fit limiting conditions, opportunities, and hypothetical contingencies into the multidimensional facets characteristic of the artifactual nature of human habitation" (V. Ostrom 1997a, 98–100, 105). In turn, different conceptualizations lead to different analytical techniques, writes Elinor Ostrom (1982, 17). In brief, there is a logic connecting the fact of the diversity and uncertainty of social life to the pluralism of conceptualizations and theories, and from there to the pluralism of methods and techniques of social sciences.

Contrast this view with what critics like Bromley (2006), Lawson (2003), or Clarke and Primo (2012) dub the "commitment to deduction," the notion that "there is but one way of knowing," a situation that is one of the "unfortunate legacies of logical positivism." For years and years, writes Bromley, "generations of economists have been taught that there is only one way to truth—relentless adherence to what has come to be called *the* scientific method (as if there were but one)" (2006, 88–89). That was the tenor of the intellectual current the Bloomington scholars had to work against. Instead of being fixated on a particular tool (and the recipes of the day about what is appropriate and not appropriate research), the Ostroms have systematically followed an approach in which the main driver of the inquiry was not methodology or the philosophical assumptions fashionable within the relevant epistemic community. The context of discovery, of the heuristics and hypothesis-building strategies, was for them as important as the context of verification. The pluralism of methods and approaches, a key theme at the core of their perspective and inspired by their research experience in various settings, their reading of non-mainstream philosophy of science, and their scholarly intuitions, converges in an unambiguous way with the spirit of pragmatist philosophy. If epistemic monism and exclusivism are the outcome of logical positivism and related doctrines, pluralism of method and approach is intrinsic to the pragmatist paradigm. The Ostroms' attitude seems to reflect the spirit of pragmatic pluralism: Scholars and researchers have to use different standards and methods as a function of the situation and the available data, and if an epistemological doctrine frowns on that, so much the worse for that doctrine. Today, current developments in both cognitive sciences and the philosophy of science seem to validate that position.

Reconstructed Institutionalism and Varieties of Pragmatism

Looking beyond the methodological and epistemological aspect, a question of interest is what is the substantive impact of this reorientation and recalibration on pragmatist grounds of the core ideas and approaches in political economy and institutional theory. A closer look at Bromley's elaboration of the notion of "volitional institutionalism" (2006) gives a more concrete sense of pragmatism's ramifications in institutional theory. At the same time, his effort is both an example of what it means to rethink the foundations of institutionalism (and for that matter, of economics and political sciences) and an early warning about the limits and possible traps in such an enterprise.

Pivoting on the notion of "*volitional* institutionalism" as the concept that captures best the implications of the pragmatist position for institutional theory, Bromley's book makes "human will in action, looking to the future, struggling with the perplexing problem of how that future ought to unfold" the centerpiece of his reconstruction of institutional theory. From the very beginning, this future and action-oriented perspective is identified as "not a plausible domain for mechanistic Paretian truth rules about what is claimed to be socially preferred. It is, instead, a domain for articulating reasons—reasons for various images of plausible ends, and reasons for various images of plausible means" (Bromley 2006, 215–16). The idea is that in institutional theory and economics in general, explanation has to identify and deal with "reasons," something that goes beyond mere (deterministically conceptualized) "causes." Institutional, economic, social facts are the result of human judgments, decisions, and actions. Without looking into the reasons people have for their actions (albeit in many cases they may be rationalizations or self-deceptive), one is unable to go beyond mere speculation. And in this respect the question is: Are the axiomatic, maximization postulates and the covering laws of the mainstream able to deal with reasons in all their heterogeneity? Are they able to capture correctly or at least realistically the multiple ways reasons operate as causes of action, social order, and change? On the other hand, a methodology based in pragmatism seems well suited for this task. Bromley (2006, 211–17) explains that pragmatist-inspired abductivist logic, once applied, will indicate several plausible reasons for the phenomena in question and will lead researchers to investigate them. Abduction changes the angle of the approach and, in doing that, creates room for real explanations, not just self-referential procedures.

In the emerging approach, microfoundations come to be predicated on the distinction between explanations that are mechanical-causal and explanations that focus on reasons and intentions. Focusing on reasons as causes of the action to be explained, we come immediately to the core of pragmatism's conception of individual action (Boettke, Lavoie, and Storr 2004). It has two major elements: (*a*) reasons articulated as ideas and future-oriented images and (*b*) volition based on them. First, in volitional institutionalism, ideas, beliefs, expectations, and "plausible descriptions of reasons for particular actions and decisions" take center stage. Because all action is about a future that "entails new circumstances" and in relationship with which individuals create images and operate on them as possible futures, the challenge of what in chapter 5 we called "the shadow of the future" emerges as a central theme from the very beginning, without any ambiguity. Second, Bromley's interpretation links the issue of ideas and the future with that of volition. Images of the future engender purposes for action: "These created imaginings comprise—indeed inform—the volitional premises of those contemplating particular actions" (Bromley 2006, 220). Everything considered, these basic observations constitute by all accounts a powerful and distinctive point of departure for a bottom-up reconstruction of institutional theory.

Starting with that basis, one may develop the broad outlines of a theory of institutions and of institutional change. The approach advocated by Bromley liberates the theory of institutional change from the remaining shackles imposed by the neoclassical paradigm. Current approaches, he writes, "fail to offer an understanding of institutional change because they are intent on embedding institutional change in the same mechanistic choice-theoretic algorithms that are thought to explain individual choice" (Bromley 2006, 219). Volitional pragmatism "does not close doors on possible hypotheses." It simply approaches the study of institutions and institutional change "with an open and enabling epistemology." The "epistemic turn" it advances "takes us away from the mechanism of logical positivism and redirects us toward the quest for—and articulation of—reasons that constitutes the core of pragmatism" (215).

Following the logic of volitional institutionalism, Bromley identifies public policy ("collective action in restraint, liberation, and expansion of individual action") as a major determinant of the configurations of "provisioning" strategies and arrangements of a given society. This specific and intricate form of collective action, public policy, is a major force operating at the institutional foundations of an economy, "altering the realms of choice—fields of action— for individuals" (Bromley 2006, 215). One may be able to recognize in this description the joint operation of what the Ostroms call the public choice and constitutional choice levels. The ensuing conclusions are alike: A major (if not the major) task of institutional theory, and political economy in general, should be developing an account of how collective action in public policy actually proceeds, "an account of how individuals and groups arrive at decisions about the nature and structure of those working rules and property relations that will restrain, liberate, and expand their range of volitional choice and action."

Bromley's attempt to reorient our take on institutional theory via a pragmatist reconstruction of its philosophical basis opens up an avenue that seems to be—at least prima facie—rather promising. It involves, as we have seen above, a focus on reasons as causes, ideas in action and expectations, on the problem of prediction versus control of the future, and on public reasons and collective action as foundational for institutional arrangements and their performance. But there is another task that takes, at least in an epistemological sense, precedence. This task is related to the specifics of the pragmatist philosophical basis on which the theoretical and analytical constructions are to take place, and it is important to at least mention it.

Pragmatist philosophy, broadly defined, is no doubt an inspiration and a reference point. But if one wants to use it for ambitious goals of reconstructing social science paradigms, one needs to be more specific regarding the features of the type of pragmatism mobilized for these purposes. In this respect it is crucial to note that in the contemporary pragmatist tradition a gap has been opened for quite a while between two forms of pragmatism: on the one hand what might be called a "pragmatism of the left" and on the other hand a "pragmatism of the right." The first is associated with William James,

F. C. S. Schiller, and Richard Rorty, the second with C. S. Peirce, C. I. Lewis, Nicholas Rescher, Hilary Putnam, and Susan Haak. Today, indeed, under the umbrella of the same concept, two rather different philosophies coexist.

As already discussed, the defining innovation of pragmatism broadly defined is that it introduced as an explicit criterion in philosophy the standard of the practical and operational level, of "what works." But, as Rescher (1999, 65–68) explains, that standard invites the next question: For whom? Different people, different groups, have different objectives and preferences while acting and applying the criteria in different circumstances. This is the point where the two brands of pragmatisms separate. One type of pragmatism remains focused on subjective, individual, and psychocultural variation. Epistemic impersonal standards are abandoned and cast under the shadow of subjectivism and relativism. This leads to a form of relativism in which the ideal of objectivity is lost. Central to the pragmatism of the left is "its dismissal of the traditional theory of knowledge's insistence upon judging issues by impersonal or of any rate person-indifferent standards" (Rescher 1999, 67). Pragmatic efficacy (the "what works" criterion) is something to be applied and assessed in personal, individual, and social convention terms.

On the other side, the pragmatism of the right accepts the reality of diversity and subjectivism but goes beyond conclusion. It sees pragmatism's concern for efficacy as being not subjective and individualist, but rather as "collective, across-the-board human enterprises whose rationale is rooted in the nature of the human condition at large" (Rescher 1999, 67). It anchors itself not in subjectivity but in intersubjectivity, not in social convention but in empirical knowledge. The ultimate reference point is nature and empirical reality: "We may propose, but nature disposes—it is reality not we ourselves that is the arbiter of what works in relation to our actions in the world. Pragmatism is a road that leads not to subjectivity but to objectivity; it speaks not for relativistic preferences but for objective constraints" (Rescher 1999, 66). Such an approach looks to pragmatism as a "reality principle." What works cannot be a mere function of personal and local wants and preferences, objectives, and strategies. The pragmatism of the right is global and universalist. The reference group based on which the "what works" criterion is applied is the global community of rational people. That is to say, the idea of universal rationality is represented by a global community with generic needs aiming at objectivistic and universalistic judgment, via impersonal standards.

Looking at efforts toward integrating institutionalism and pragmatism in the light of the tension between the two schools of thought, it is conspicuous that the pragmatism of the left seems to have the upper hand. An overview of the bibliographies of the recent works linking institutional theory to pragmatism reveals that when one goes beyond the introduction of the basic principles and the elementary standard references, and moves toward a more elaborated and sophisticated treatment, the references to the pragmatism of the left become overwhelming. That leads to an unnecessary weakness or vulnerability, exactly in the sensitive area where the pragmatist contribution is mostly needed: epistemological foundations. Bromley's effort, for instance, is in many respects self-undermining precisely because of its reliance on a version of pragmatism that has a very limited epistemic carrying capacity for the very purposes of institutional analysis he advances. One cannot build a social science (even more, a science that gives priority to practice and institutional design) on an idiosyncratic philosophical basis of irony, discourse, and conversation, theorized as substitutes for the confrontation with the test of empirical reality or, for that matter, on the use of subjectivism and relativism invoked as an easy epistemological way out from the grand problems of validity, realism, and objectivity.

One may conjecture that as the research institutionalist agenda advances, the fact that a social science research program cannot rely on an epistemic strategy that tries to substitute the expediencies of practical context for truth, will become clearer and clearer, especially when it is better understood that a superior alternative is available. Moreover, pragmatism understood as a positive doctrine, "not one that *substitutes* practical efficacy for truth, but one that involves practice as our best available *evidential test* of truth" (Rescher 1999, 67), is, after all, congenial to the natural way of thinking of most institutionalist scholars. We have seen that the developments surrounding social sciences, in philosophy, cognitive sciences, psychology, all invite or press in this direction. So the question is not whether the efforts to integrate institutionalism and a science-friendly form of pragmatism are worthwhile and promising. The question is what the best paths are for these efforts.

Institutionalism and Pragmatism: Themes and Directions

This chapter started with the idea that Ostrom's institutionalism challenges us in more than one way to rethink the foundations of our theorizing, inviting a re-evaluation of how we build the interface between philosophy and social sciences. It has argued that, at a closer look, an underlying theme, a certain philosophical profile, is emerging, and that this profile matches well with that of the pragmatist philosophical tradition. Most probably, the pragmatist-institutionalist junction is not the sole possible alternative in an evolving intellectual and scientific climate that forces institutionalism to adjust and redefine its foundations. Yet, as far as one can see, at this point no better alternative is in sight. The reconstruction of institutionalism away from positivism and neoclassical orthodoxies is a work in progress. Further development and calibration is needed, both on the institutionalist theory side and on the pragmatist social philosophy side. As this chapter has demonstrated, the directions are rather clear, and one may say that on the institutionalist side, the Ostroms' work, with its realism, fallibilism, pluralism of method, recognition of the role of reasons and ideas in social action, robust empiricism, and focus on practice and the applied level, has contributed substantially to the creation of propitious conditions for the next steps.

Perhaps one of the most constructive ways to conclude this rapid but intensive itinerary at the interface between institutionalist political economy and pragmatist philosophy is to briefly review a question that comes naturally: what will be the major themes defining the next stage in the emergence of this avatar of institutionalist political economy, framed from a pragmatist perspective? Some aspects of the answer have already become salient and have been touched on from various angles in this book. Probably the clearest preview, however, is to be found in Jack Knight's and James Johnson's *The Priority of Democracy* (2011), a work that has been explicitly mentioned here for its multiple contributions to the advancement of the agenda. The fact that Knight and Johnson's outlook converges in such a large measure with how things are seen from the Ostromian perspective discussed in the present book (although the two approaches have been developed independently, from two different quarters of the institutionalist camp) should be seen as an encouraging signal: It may be an indication that institutionalism is a vibrant and cumulative progressive research program, and its new opening cycle of research is evolving, led by a coherent internal logic linking organically the growth of one stage of evolution with the next. Setting aside speculations regarding the significance of this convergence, it looks like parallel efforts to systematize and simultaneously redefine institutional theory predicated on a pragmatist perspective bring to the fore three major themes: the epistemic theme, the heterogeneity and diversity theme, and the social-institutional process theme. All have a strong normative significance. In fact, one of the main features of the pragmatism-inspired perspective is that in its light, political economy is no longer a domain precariously straddling predictive science and moral philosophy, as James Buchanan described it. It is a combination of both, requiring the revision of our notions of both what moral philosophy is and what predictive science is and is not.

On the epistemic front, at the most basic level, the epistemological relativism and the skepticism associated with the dominant interpretation of pragmatism is rejected: we live in a world that can be known in ways that allow us to operate largely successfully in it. Yet—and this is the second level—we are fallible: Errors and imperfections plague our knowledge, judgment, and decision-making. This means that, at the third level, we need to find inter-subjective, collective, institutional ways to cope with this intrinsic human proneness to error. Institutions need to be flexible, following the ongoing adjustment and change of our beliefs, and be prepared for the consequences following from that evolution. Needless to say, this requirement implies an instrumentalist-consequentialist view of institutions.

These notions are reinforced by the second theme. Diversity is a social fact. Hence realism requires we take a step away from the academic conven-tional wisdom that presume homogeneity and consensus. In large measure, institutions may be seen as tools for human beings to deal with the challenges and opportunities raised by heterogeneity and the array of problems deriving from that. The best principle of applying this challenge, given the diversity of conditions and situations, is experimentalism—working through a variety of processes of problem solving, by trial and error. "Institutional arrangement that can exploit the virtues of diversity," explain Knight and Johnson (2011, 43), "will be more likely to generate better social and political outcomes than arrangements that cannot."

The idea of assessment of outcomes and institutions introduces into the picture the problem of criteria. In a pluralist world, as realistically seen through pragmatist lenses, there are no foundational criteria. There is no one single, ultimate metric for institutional choice. Fairness, efficiency, distributive jus-tice, and freedom compete for preeminence as a function of circumstances, situation, and context. That leads indeed to disagreement, tensions, bargain-ing, and conflict. Hence, the third major theme or direction: The notion that the solution and the criteria themselves for assessing performance are to be derived not from abstract blueprints based on a "view from nowhere" or on God's-eye theories but from endogenous social-political-institutional process of communication, bargaining, and discovery, in which the members of the society or community get engaged in their attempts to find solutions. It is a collective discovery and choice process in which politics, ideas, and insti-tutions intertwine. In fact, this is by far the most far-reaching thesis of the emerging institutionalism of diversity, heterogeneity, and pluralism and is, by all accounts, an idea also growing from the core insights of the pragmatist social philosophy:

In the face of what they see as reasonable disagreement, pragmatists believe that there is no *ex ante* way to resolve these differences and tensions. And so they conclude that the criteria of institutional choice must be determined by those who are involved in the relevant social interaction in accordance with their own interests, attachments, and commitments. That is, the participants themselves must determine what constitutes the "best" consequences in any particular situation. In doing so, they must balance the various factors by which they assess the relevant consequences and derive a workable standard for particular cases, hence the political nature of the experimental process. (Knight and Johnson 2012, 47)

These are, in a nutshell, the three directions that seem at this point to emerge as the frontline in the ongoing intellectual consolidation of the pragmatist-based institutionalism: the epistemic, cognitive, and social organization of fallible knowledge of fallible but capable human beings operating in fallible institutional systems; heterogeneity and social diversity as both problems and resources for institutional design; and last but not least, the analytical and normative meshing of knowledge, power, and institutions in complex social processes meant to coordinate humans in "first order" and "second order" tasks. A research agenda organized around them seems to ensure continuity with the substantive advancements in our understanding of institutions and institutional order brought by the previous generations of institutionalist scholars, as well as the needed change leading to a revamping and relaunching of the institutionalist agenda, in the context of the new intellectual, social, cultural, and political circumstances of the 21st century.

Conclusion

THE INTELLECTUAL ITINERARY charted in this book documents how and why the research agenda advanced by the Ostroms and their associates is contributing to the emergence of a new chapter in thinking and theorizing about collective action, governance, and institutional arrangements. We have seen how the challenges clustered around the themes of heterogeneity and institutional diversity (chapter 1), polycentricity (chapter 2), institutional mapping (chapter 3), resilience (chapter 4), and institutional design and predictability (chapter 5) set the stage for a reassessment and reconstruction of our approaches to institutional theory, as well as to some of the dearest and deepest philosophical assumptions behind our methods and theories. Thus, step by step and piece by piece, we have seen that the Ostroms institutionalism looks like a broad intellectual enterprise redefining by doing, hands on, the relationship between predictive science and social and moral philosophy. It is an enterprise of strong but unassuming radicalism that persistently invites us to reconsider the very foundations and significance of our scientific efforts.

The depth and boldness of the project are revealed only when we single out the specific assumptions and perspectives challenged, as well as the full measure in which that challenge upholds a radical departure from powerful ideas tacitly framing a vast part of modern political economy. The list is remarkable, but a cluster of related candidates makes the top of it, in any account: agent and institutional homogenization as a theoretical and methodological default position; centralization and monocentrism as key principles of governance; and "seeing like a state" as an acquired *forma mentis* in thinking about political and economic affairs.

The typical strategy of dealing with the challenge of heterogeneity comes easily as one of the top contenders. The homogenization by assumption of social agents, the rhetorical trick by which homogeneity is nominally recognized as a fact and a problem but then, in the next move, reduced to a modal profile, a homogenous "representative agent," with minimalist formal features, is both popular and influential. Versions of the strategy, operating at different levels and on different aspects of heterogeneity, are prevalent, from economics and public choice to political science and social philosophy. The logic of the Ostromian perspective challenges that strategy. Furthermore, it explicitly links the problem of heterogeneity to that of institutional diversity: Because institutional arrangements in any society emerge largely as a response to heterogeneity, and in turn are conditions of heterogeneity, institutional diversity should be a central (if not the central) theme of institutional theory. Yet that doesn't seem to be the case in the literature. Models of "markets and hierarchies" remain pivotal, although the theoretical lenses of the theory of the market or the theory of the state are obviously unable to capture and illuminate the wide diversity of existing and possible institutional arrangements. A replacement of the classical dichotomous typology (markets and states) with a new trinity (markets, states, and networks) does not seem an adequate solution. By refusing to accept such solutions, the Ostromian approach looks commonsensical. Yet, in relationship with the prevalent views, it is radical. Bloomington institutionalism is ready to take institutional diversity seriously and to follow to the end its analytical and normative logic.

The theme of institutional diversity leads to the next top contender on the list: the bias toward centralization and against polycentric, decentralized arrangements. When it comes to governance in complex social systems, the ideal of monocentrism (usually thought of as an idealized model or image of the nation-state) seems to have become the default mode in thinking about governance. The Ostroms challenge that. They advance instead the notion of polycentrism. Even before being a normative challenge, polycentricity is a challenge on descriptive, positive grounds. The elemental starting point is the basic condition of complex human societies. In real life there are multiple, competing, and overlapping action arenas, institutional levels, and sources of decision-making and authority, from families, communities, and religious organizations to nations and states. None of them has absolute power and authority over the life of an individual in all aspects, at all times, and in any circumstance. This dispersion of action arenas and authority is a social fact, a feature defining human societies of a certain complexity and development. Thinking about it as being created, granted, sanctioned by (and depending on) a centralized, ultimate, and unique all-monitoring source of authority and power violates principles of positive political economy before violating any normative principle. The image emerging is one of a conglomerate of diverse institutions, materializing various degrees and forms of decentralization and centralization through functional differentiation and historical accidents, in an ongoing process of change, while inside this process, the typical institutional forms of the national state, markets, or democracy take shape, or decline and fade away, form and reform, as time goes by. A governance system, polycentric governance, having properties favorable to institutional performance and human flourishing, may emerge out of these processes under certain conditions.

The polycentrism advanced by the Ostroms thus suggests to be cautious when advancing claims of preeminence for various institutions, be they the democratic state or the free market. Again, that may sound commonsensical, but when compared with the prevalent views, it is rather radical. We should avoid looking at the world through one and only one pair of conceptual lenses. And we should avoid thinking about governance having in mind one and only one institutional arrangement. The retreat from pluralism is dangerous, both on analytical and on normative grounds. With this remark, we have reached our third member of the list: "seeing like a state."

Reading through the academic literature dedicated to governance, one cannot avoid the feeling that a large part of it is written as if the public choice revolution had never taken place, as if no new insights regarding the potential and the limits of centralized, state-centered, technocratic, and bureaucratic government have been brought to the fore in the last several decades. One discovers a genre in itself, of a state-centered worldview, having the state and its personnel as an audience and beneficiary, with problem definitions framed on statist lines and with diagnosis and solutions suggesting state interventions, using state-based instruments and powers. In brief, something developed from a state-centric perspective, for a state-centric perspective, brushing aside a large part of the empirical and theoretical knowledge available on the nature, functioning, and performance of this particular institutional arrangement called "the modern state." On the other side, the Ostroms introduce a public-choice-inspired, post-public-choice attitude, an attempt to rethink the theory and practice of governance, as if public choice has made a difference. Their logic is one of incorporating the first- and second-generation public choice insights and lessons and reconsidering institutional theory and the problems of governance in that light. That means simply to follow the implications of those lessons and attempt to substitute for the state-centered view a pluralist one. It is a reasonable idea of "institutional portfolio diversification" in the context in which the vulnerabilities and dangers of relying on only one institutional arrangement have become so obvious. Yet again, this is an idea that may sound commonsensical, but when compared with the prevalent views, is rather radical.

How powerful, subtle, and profound is the intellectual current against which the Ostromian attempt runs is best illustrated by the reception of the Ostroms' work itself. If anything, their work demonstrated that "seeing like a state" is not an unavoidable way to think about collective action problems and their solutions. Collective action solutions do not necessarily involve seeing like a state, acting like a state, mobilizing the state. Yet, surprisingly often, one finds out that studies like those on the tragedy of the commons and their solutions are read as a rejection of decentralization and a vindication of centralization. Despite the explicit and persistent efforts of the Ostroms to disentangle the idea of collective action from that of "The State" and to demonstrate that successful collective action doesn't need a Leviathan, again and again one finds the Ostroms' work invoked to support state-sponsored arrangements, wrapped in vague notions of "democracy" and "participation," having nothing to do with the spirit or the letter of that work—and all that done, by all accounts, in good faith, so profound is the power of the "seeing like a state" *forma mentis* among an important part of the relevant epistemic community. In brief, the Ostroms' attempt to follow up on the public choice revolution and to rethink governance away from a state-centered view on pluralist, polycentric lines, remains a work in progress and continues to sound as radical today as thirty years ago.

Looking back, by their own account, the Ostroms saw their lifetime endeavors as been part of a long and illustrious intellectual tradition contributing to the "science and art of the association," that indispensable constituent of a self-governing society of free individuals. Considered in this light, their work has been a continuous effort to articulate an alternative way of looking at governance and institutional order: probably "seeing like a citizen" is one good contender for a name for it; "seeing like a self-governing human being" is another. Their endeavors at their Indiana University Bloomington Workshop were driven by two convictions. The first is that one cannot build a self-governing society of free individuals when the prevalent mode of thinking about institutional order and governance is done by elites who think like a state and strive for monocentrism. The second is that the ideal of a society of self-governing, fallible, but capable human beings, able to master the "art and science of the association," is worth pursuing because in it lies a powerful self-fulfilling prophecy. In the end, it is all about preserving, developing, and disseminating as much as possible the knowledge of this unique and fragile but vital "art and science":

> The work that we have done at the Workshop is deeply rooted in the central tradition of human and social studies. There is no better testimony for that than the questions that structure our work: How can fallible human beings achieve and sustain self-governing entities and self-governing ways of life? How can individuals influence the rules that structure their lives? Similar questions were asked by Aristotle and other foundational social and political philosophers. These were

the concerns of Madison, Hamilton and de Tocqueville. Today these central questions unite political scientists, economists, geographers, sociologists, psychologists, anthropologists, and historians who study the effect of diverse rules on human behavior in various institutional contexts, countries or at different geographic scales. Moreover one of our greatest priorities at the Workshop has been to ensure that our research contributes to the education of future citizens, entrepreneurs in the public and private spheres, and officials at all levels of government. We have a distinct obligation to participate in this educational process as well as to engage in the research enterprise so that we build a cumulative knowledge base that may be used to sustain democratic life. Self-governing, democratic systems are always fragile enterprises. Future citizens need to understand that they participate in the constitution and reconstitution of rule-governed polities. And they need to learn the "art and science of association." If we fail in this, all our investigations and theoretical efforts are useless. (E. Ostrom in Aligica and Boettke 2009, 159)

References

Abbott, Andrew. 1997. "Of Time and Space: The Contemporary Relevance of the Chicago School." *Social Forces* 75(4): 1149–82.

Abelson, Robert P., and Roger C. Schank. 1977. *Scripts, Plans, Goals, and Understanding: An Inquiry into Human Knowledge Structures.* Hillsdale, NJ: Lawrence Erlbaum Associates.

Adger, W. Neil. 2000. "Social and Ecological Resilience: Are They Related?" *Progress in Human Geography* 24(3): 347–64.

Agarwal, B. 1998. "Environmental management, equity and ecofeminism: Debating India's Experience". *Journal of Peasant Studies* 25(4, July): 55–95.

Alesina, Alberto, Reza Baqir, and William Easterly. 1999. "Public Goods and Ethnic Divisions." *Quarterly Journal of Economics* 14(4): 1243–84.

Alesina, Alberto, and Eliana La Ferrara. 2000. "Participation in Heterogeneous Communities." *Quarterly Journal of Economics* 115(3): 847–904.

Aligica, Paul D. 2003. *Rethinking Institutional Analysis and Development: The Bloomington School. Interviews with Vincent Ostrom and Elinor Ostrom with Introductory Notes by Gordon Tullock and Vernon Smith.* Arlington, VA: George Mason University.

Aligica, Paul D. 2009. "Social Predictions, Institutional Design and Prestige Loops." *Futures* 41(3): 147–155.

Aligica, Paul D., and Peter J. Boettke. 2009. *Challenging Institutional Analysis and Development: The Bloomington School.* New York: Routledge.

Aligica, Paul D., and Peter J. Boettke. 2011a. "Institutional Design and Ideas-Driven Social Change: Notes from an Ostromian Perspective." *Good Society* 20(1): 50–66.

Aligica, Paul D., and Peter J. Boettke. 2011b. "The Two Social Philosophies of Ostroms' Institutionalism." *Policy Studies Journal* 39(1): 29–49.

Allport, Floyd H. 1962. "A Structuronomic Conception of Behavior: Individual and Collective: I." *Journal of Abnormal and Social Psychology* 64(1): 3–30.

Anderson, Christopher J., and Aida Paskeviciute. 2006. "How Ethnic and Linguistic Heterogeneity Influence the Prospects for Civil Society: A Comparative Study of Citizenship Behavior." *Journal of Politics* 68(4): 783–802.

Andersson, Krister, and Agrawal, A. 2010. "Inequalities, Institutions, and Forest Outcomes." http://sobek.colorado.edu/~anderssk/Andersson&Agrawal_GEC.pdf

Ansell, Christopher K. 2011. *Pragmatist Democracy: Evolutionary Learning as Public Philosophy*. New York: Oxford University Press.

Appleyard, David L. 1987. "A Grammatical Sketch of Khamtanga—I." *Bulletin of the School of Oriental and African Studies* 50(2): 241–66.

Aquino, Karl, Victoria Steisel, and Avi Kay. 1992. "The Effects of Resource Distribution, Voice, and Decision Framing on the Provision of Public Goods." *Journal of Conflict Resolution* 36(4): 665–87.

Arce, Daniel G. 2000. "The Evolution of Heterogeneity in Biodiversity and Environmental Regimes." *Journal of Conflict Resolution* 44(6): 753–72.

Arce, Daniel G. 2001. "Leadership and the Aggregation of International Collective Action." *Oxford Economic Papers* 53(1): 114–37.

Arthur, W. Brian. 1997. "Beyond Rational Expectations: Indeterminacy in Economic and Financial Markets." In *Frontiers of the New Institutional Economics*, edited by John N. Drobak and John V. Nye: 291–305. San Diego: Academic Press.

Axtell, Robert L. 2003. "Economics as Distributed Computation." In *Meeting the Challenge of Social Problems via Agent-Based Simulation*, edited by Takao Terano, Hiroshi Deguchi, and Keiki Takadama: 1–22. Tokyo: Springer.

Azevedo, Jane. 1997. *Mapping Reality: An Evolutionary Realist Methodology for the Natural and Social Sciences*. Albany: SUNY Series in the Philosophy of the Social Sciences.

Baland, J.-M., Bardhan, P., & Bowles, S. (Eds.). 2007. *Inequality, Cooperation, and Environmental Sustainability*. Delhi: Oxford University Press.

Baert, Patrick. 2005. *Philosophy of the Social Sciences: Towards Pragmatism*. Cambridge: Polity Press.

Bak, Per. 1996. *How Nature Works: The Science of Self-Organized Criticality*. New York: Copernicus.

Baland, Jean-Marie, and Jean-Philippe Platteau. 1996. *Halting Degradation of Natural Resources: Is There a Role for Rural Communities?* Rome: Food and Agricultural Organization and Oxford University Press.

Baland, Jean-Marie, and Jean-Philippe Platteau. 1999. "The Ambiguous Impact of Inequality on Local Resource Management." *World Development* 27(5): 773–88.

Bardhan, Pranab, and Jeff Dayton-Johnson. 2002. "Unequal Irrigators: Heterogeneity and Commons Management in Large-Scale Multi-variate Research." In *The Drama of the Commons*, edited by Elinor Ostrom, Thomas Dietz, Nives Dolsak, Paul C. Stern, Susan Stonich, and Elke U. Weber. Washington, DC: National Academy Press.

Barry, Norman. 1988. *The Invisible Hand in Economics and Politics: A Study in the Two Conflicting Explanations of Society: End-States and Processes*. London: Institute of Economic Affairs.

Béland, Daniel, and Robert H. Cox, eds. 2011. *Ideas and Politics in Social Science Research*. New York: Oxford University Press.

Bellamy, Richard. 1999. *Liberalism and Pluralism: Towards a Politics of Compromise*. New York: Routledge.

Berger, Helge, and Mark Spoerer. 2001. "Economic Crises and the European Revolutions of 1848." *Journal of Economic History* 61(2): 293–326.

Berger, Peter L., and Thomas Luckmann. 1967. *The Social Construction of Reality: A Treatise in the Sociology of Knowledge*. Garden City, NJ: Doubleday.

Berkes, Fikret, Johan Colding, and Carl Folke, eds. 2003. *Navigating Social-Ecological Systems: Building Resilience for Complexity and Change*. New York: Cambridge University Press.

Berkes, Fikret, and Carl Folke, eds. 1998. *Linking Social and Ecological Systems: Management Practices and Social Mechanisms for Building Resilience*. Cambridge: Cambridge University Press.

Berkes, Fikret, and Nancy J. Turner. 2006. "Knowledge, Learning, and the Evolution of Conservation Practice for Social-Ecological System Resilience." *Human Ecology* 34(4): 479–94.

Biderman, Albert D. 1969. "On the Influence, Affluence and Congruence of Phenomena in the Social Sciences." *American Sociologist* 4(2): 128–30.

Bish, Robert L. 1971. *The Public Economy of Metropolitan Areas*. Chicago: Markham.

Bish, Robert L. 1999. "Federalist Theory and Polycentricity: Learning from Local Governments." In *Limiting Leviathan*, edited by Donald P. Racheter and Richard E. Wagner: 203–20. Cheltenham, UK: Edward Elgar.

Blomquist, William A. 1992. *Dividing the Waters: Governing Groundwater in Southern California*. San Francisco: ICS Press.

Blomquist, William A., and Peter deLeon. 2011. "The Design and Promise of the Institutional Analysis and Development Framework." *Policy Studies Journal* 39(1): 1–7.

Blomquist, William A., Edella Schlager, and Tanya Heikkila. 2004. *Common Waters, Diverging Streams: Linking Institutions and Water Management in Arizona, California, and Colorado*. Washington, DC: Resources for the Future.

Bloor, David. 1976. *Knowledge and Social Imagery*. Chicago: University of Chicago Press.

Boettke, Peter J. 2005. "Anarchism as a Progressive Research Program in Political Economy." In *Anarchy, State and Public Choice*, edited by Edward Stringham: 206–19. Cheltenham, UK: Edward Elgar.

Boettke, Peter J. 2010. "Is the Only Form of 'Reasonable Regulation' Self Regulation? Lessons from Lin Ostrom on Regulating the Commons and Cultivativing Citizens." *Public Choice* 143(3): 283–91.

Boettke, Peter J. 2012. *Living Economics: Yesterday, Today, and Tomorrow*. Oakland: Independent Institute.

Boettke, Peter J., and Chris Coyne. 2005. "Methodological Individualism, Spontaneous Order and the Research Program of the Workshop in Political Philosophy and Policy Analysis." *Journal of Economic Behavior and Organization* 57(2): 145–58.

Boettke, Peter J., Don Lavoie, and Virgil Storr. 2004. "The Subjectivist Methodology of Austrian Economics and Dewey's Theory of Inquiry." In *Dewey, Pragmatism and Economic Methodology*, edited by Elias Khalil: 327–56. London: Routledge.

Boettke, Peter J., and David L Prychitko. 1994. *Market Process: Essays in Contemporary Austrian Economics*. Cheltenham, UK: Edward Elgar.

Bornstein, Morris. 1994. *Comparative Economic Systems: Models and Cases*. 7th ed. Boston: Irwin.

Boudon, Raymond. 1977. *Effets pervers et ordre social*. Paris: Presses Universitaires de France.

Boyte, Harry. 2011. "Public Work and the Politics of the Commons." *Good Society* 20(1): 84–102.

Brennan, Geoffrey H., and Loren E. Lomasky. 1989. *Politics and Process: New Essays in Democratic Thought*. Cambridge: Cambridge University Press.

Bromley, Daniel W. 2006. *Sufficient Reason: Volitional Pragmatism and the Meaning of Economic Institutions*. Princeton, NJ: Princeton University Press.

Brugha, Ruairi, and Zsuzsa Varvasovszky. 2000. "Stakeholder Analysis: A Review." *Health Policy and Planning* 15(3): 239–46.

Buchanan, James M. 1975. *The Limits of Liberty: Between Anarchy and Leviathan*. Indianapolis: Liberty Fund.

Buchanan, James M. 2000. *Economics: Between Predictive Science and Moral Philosophy*. College Station: Texas A&M University Press.

Buck, Roger C. 1963. "Reflexive Predictions." *Philosophy of Science* 30(4): 359–69.

Buck, Roger C. 1969. "Do Reflexive Predictions Pose Special Problems for the Social Scientist?" In *The Nature and Scope of Social Science*, edited by L. Krimerman: 153–62. New York: Meredith.

Bulmer, Martin. 1984. *The Chicago School of Sociology: Institutionalisation, Diversity, and the Rise of Sociological Research*. Chicago: University of Chicago Press.

Burns, Tom R., and Helena Flam. 1987. *The Shaping of Social Organization: Social Rule System Theory with Applications*. London: Sage Publications.

Carlson, Jean M., and John Doyle. 1999. "Highly Optimized Tolerance: A Mechanism for Power Laws in Designed Systems." *Physical Review E* 60(2): 1412–27.

Carlson, Jean M., and John Doyle. 2002. "Complexity and Robustness." *PNAS* 99: 2538–45.

Carpenter, Steve R., Brian H. Walker, J. Marty Anderies, and Nick Abel. 2001. "From Metaphor to Measurement: Resilience of What to What?" *Ecosystems* 4: 765–81.

Carr, Craig. 2010. *Liberalism and Pluralism: The Politics of E Pluribus Unum*. New York: Palgrave Macmillan.

Cerny, Philip G. 1995. "Globalization and the Changing Logic of Collective Action." *International Organization* 49(4): 595–625.

Chan, Kenneth S., Stuart Mestelman, Rob Moir, and R. Andrew Muller. 1999. "Heterogeneity and the Voluntary Provision of Public Goods." *Experimental Economics* 2(1): 5–30.

Chayes, Abram. 1976. "The Role of the Judge in Public Law Litigation." *Harvard Law Review* 89(7): 1281–84.

Cherry, Todd L., Stephan Kroll, and Jason F. Shogren. 2005. "The Impact of Endowment Heterogeneity and Origin on Public Good Contributions: Evidence from the Lab." *Journal of Economic Behavior & Organization* 57: 357–65.

Clarke, Kevin A., and David M. Primo. 2012. *A Model Discipline*. New York: Oxford University Press.

Coats, Alfred W. 1993. *The Sociology and Professionalization of Economics*. New York: Routledge.

Colella, E. Paul. 1992. *C. I. Lewis and the Social Theory of Conceptualistic Pragmatism: The Individual and the Good Social Order*. San Francisco: Mellen Research University Press.

Coleman, James S. 1964. *Introduction to Mathematical Sociology*. London: Free Press of Glencoe.

Commons, John R. [1924] 1968. *Legal Foundations of Capitalism*. New York: Macmillan.

Costa, Dora, and and Matthew Kahn. 2003. "Civic Engagement and Community Heterogeneity: An Economist's Perspective." http://web.mit.edu/costa/www/costa.kahn.1.4pdf.pdf

Coyne, Christopher, and J. Lemke. 2011. "Polycentricity in Disaster Relief." *Studies in Emergent Orders* 3: 45–57.

Crawford, Sue E., and Elinor Ostrom. 1995. "A Grammar of Institutions." *American Political Science Review* 89(3): 582–600.

Crutchfield, James P., and Peter Schuster, eds. 2003. *Evolutionary Dynamics: Exploring the Interplay of Selection, Accident, Neutrality, and Function*. New York: Oxford University Press.

D'Agostiono, Fred. 2003. *Incommensurability and Commensuration*. Aldershot: Ashgate.

Dahl, Robert A. 1971. *Polyarchy: Participation and Opposition*. New Haven: Yale University Press.

David, Paul A. 1994. "Why Are Institutions the Carriers of History? Path Dependence and the Evolution of Conventions, Organizations and Institutions." *Structural Change and Economic Dynamics* 5(2): 205–20.

Davoudi, Simin. 2002. "Polycentricity—Modelling or Determining Reality?" *Town and Country Planning* 71(4): 114–17.

Denzau, Arthur T., and Douglass C. North. 1994. "Shared Mental Models: Ideologies and Institutions." *Kyklos* 47(1): 3–31.

Devletoglou, Evangelos A. 1961. "Correct Public Prediction and the Stability of Equilibrium." *Journal of Political Economy* 69(2): 142–61.

Dewey, John. 1927. *The Public and Its Problems*. New York: Holt.

Dewey, John. 1938. *Logic: The Theory of Inquiry*. New York: Saerchinger Press.

Dewey, John. 1998. "Social Science and Social Control." In *The Essential Dewey*, vol. 1: *Pragmatism, Education, Democracy*, edited by Larry A. Hickman and Thomas M. Alexander: 369-372. Bloomington: Indiana University Press.

Diamond, Jared M. 2005. *Collapse: How Societies Choose to Fail or Succeed*. New York: Viking Press.

Eccles, Robert G., and Nitin Nohria. 1992. *Beyond the Hype*. Cambridge: Harvard Business School Press.

Eggertsson, Thrainn. 1997. "Rethinking the Theory of Economic Policy: Some Implications of the New Institutionalism." In *Transforming Post-Communist Political Economies*, edited by Joan M. Nelson, Charles Tilly, and Lee Walker: 61–79. Washington, DC: National Academy Press.

Elkin, Stephen L., and Karol E. Soltan, eds. 1999. *Citizen Competence and Democratic Institutions*. University Park: Pennsylvania State University.

Elster, Jon. 1989. *The Cement of Society*. Cambridge: Cambridge University Press.

Engel, Christoph. 2005. *Generating Predictability*. Cambridge: Cambridge University Press.

Faris, Robert E. L. 1967. *Chicago Sociology, 1920–1932*. Chicago: University of Chicago Press.

Farr, James. 1985. "Situational Analysis: Explanation in Political Science." *Journal of Politics* 47(4): 1085–1107.

Feyerabend, Paul K. 1975. *Against Method: Outline of an Anarchistic Theory of Knowledge*. London: Humanities Press.

Folke, Carl. 2006. "Resilience: The Emergence of a Perspective for Social-Ecological Systems Analyses." *Global Environmental Change* 16(3): 253–67.

Folke, Carl, Steve Carpenter, Thomas Elmqvist, Lance Gunderson, Crawford S. Holling, and Brian Walker. 2002. "Resilience and Sustainable Development: Building Adaptive Capacity in a World of Transformations." *Ambio* 31(5): 437–40.

Fuller, Lon L. 1978. "The Forms and Limits of Adjudication." *Harvard Law Review* 92(2): 353–409.

Galatin, Malcolm. 1976. "Optimal Forecasting in Models with Uncertainty When the Outcome Is Influenced by the Forecast." *Economic Journal* 86(342): 278–95.

Galston, William. 2002. *Liberal Pluralism: The Implications of Value Pluralism for Poltical Theory and Practice*. New York: Cambridge University Press.

Gaus, Gerald. 2003. *Contemporary Theories of Liberalism: Public Reason as a Post Enlightenment Project*. London: Sage Publications.

Gaus, Gerald. 2011. "Between Discovery and Choice: The General Will in a Diverse Society." Working paper, http://www.gaus.biz/Discovery.pdf.

Gaus, Gerald. 2011. *The Order of Public Reason: A Theory of Freedom and Morality in a Diverse and Bounded World*. Cambridge: Cambridge University Press.

Gerring, John. 2001. *Social Science Methodology: A Criterial Framework*. New York: Cambridge University Press.

Gibson, Clark C., Margaret A. McKean, and Elinor Ostrom. 2000. *People and Forests: Communities, Institutions, and Governance Politics, Science, and the Environment.* Cambridge: MIT Press.

Gigerenzer, Gerd. 2000. *Adaptive Thinking: Rationality in the Real World.* New York: Oxford University Press.

Gigerenzer, Gerd. 2008. *Rationality for Mortals: How People Cope with Uncertainty.* New York: Oxford University Press.

Gigerenzer, Gerd, Zeno Swijtink, Theodore Porter, Lorraine J. Daston, John Beatty, and Lorenz Krueger. 1989. *The Empire of Chance: How Probability Changed Science and Everyday Life.* Cambridge: Cambridge University Press.

Gigerenzer, Gerd, and Murray J. David. 1987. *Cognition as Intuitive Statistics.* London: L. Erlbaum Associates.

Glaeser, Edward L., David I. Laibson, Jose A. Scheinkman, and Christine L. Soutter. 2000. "Measuring Trust." *Quarterly Journal of Economics* 15(3): 811–46.

Goertz, Gary. 2007. *Social Science Concepts: A User's Guide.* Princeton: Princeton University Press.

Goffman, Erving. 1974. *Frame Analysis: An Essay on the Organization of Experience.* New York: Harper & Row.

Goldstone, Jack A. 1997. "Methodological Issues in Comparative Macrosociology." *Comparative Social Research* 16(1): 107–20.

Goldstone, Jack A. 1998. "Initial Conditions, General Laws, Path Dependence, and Explanation in Historical Sociology." *American Journal of Sociology* 104(3): 829–45.

Goldstone, Jack A. 2004. "Reasoning about History, Sociologically." *Sociological Methodology* 34(1): 35–61.

Goldstone, Jack A. 2008. *Why Europe: The Rise of the West in World History, 1500–1850.* New York: McGraw Hill Higher Education.

Goodin, Robert E., ed. 1996. *The Theory of Institutional Design.* New York: Cambridge University Press.

Gordon, Scott. 1991. *The History and Philosophy of Social Science.* New York: Routledge.

Gray, Peter. 1999. *Famine, Land and Politics: British Government and Irish Society, 1843–50.* Portland: Irish Academic Press.

Gregory, Paul R., and Robert C. Stuart. 1999. *Comparative Economic Systems.* Boston: Houghton Mifflin.

Groenewegen, John. 2011. "The Bloomington School and American Institutionalism." *Good Society* 20(1): 15–36.

Groenewegen, John, and Jack Vromen. 1995. "Making a Case for Theoretical Pluralism." In *Transaction Cost Economics and Beyond*, edited by John Groenewegen: 365–80. Boston: Kluwer.

Gross, Niel. 2009. "A Pragmatist Theory of Social Mechanisms." *American Sociological Review* 74(3): 358–79.

Grunberg, Emile. 1985. "Predictability and Reflexivity." *American Journal of Economics and Sociology* 45(4): 475–88.

Grunberg, Emile, and Franco Modigliani. 1954. "The Predictability of Social Events."
    Journal of Political Economy 62(6): 465–78.

Grunberg, Emile, and Franco Modigliani. 1963. "Economic Forecasting When the
    Subject of the Forecast Is Influenced by the Forecast: Comment." *American
    Economic Review* 53(4): 734–37.

Grunberg, Emile, and Franco Modigliani. 1965. "Reflexive Prediction." *Philosophy of
    Science* 32(2): 173–74.

Gunderson, Lance H. 2000. "Ecological Resilience: In Theory and Application."
    Annual Review of Ecology and Systematics 31(1): 425–39.

Gunderson, Lance H., and Crawford S. Holling. 2002. *Panarchy: Understanding
    Transformations in Human and Natural Systems.* Washington, DC: Island Press.

Habyarimana, James, Macartan Humphreys, Daniel Posner, and Jeremy M.
    Weinstein. 2009. *Coethnicity: Diversity and the Dilemmas of Collective Action.*
    New York: Russell Sage Foundation.

Habermas, Jürgen. 1973. *Theory and Practice.* Boston: Beacon Press.

Hackett, Steven, Edella Schlager, and James Walker. 1994. "The Role of
    Communication in Resolving Commons Dilemmas: Experimental Evidence
    with Heterogeneous Appropriators." *Journal of Environmental Economics and
    Management* 27(2): 99–126.

Hague, Cliff, and Karryn Kirk. 2003. *Polycentricity Scoping Study.* Edinburgh: School
    of the Built Environment, Heriot-Watt University.

Hands, D. Wade. 1998. "Reflexivity." In *The Handbook of Economic Methodology,*
    edited by John B. Davis, D. Wade Hands, and Uskali Maki: 413–16.
    Chelthenham: Edward Elgar.

Hansen, Alvin H. 1963. *Monetary Theory and Fiscal Policy.* New York: McGraw-Hill.

Hayek, Friedrich A. 1945. "Use of Knowledge in Society." *American Economic Review*
    35(4): 519–30.

Hayek, Friedrich A. 1952. *The Counter-revolution of Science: Studies on the Abuse of
    Reason.* New York: Free Press of Glencoe.

Hayek, Friedrich A. 1973. *Law, Legislation and Liberty.* Vol. 1: *Rules and Order.*
    Chicago: University of Chicago Press.

Hayek, Friedrich A. 1976. *Law, Legislation and Liberty.* Vol. 2: *The Mirage of Social
    Justice.* Chicago: University of Chicago Press.

Hayek, Friedrich A. 1979. *Law, Legislation and Liberty.* Vol. 3: *The Political Order of a
    Free People.* Chicago: University of Chicago Press.

Heckathorn, Douglas D. 1993. "Collective Action and Group Heterogeneity: Voluntary
    Provision versus Selective Incentives." *American Sociological Review* 58(3): 329–50.

Heiner, Ronald A. 1989. "The Origin of Predictable Dynamic Behavior." *Journal of
    Economic Behavior & Organization* 12(2): 233–57.

Heise, David R. 1979. *Understanding Events: Affect and the Construction of Social
    Action.* New York: Cambridge University Press.

Henshel, Richard L. 1971. "Sociology and Prediction." *American Sociologist* 6(3): 213–20.

Henshel, Richard L. 1975. "Effects of Disciplinary Prestige on Predictive Accuracy: Distortions from Feedback Loops." *Futures* 7(2): 92–106.

Henshel, Richard L. 1976. *On the Future of Social Prediction.* Indianapolis: Bobbs-Merrill Company, Inc.

Henshel, Richard L. 1982. "The Boundary of the Self-Fulfilling Prophecy and the Dilemma of Social Prediction." *British Journal of Sociology* 33(4): 511–28.

Henshel, Richard L. 1990. "Credibility and Confidence Loops in Social Prediction." In *Self-Referencing in Social Systems,* edited by Felix Geyer and Johannes van der Zouwen: 31–58. Salinas: Intersystems Publications.

Henshel, Richard L. 1993. "Do Self-Fulfilling Prophecies Improve or Degrade Predictive Accuracy? How Sociology and Economics Can Disagree and Both Be Right." *Journal of Socio-Economics* 22(2): 85–104.

Henshel, Richard L., and L. Kennedy. 1973. "Self-Altering Prophecies: Consequences for the Feasibility of Social Prediction." *General Systems* 18: 119–26.

Herzberg, Roberta L. 2005. "The Impact of Vincent Ostrom's Scholarship." *Journal of Economic Organization and Behavior* 57: 173–88.

Hintikka, Jaakko. 1998. "What Is Abduction? The Fundamental Problem of Contemporary Epistemology." *Transactions of the Charles S. Peirce Society* 34(3): 503–33.

Holling, Crawford S. 1973. "Resilience and Stability of Ecological Systems." *Annual Review of Ecology and Systematics* 4(1): 1–23.

Holling, Crawford S. 1996. "Surprise for Science, Resilience for Ecosystems, and Incentives for People." *Ecological Applications* 6(3): 733–35.

Holling, Crawford S. 2001. "Understanding the Complexity of Economic, Ecological, and Social Systems." *Ecosystems* 4(5): 390–405.

Holling, Crawford S., D. W. Schindler, Brian W. Walker, and Jonathan Roughgarden. 1995. "Biodiversity in the Functioning of Ecosystems: An Ecological Synthesis." In *Biodiversity Loss: Economic and Ecological Issues,* edited by Charles Perrings, Karl-Goran Mäler, Carl Folke, Crawford S. Holling, and Bengt-Owe Jansson: 44–83. Cambridge: Cambridge University Press.

Holmwood, John. 2011. "Pragmatism and the Prospects of Sociological Theory" *Journal of Classical Sociology* 1: 15–30.

Horowitz, Donald L. 1977. *The Courts and Social Policy.* Washington, DC: Brookings Institution Press.

Institute for Local Self-Government. 1970. *Special Districts or Special Dynasties?* Berkeley, CA: Institute for Local Self-Government.

Janssen, Marco A. 2001. "A Future of Surprises." In *Panarchy: Understanding Transformations in Human and Natural Systems,* edited by Lance H. Gunderson and Crawford S. Holling: 241–60. Washington, DC: Island Press.

Janssen, Marco A., John M. Anderies, and Elinor Ostrom. 2004. "A Framework to Analyze the Robustness of Social-Ecological Systems from an Institutional Perspective." *Ecology and Society* 9(1): 18.

Janssen, Marco A., John M. Anderies, and Elinor Ostrom. 2007. "Robustness of Social-Ecological Systems to Spatial and Temporal Variability." *Society and Natural Resources* 20(4): 307–22.

Janssen, Marco A., Oran R. Young, Frans Berkhout, Gilberto C. Gallopin, Elinor Ostrom, and Sander van der Leeuw. 2006. "The Globalization of Socio-Ecological Systems: An Agenda for Scientific Research." *Global Environmental Change* 16(3): 304–16.

Joas, Hans. 1993. *Pragmatism and Social Theory.* Chicago: University of Chicago Press.

Johnson, D. Gale. 2000. "Population, Food, and Knowledge." *American Economic Review* 90(1): 1–14.

Johnson, James. 2006. "Consequences of Positivism: A Pragmatist Assessment." *Comparative Political Studies* 39:224–52.

Jones, Eric C. 2004. "Wealth-Based Trust and the Development of Collective Action." *World Development* 32(4): 691–711.

Kahn, Herman. 2009. *The Essential Herman Kahn: In Defense of Thinking,* edited by Paul D. Aligica and Kenneth R. Weinstein: 9–27. Lanham, MD: Lexington Books.

Kemp, Murray C. 1962. "Economic Forecasting When the Subject of the Forecast is Influenced by the Forecast." *American Economic Review* 52(3): 492–96.

Keohane, Robert O. 2002. *Power and Governance in a Partially Globalized World.* New York: Routledge.

Keohane, Robert O., and Joseph S. Nye. 1977. *Power and Interdependence: World Politics in Transition.* Boston: Little, Brown.

Keohane, Robert O., and Elinor Ostrom. 1995. *Local Commons and Global Interdependence Heterogeneity and Cooperation in Two Domains.* New York: Sage Publications.

Keohane, Robert O., and Kal Raustiala. 2009. *Toward a Post-Kyoto Climate Change Architecture: A Political Analysis.* Cambridge: Cambridge University Press.

Keohane, Robert O., and David G. Victor. 2011. "The Regime Complex for Climate Change." *American Politcal Science Review* 9(1): 7–23.

King, J. 2006. "Polycentricity and Resource Allocation: A Critique and Refinement." Oxford Jurisprudence Discussion Group.

Kiser, Larry L., and Elinor Ostrom. 1982. "The Three Worlds of Action: A Meta-theoretical Synthesis of Institutional Approaches." In *Strategies of Political Inquiry,* edited by Elinor Ostrom: 179–222. Beverly Hills, CA: Sage Publications.

Klein, Daniel. 2012. *Knowledge and Coordination: A Liberal Interpretation.* New York: Oxford University Press.

Kliemt, Hartmut. 2011. "Tayloring Game Theory the Ostrom Way." *Good Society* 20(1): 37–50.

Kling, Arnold, and Nick Schulz. 2009. *From Poverty to Prosperity: Intangible Assets, Hidden Liabilities and the Lasting Triumph over Scarcity.* New York: Encounter Books.

Kloppenberg, James T. 2000. *The Virtues of Liberalism.* New York: Oxford University Press.

Knight, Jack, and James Johnson. 1996. "The Political Consequences of Pragmatism." *Political Theory* 24(1): 68–96.

Knight, Jack, and James Johnson. 2011. *The Priority of Democracy: Political Consequences of Pragmatism.* Princeton, NJ: Princeton University Press.

Koestler, Arthur. 1973. "The Tree and the Candle." In *Unity through Diversity*, edited by William Gray and Nicholas Rizzo: 284–314. New York: Gordon and Breach Science Publishers.

Koremenos, Barbara, Charles Lipson, and Duncan Snidal, eds. 2001. *The Rational Design of International Institutions.* Special issue of the journal, *International Organization*, New York: Cambridge University Press.

Krishna, Daya. 1971. "The Self-Fulfilling Prophecy." *American Sociological Review* 36(6): 1104–7.

Krugman, Paul. 1991. "History versus Expectations." *Quarterly Journal of Economics* 106(2): 651–67.

Kuhn, Thomas. 1970. *The Structure of Scientific Revolutions.* Chicago: University of Chicago Press.

Kukathas, Chandran. 1999. *The Liberal Archipelago.* Oxford: Oxford University Press.

Kukathas, Chandran. 2009. "Two Constructions of Libertarianism." *Libertarian Papers* 1(11): 1–13.

Lakatos, Imre. 1970. "Falsification and the Methodology of Scientific Research Programmes." In *Criticism and the Growth of Knowledge*, edited by Imre Lakatos and Alan Musgrave: 91–95. Cambridge: Cambridge University Press.

Lakatos, Imre. 1971. "History of Science and Its Rational Reconstructions." In *Boston Studies in the Philosophy of Science*, vol. 8, edited by Robert S. Cohen and Mark W. Wartofsky: 91–136. Dordrecht: D. Reidel.

Lakatos, Imre. 1976. *Proofs and Refutations.* Cambridge: Cambridge University Press.

Lange, Oskar. 1938. *On the Economic Theory of Socialism.* Minneapolis: University of Minnesota Press.

Lassman, Peter. 2011. *Pluralism.* Cambridge: Polity Press.

Laudan, Larry. 1981. *Science and Hypothesis: Historical Essays on Scientific Methodology.* Dordrecht: D. Reidel.

Lawson, Tony. 2003. *Reorienting Economics.* London: Routledge.

Leeson, Peter T. 2005. "Do Contracts Require Formal Enforcement?" In *Anarchy, State, and Public Choice*, edited by Edward Stringham: 67–76. Cheltenham, UK: Edward Elgar Publishing.

Leeson, Peter T. 2009. "The Laws of Lawlessness." *Journal of Legal Studies* 38(2): 471–503.

Levati, M. Vittoria, Matthias Sutter, and Eline van der Heijden. 2007. "Leading by Example in a Public Goods Experiment with Heterogeneity and Incomplete Information." *Journal of Conflict Resolution* 51(5): 793–818.

Levine, Peter. 2011. "Seeing Like a Citizen: The Contributions of Elinor Ostrom to 'Civic Studies.'" *Good Society* 20(1): 3–15.

Levy, Jascob. 2000. *The Multiculturalism of Fear.* Oxford: Oxford University Press.

Lewis, Clarence I. 1957. *Our Social Inheritance.* Bloomington: Indiana University Press.

Lindblom, Charles E., and Edward J. Woodhouse. 1993. *The Policy-Making Process.* 3rd ed. Englewood Cliffs, NJ:: Prentice Hall.

Liu, Jianguo, Thomas Dietz, Stephen R. Carpenter, Marina Alberti, Carl Folke, Emilio Moran, Alice N. Pell, Peter Deadman, Timothy Kratz, Jane Lubchenco, Elinor Ostrom, Zhiyun Ouyang, William Provencher, Charles L. Redman, Stephen H. Schneider, and William W. Taylor. 2007a. "Complexity of Coupled Human and Natural Systems." *Science* 317(5844): 1513–16.

Liu, Jianguo, Thomas Dietz, Stephen R. Carpenter, Marina Alberti, Carl Folke, Emilio Moran, Alice N. Pell, Peter Deadman, Timothy Kratz, Jane Lubchenco, Elinor Ostrom, Zhiyun Ouyang, William Provencher, Charles L. Redman, Stephen H. Schneider, and William W. Taylor. 2007b. "Coupled Human and Natural Systems." *Ambio* 36(8): 639–49.

Lucas, Robert E. 1976. "Econometric Policy Evaluation: A Critique." *Carnegie-Rochester Conference Series on Public Policy* 1(1): 19–46.

Lucas, Robert E. 1988. "On the Mechanics of Economic Development." *Journal of Monetary Economics* 22(1): 3–42.

Lukes, Steve. 2003. *Liberals and Cannibals.* London: Verso.

Luttmer, Erzo F. P. 2001. "Group Loyalty and the Taste for Redistribution." *Journal of Political Economy* 109(3): 500–528.

MacKenzie, Donald. 2006. *An Engine, Not a Camera: How Financial Models Shape Markets.* Cambridge: MIT Press.

MacKenzie, Donald, Fabian Muniesa, and Lucia Siu. 2007. *Do Economists Make Markets? On the Performativity of Economics.* Princeton, NJ: Princeton University Press.

Mahoney, James. 2000. "Path Dependence in Historical Sociology." *Theory and Society* 29(4): 507–48.

Mandelbrot, Benoit B., and Richard L. Hudson. 2004. *The (Mis)behavior of Markets: A Fractal View of Risk, Ruin, and Reward.* New York: Basic Books.

Martin, Lisa L. 1994. "Heterogeneity, Linkage and Commons Problems." *Journal of Theoretical Politics* 6(4): 475–95.

McGinnis, Michael D. 1999a. *Polycentric Governance and Development: Readings from the Workshop in Political Theory and Policy Analysis.* Ann Arbor: University of Michigan Press.

McGinnis, Michael D. 1999b. *Polycentricity and Local Public Economies: Readings from the Workshop in Political Theory and Policy Analysis*. Ann Arbor: University of Michigan Press.

McGinnis, Michael D. 2000. *Polycentric Games and Institutions: Readings from the Workshop in Political Theory and Policy Analysis*. Ann Arbor: University of Michigan Press.

McGinnis, Michael D. 2005. "Self-Governance, Polycentrism, and Federalism: Recurring Themes in Vincent Ostrom's Scholarly Oeuvre." *Journal of Economic Behavior and Organization* 57(2): 173–88.

McGinnis, Michael D. 2011. "An Introduction to IAD and the Language of the Ostrom Workshop: A Simple Guide to a Complex Framework." *Policy Studies Journal* 39(1): 163–77.

McGinnis, Michael D. 2012. "Comment on Polycentricity and Democracy." Manuscript, George Mason University.

McGinnis, Michael D., and Elinor Ostrom. 1996. "Design Principles for Local and Global Commons." In *The International Political Economy and International Institutions*, vol. 2, edited by Oran R. Young: 465–93. Cheltenham, UK: Edward Elgar.

McGinnis, Michael D., and James M. Walker. 2010. "Foundations of the Ostrom Workshop: Institutional Analysis, Polycentricity, and Self-Governance of the Commons." *Public Choice* 143(3): 293–301.

Merton, Robert K. 1936. "The Unanticipated Consequences of Purposive Social Action." *American Sociological Review* 1(6): 894–904.

Merton, Robert K. 1948. "The Self-Fulfilling Prophecy." *Antioch Review* 8(2): 193–210.

Miguel, Edward and Mary Kay Gugerty. 2002. "Ethnic Diversity, Social Sanctions, and Public Goods in Kenya." Unpublished manuscript. University of California, Berkeley.

Miller, John H., and Scott E. Page. 2007. *Complex Adaptive Systems: An Introduction to Computational Models of Social Life*. Princeton, NJ: Princeton University Press.

Mises, Ludwig von. [1922] 1981. *Socialism: An Economic and Sociological Analysis*. Indianapolis: Liberty Fund.

Monmonier, Mark. 1993. *Mapping It Out: Expository Cartography for the Humanities and Social Sciences*. Chicago: University of Chicago Press.

Moon, Donald. 1975. "The Logic of Political Inquiry." In *Political Science: Scope and Theory*, vol. 1, edited by Fred I. Greenstein and Nelson W. Polsby: 131–228. Reading, MA: Addison-Wesley.

Morgan, Peter, and Suzanne Taschereau. 1996. "Capacity and Institutional Assessment: Frameworks, Methods and Tools for Analysis." Prepared for CIDA Policy Branch.

Muldoon, Ryan. 2009. "Diversity and the Social Contract." PhD diss., http://www.sas.upenn.edu/~rmuldoon/DiversityandtheSocialContract.pdf.

Muldoon, Ryan, Michael Borgida, and Michael Cuffaro. 2012. "The Conditions of Tolerance." *Politics, Philosophy, & Economics* 11(3): 322–44.

Mullins, Phil. 2002. "Peirce's Abduction and Polanyi's Tacit Knowing." *Journal of Speculative Philosophy*, n.s. 16(3): 198–224.

Munger, Michael. 2010. "Endless Forms Most Beautiful and Most Wonderful: Elinor Ostrom and the Diversity of Institutions." *Public Choice* 143(3): 263–68.

Musgrave, A. 1961. "Evidential Support, Falsification, Heuristics, and Anarchism." In "Rational Expectations and the Theory of Price Movements," edited by G. Radnitzky and J. Muth, *Econometrica* 29(3): 315–35.

Nagel, Ernest. 1961. *The Structure of Science.* New York: Harcourt, Brace & World.

Newey, Glen. 2001. *After Politics: The Rejection of Politics in Contemporary Liberal Philosophy.* Houndmills, Basingstoke: Palgrave.

Nickles, Thomas. 1987. "Lakatosian Heuristics and Epistemic Support." *British Journal for the Philosophy of Science* 38(2): 181–205.

North, Douglass C., ed. 1997. *Transforming Post-Communist Political Economies.* Washington, DC: National Resource Council, National Academy of Sciences.

North, Douglass C. 2005. *Understanding the Process of Economic Change.* Princeton, NJ: Princeton University Press.

Nozick, Robert. 1974. *Anarchy, State, and Utopia.* New York: Basic Books.

Oakerson, Ronald J. 1999. *Governing Local Public Economies: Creating the Civic Metropolis.* San Francisco: ICS Press.

Oberschall, Anthony. 2004. "Explaining Terrorism: The Contribution of Collective Action Theory." *Sociological Theory* 22(1): 26–37.

O'Driscoll, Gerald P. 1977. *Economics as a Coordination Problem: The Contributions of Friedrich A. Hayek.* Kansas City, KS: Sheed Andrews and McMeel.

O'Driscoll, Gerald P., Mario J. Rizzo. 1985. *The Economics of Time and Ignorance.* Oxford: Blackwell.

Oliver, Pamela E., and Gerald Marwell. 2001. "Whatever Happened to Critical Mass Theory? A Retrospective and Assessment." *Sociological Theory* 19(3): 292–311.

Oliver, Pamela, E., Gerald Marwell, and Ruy Teixeira. 1985. "A Theory of the Critical Mass. I. Interdependence, Group Heterogeneity, and the Productionof Collective Action." *American Journal of Sociology* 91(3): 522–56.

Olson, Mancur. 1993. "Dictatorship, Democracy, and Development." *American Political Science Review* 87(3): 567–76.

Olsson, Per, Carl Folke, and Fikret Berkes. 2004. "Adaptive Comanagement for Building Resilience in Social-Ecological Systems." *Environmental Management* 34(1): 75–90.

Ormerod, Richard. 2006. "The History and Ideas of Pragmatism." *Journal of the Operational Research Society* 57(8): 892–909.

O'Rourke, Kevin H. 1994. "The Economic Impact of the Famine in the Short and Long Run." *American Economic Review* 82(2): 309–13.

Ostrom, Elinor. 1972. "Metropolitan Reform: Propositions Derived from Two Traditions." *Social Science Quarterly* 53(3): 474–93.

Ostrom, Elinor, ed. 1982. *Strategies of Political Inquiry*. Beverly Hills, CA: Sage Publications.

Ostrom, Elinor. 1986. "An Agenda for the Study of Institutions." *Public Choice* 48(1): 3–25.

Ostrom, Elinor. 1990. *Governing the Commons: The Evolution of Institutions for Collective Action*. New York: Cambridge University Press.

Ostrom, Elinor. 1991. "Rational-Choice Theory and Institutional Analysis: Towards Complementarity." *American Political Science Review* 85(1): 237–50.

Ostrom, Elinor. 1992. *Crafting Institutions for Self-Governing Irrigation Systems*. San Francisco: ICS Press.

Ostrom, Elinor. 1994. *Neither Market Nor State: Governance of Common-Pool Resources in the Twenty-First Century*. Washington, DC: International Food Policy Research Institute.

Ostrom, Elinor. 1997. "A Behavioral Approach to the Rational Choice Theory of Collective Action." Presidential Address, American Political Science Association, Indiana University.

Ostrom, Elinor. 1998. "The Comparative Study of Public Economies." Presented upon Acceptance of the Frank E. Seidman Distinguished Award in Political Economy. Memphis, TN, P. K. Seidman Foundation.

Ostrom, Elinor. 2000. "Collective Action and the Evolution of Social Norms." *Journal of Economic Perspectives* 14(3): 137–58.

Ostrom, Elinor. 2005. *Understanding Institutional Diversity*. Princeton, NJ: Princeton University Press.

Ostrom, Elinor. 2008. "Developing a Method for Analyzing Institutional Change." In *Alternative Institutional Structures: Evolution and Impact*, edited by Sandra Batie and Nicholas Mercuro: 48–77. London: Routledge.

Ostrom, Elinor. 2009. "Postscript: Rethinking Institutional Analysis and Development. Dialogues with Vincent and Elinor Ostrom." In *Challenging Institutional Analysis and Development: The Bloomington School*, edited by Paul D. Aligica and Peter J. Boettke: 142–60. London: Routledge.

Ostrom, Elinor, Thomas Dietz, and Paul C. Stern. 2003. "The Struggle to Govern the Commons." *Science* 302(5652): 1907–12.

Ostrom, Elinor, Roy Gardner, and James Walker. 1994. *Rules, Games, and Common-Pool Resources*. Ann Arbor: University of Michigan Press.

Ostrom, Elinor, and Charlotte Hess, eds. 2007. *Understanding Knowledge as a Commons: From Theory to Practice*. Cambridge: MIT Press.

Ostrom, Elinor, and Vincent Ostrom. 2004. "The Quest for Meaning in Public Choice." *American Journal of Economics and Sociology* 63(1): 105–47.

Ostrom, Elinor, and Roger B. Parks. 1973a. "Neither Gargantua nor the Land of Lilliputs: Conjectures on Mixed Systems of Metropolitan Organization." In

Polycentricity and Local Public Economies: Readings from the Workshop in Political Theory and Policy Analysis, edited by Michael D. McGinnis: 284–305. Ann Arbor: University of Michigan Press.

Ostrom, Elinor, and Roger B. Parks. 1973b. "Suburban Police Departments: Too Many and Too Small?" In *The Urbanization of the Suburbs*, edited by Louis H. Masotti and Jeffrey K. Hadden: 367–402. Beverly Hills, CA: Sage Publications.

Ostrom, Elinor, Roger B. Parks, and Gordon P. Whitaker. 1973. "Do We Really Want to Consolidate Urban Police Forces? A Reappraisal of Some Old Assertions." *Public Administration Review* 33(5): 423–32.

Ostrom Elinor, Roger B. Parks, and Gordon P. Whitaker. 1978. *Patterns of Metropolitan Policing*. Cambridge: Ballinger.

Ostrom, Elinor, Larry Schroeder, and Susan Wynne. 2003. "Analyzing the Performance of Alternative Institutional Arrangements for Sustaining Rural Infrastructure in Developing Countries." *Journal of Public Administration Research and Theory* 3(1): 11–45.

Ostrom, Elinor, and James Walker, eds. 2003. *Trust and Reciprocity: Interdisciplinary Lessons from Experimental Research*. New York: Russell Sage Foundation.

Ostrom, Vincent. 1972. "Polycentricity." Workshop Working Paper Series, Workshop in Political Theory and Policy Analysis, Presented at Annual Meeting of the American Political Science Association, September 5–9.

Ostrom, Vincent. 1973. "Order and Change Amid Increasing Relative Ignorance," *Workshop Working Paper Series, Workshop in Political Theory and Policy Analysis*, Indiana University, Bloomington.

Ostrom, Vincent. 1980. *Leviathan and Democracy*. Bloomington: Workshop in Political Theory and Policy Analysis, Indiana University.

Ostrom, Vincent. 1984. "The Meaning of Value Terms." *American Behavioral Scientist* 28(2): 249–62.

Ostrom, Vincent. 1986. "The Constitutional Level of Analysis: A Challenge." Bloomington: Workshop Working Paper Series, Workshop in Political Theory and Policy Analysis, Indiana University.

Ostrom, Vincent. 1990. "Problems of Cognition as a Challenge to Policy Analysts and Democratic Societies." *Journal of Theoretical Politics* 2(3): 243–62.

Ostrom, Vincent. 1991. *The Meaning of American Federalism: Constituting a Self-Governing Society*. San Francisco: ICS Press.

Ostrom, Vincent. 1993. "Opportunity, Diversity and Complexity." In *Rethinking Institutional Analysis and Development: Issues, Alternatives, and Choices*, edited by Vincent Ostrom, David Feeny, and Hartmut Picht: 389–407. San Francisco: ICS Press, Institute for Contemporary Studies.

Ostrom, Vincent. 1997. *The Meaning of Democracy and the Vulnerability of Democracies: A Response to Tocqueville's Challenge*. Ann Arbor: University of Michigan Press.

Ostrom, Vincent. 1999a. "Cryptoimperialism, Predatory States, and Self-Governance." In *Polycentric Governance and Development: Readings from the Workshop in Political Theory and Policy Analysis*, edited by Michael D. McGinnis: 166–85. Ann Arbor: University of Michigan Press.

Ostrom, Vincent. 1999b. "Public Goods and Public Choices." In *Polycentricity and Local Public Economies: Readings from the Workshop in Political Theory and Policy Analysis*, edited by Michael D. McGinnis: 75–103. Ann Arbor: University of Michigan Press.

Ostrom, Vincent. [1973] 2008. *The Intellectual Crisis in American Public Administration.* 3rd ed. Tuscaloosa: University of Alabama Press.

Ostrom, Vincent. [1971] 2008. *The Political Theory of a Compound Republic.* 3rd ed. New Brunswick, NJ: Transaction.

Ostrom, Vincent, Robert Bish, and Elinor Ostrom. 1988. *Local Government in the United States.* San Francisco: ICS Press.

Ostrom, Vincent, and Elinor Ostrom. 1965. "A Behavioral Approach to the Study of Intergovernmental Relations." *Annals of the American Academy of Political and Social Science* 359(1): 135–46.

Ostrom, Vincent, Charles M. Tiebout, and Robert Warren. 1961. "The Organization of Government in Metropolitan Areas: A Theoretical Inquiry." *American Political Science Review,* 55: 831–42.

Page, Scott E. 2007. *The Difference: How the Power of Diversity Creates Better Groups, Firms, Schools, and Societies.* Princeton, NJ: Princeton University Press.

Page, Scott E. 2010. *Diversity and Complexity.* Princeton, NJ: Princeton University Press.

Page, Scott, 2010b, "Complexity in Social, Political, and Economic Systems." American Economic Association, Ten Years and Beyond: Economists Answer NSF's Call for Long-Term Research Agendas, http://papers.ssrn.com/sol3/papers.cfm?abstract_id=1889359

Peirce, Charles S. 1998. *The Collected Papers of Charles Sanders Peirce.* Edited by Charles Hartshorne, Paul Weiss, and Arthur W. Burks. Cambridge: Harvard University Press.

Pennington, Mark. 2011. *Robust Political Economy.* Cheltenham, UK: Edward Elgar.

Pierson, Paul. 2000. "Increasing Returns, Path Dependence, and the Study of Politics." *American Political Science Review* 94(2): 251–67.

Polanyi, Michael. 1951. *The Logic of Liberty.* Chicago: University of Chicago Press.

Polanyi, Michael. 1962. "The Republic of Science: Its Political and Economic Theory." *Minerva* 1: 54–74.

Polanyi, Michael, and Harry Prosch. 1975. *Meaning.* Chicago: University of Chicago Press.

Polski, Margaret M., and Elinor Ostrom. 1999. "An Institutional Framework for Policy Analysis and Design." Workshop in Political Theory and Policy Analysis, Department of Political Science, Indiana University.

Popper, Karl R. 1964. *The Poverty of Historicism.* London: HarperCollins.

Popper, Karl R. 1976. *Unended Quest: An Intellectual Autobiography.* London: Fontana.

Posner, Richard A. 2003. *Law, Pragmatism, and Democracy.* Cambridge: Harvard University Press.

Poteete, Amy R., and Elinor Ostrom. 2004. "Heterogeneity, Group Size, and Collective Action: The Role of Institutions in Forest Management." *Development and Change* 35(3):435–61.

Poteete, A., M. Janssen, and E. Ostrom. 2010. *Working Together:Collective Action, the Commons, and Multiple Methods in Practice.* Princeton: Princeton University Press.

Poterba, James M. 1997. "Demographic Structure and the Political Economy of Public Education." *Journal of Policy Analysis and Management* 6(1): 48–66.

Powell, Benjamin, and Edward P. Stringham. 2009. "Public Choice and the Economic Analysis of Anarchy: A Survey." *Public Choice* 140(3): 503–38.

Pritchard, Lowell, Jr., John Colding, Fikret Berkes, Uno Svedin, and Carl Folke. 1998. "The Problem of Fit Between Ecosystems and Institutions." IHDP Working Paper, International Human Dimensions Program.

Prosch, Harry. 1986. *Michael Polanyi: A Critical Exposition.* Albany: State University of New York Press.

Pryor, Frederic L. 2005. *A Guidebook to the Comparative Study of Economic Systems.* Cambridge: Cambridge University Press.

Putnam, Hilary. 1992. "A Reconsideration of Deweyan Democracy." In Putnam, *Renewing Philosophy.* Cambridge: Harvard University Press.

Raiffa, Howard. 1982. *The Art and Science of Negotiation.* Cambridge: Harvard University Press.

Raub, Werner, and Thomas Voss. 1986. "Conditions for Cooperation in Problematic Social Situations." In *Paradoxical Effects of Social Behavior,* edited by Andreas Diekmann and Peter Mitter: 85–104. Heildelberg: Physica-Verlag.

Rescher, Nicholas. 1977. *Methodological Pragmatism: A Systems-Theoretic Approach to the Theory of Knowledge.* London: Blackwell.

Rescher, Nicholas. 1979. *Cognitive Systematization: A Systems-Theoretic Approach to a Coherentistic Theory of Knowledge.* Totowa, NJ: Rowman and Littlefield.

Rescher, Nicholas. 1980. *Induction: An Essay on the Justification of Inductive Reasoning.* Oxford: Blackwell.

Rescher, Nicolas. 1993. *Pluralism: Against the Demand for Consensus.* New York: Oxford University Press.

Rescher, Nicholas. 1999. *Realistic Pragmatism: An Introduction to Pragmatic Philosophy.* Albany: State Univeristy of New York Press.

Rescher, Nicolas. 2001. *Process Philosophy: A Survey of Basic Issues.* Pittsburgh: University of Pittsburgh Press.

Rogner, Hans-Holger. 1997. "An Assessment of World Hydrocarbon Resources." *Annual Review of Energy and the Environment* 22(1): 217–62.

Romer, Paul. 1990. "Endogenous Technological Change." *Journal of Political Economy* 98(5): 71–102.

Root, Hilton L. 2012. "No Captain at the Helm: The Network Structure of Global Political Economy." Manuscript.

Rubinstein, Robert A., Charles D. Laughlin, and John McManus. 1984. *Science as a Cognition Process*. Philadelphia: University of Pennsylvania Press.

Ruttan, Lore M. 1998. "Closing the Commons: Cooperation for Gain or Restraint?" *Human Ecology* 26(1):43–66.

Ruttan, Lore M. 2005. "Economic Heterogeneity and the Commons: Effects on Collective Action and Collective Goods Provisioning." *World Development* 36(5): 969–85.

Ruttan, Lore M. 2006. "Sociocultural Heterogeneity and the Commons." *Current Anthropology* 47(5): 843–53.

Ruttan, Lore M., and Monique Borgerhoff Mulder. 1999. "Are East African Pastoralists Truly Conservationists?" *Current Anthropology* 40(5): 621–52.

Ruttan, Vernon W. 2002. "Productivity Growth in World Agriculture: Sources and Constraints." *Journal of Economic Perspectives* 16(4): 161–84.

Sabetti, Filippo. 2008. "Normative and Empirical Inquiries into Systems of Governance." In *The Struggle to Constitute and Sustain Productive Orders*, edited by Mark Sproule-Jones, Barbara Allen, and Filippo Sabetti: 3–10. Lanham, MD: Lexington Books.

Sabetti, Fillipo. 2010. *Civilization and Self-Government*. Toronto: Lexington Books.

Sabetti, Filippo. 2011 "Constitutional Artisanship and Institutional Diversity: Elinor Ostrom, Vincent Ostrom, and the Workshop." *Good Society* 20(1): 73–84.

Sabetti, Filippo, Allen Barbara, and Mark Sproule-Jones, eds. 2009. *The Practice of Constitutional Development: Vincent Ostrom's Quest to Understand Human Affairs*. Lanham, MD: Lexington Books.

Sagoff, Mark. [1990] 2004. *Price, Principle, and the Environment*. New York: Cambridge University Press.

Sagoff, Mark. 2008. *The Economy of the Earth*. 2nd ed. Cambridge: Cambridge University Press.

Schmidtz, David. 2011. "Nonideal Theory: What It Is and What It Needs to Be." *Ethics* 121(4): 772–96.

Scott, James C. 1998. *Seeing Like a State: How Certain Schemes to Improve the Human Condition Have Failed*. New Haven: Yale University Press.

Shapiro, Michael J. 1981. *Language and Political Understanding: The Politics of Discursive Practices*. New Haven: Yale University Press.

Shermer, Michael. 2007. *The Mind of the Market: Compassionate Apes, Competitive Humans, and Other Tales from Evolutionary Economics*. New York: Henry Holt.

Sikkink, Kathryn. 1991. *Ideas and Institutions: Developmentalism in Brazil and Argentina*. Ithaca, NY: Cornell University Press.

Simon, Herbert A. 1954. "Bandwagon and Underdog Effects of Election Predictions." *Public Opinion Quarterly* 18(3): 245–53.

Simon, Herbert A. 1969. *The Science of the Artificial.* Cambridge: MIT Press.

Simon, Herbert A. 1973. "The Organization of Complex Systems." In *Hierarchy Theory: The Challenge of Complex Systems,* edited by Howard H. Pattee: 3–27. New York: Braziller.

Simon, Julian L., ed. 1995. *The State of Humanity.* Cambridge, MA: Blackwell in association with the Cato Institute.

Simon, Julian L. 1998. *The Ultimate Resource 2.* Princeton, NJ: Princeton University Press.

Smit, Barry, and Johanna Wandel. 2006. "Adaptation, Adaptive Capacity and Vulnerability." *Global Environmental Change* 16(3): 282–92.

Smith, Vernon L. 2007. *Rationality in Economics: Constructivist and Ecological Forms.* New York: Cambridge University Press.

Snidal, Duncan. 1994. "The Politics of Scope: Endogenous Actors, Heterogeneity and Institutions." *Journal of Theoretical Politics* 6(4): 449–72.

Soltan, Karol. 2011. "A Civic Science." *Good Society* 20(1): 102–19.

Sproule-Jones, Mark. 1993. *Governments at Work.* Toronto: University of Toronto Press.

Sproule-Jones, Mark, Barbara Allen, and Filippo Sabetti, eds. 2008. *The Struggle to Constitute and Sustain Productive Orders.* Lanham, MD: Lexington Books.

Stack, George J. 1978. "Reflexivity, Prediction and Paradox." *Dialogos* 13(31): 91–101.

Storr, Virgil. 2010. "The Social Construction of the Market." *Society* 47(3): 200–206.

Storr, Virgil. 2012. *Understanding the Culture of Markets.* New York: Routledge.

Talisse, Robert B. 2012. *Pluralism and Liberal Politics.* New York: Routledge.

Talisse, Robert B., and Scott F. Aikin. 2008. *Pragmatism: A Guide for the Perplexed.* New York: Continuum International Publishing Group.

Tilly, Charles. 2006. *Why?* Princeton, NJ: Princeton University Press.

Tinbergen, Jan. 1967. *Economic Policy: Principles and Design.* Chicago: Rand McNally.

Toonen, Theo 2010. "Resilience in Public Administration: The Work of Elinor and Vincent Ostrom from a Public Administration Perspective." *Public Administration Review* 70(2): 193–202.

Toulmin, Stephen E. 1977. "From Form to Function: Philosophy and History of Science in the 1950s and Now." *Daedalus* 106(3): 143–62.

Tullock, Gordon. 1972. "The Edge of the Jungle." In Tullock, *Explorations in the Theory of Anarchy.* Blacksburg, VA: Center for the Study of Public Choice.

Tullock, Gordon, Arthur Seldon, and Gordon L. Brady. 2002. *Government Failure: A Primer in Public Choice.* Washington, DC: Cato Institute.

Turnbull, David. 1989. *Maps Are Territories: Science Is an Atlas.* Chicago: University of Chicago Press.

Vanberg, Viktor. 2011. "Social Dilemmas and Self-Organization in Pre-defined and in Self-Selected Groups." *Good Society* 20(1): 67–73.

Van Dijk, Eric, and Henk Wilke. 1995. "Coordination Rules in Asymmetric Social Dilemmas: A Comparison Between Public Good Dilemmas and Resource Dilemmas." *Journal of Experimental Social Psychology* 31: 1–27.

Vedeld, Trond. 2003. "Democratic Decentralisation and Poverty Reduction: Exploring the Linkages." *Forum for Development Studies* No. 2. Oslo: Norwegian Institute for International Affaires (NUPI) and Norwegian Association for Development Research.

Veld, Roel J. 1991. *Autopoiesis and Configuration Theory: New Approaches to Societal Steering.* Dordrecht: Kluwer Academic Publishers.

Vetterling, Mary K. 1976. "More on Reflexive Predictions." *Philosophy of Science* 43(2): 278–82.

Vigdor, Jacob L. 2001. "Community Composition and Collective Action: Analyzing Initial Mail Response to the 2000 Census." Unpublished manuscript. Duke University

Vosniadou, Stellla, and Andrew Ortony. 1989. *Similarity and Analogical Reasoning.* New York: Cambridge University Press.

Wagner, Richard E. 2002. "Complexity, Governance and Constitutional Craftsmanship." *American Journal of Economics and Sociology* 61(1): 105–22.

Wagner, Richard E. 2005. "Self-Governance, Polycentrism, and Federalism: Recurring Themes in Vincent Ostrom's Scholarly Oeuvre." *Journal of Economic Behavior & Organization* 57(2):173–88.

Wagner, Richard E. 2007. *Fiscal Sociology and the Theory of Public Finance.* Cheltenham, UK: Edward Elgar.

Wagner, Richard E. 2010. *Mind, Society, and Human Action: Time and Knowledge in a Theory of Social Economy.* New York: Routledge.

Wagner, Richard E. 2011. "Democracy and Public Finance: A Polycentric, Invisible-Hand Framework." GMU Working Papers in Economics No. 11–23.

Wagner, Richard E., and Warren E. Weber. 1975. "Competition, Monopoly, and the Organization of Government in Metropolitan Areas." *Journal of Law and Economics* 18(3): 661–84.

Walker, Brian, Crawford S. Holling, Stephen R. Carpenter, and Ann Kinzig. 2004. "Resilience, Adaptability and Transformability in Social-Ecological Systems." *Ecology and Society* 9(2): 1–11.

Warr, Peter G. 1982. "Pareto Optimal Redistribution and Private Charity." *Journal of Public Economics* 19(1): 131–38.

Warr, Peter G. 1983. "The Private Provision of a Public Good Is Independent of the Distribution of Income." *Economics Letters* 13(2): 207–11.

Weimer, David L. 1995. *Institutional Design.* Boston: Kluwer Academic Publishers.

Weingast, Barry. 1995. "The Economic Role of Political Institutions." *Journal of Law, Economics and Organization* 11(1): 1–31.

Westbrook, Robert B. 1998. "Pragmatism and Democracy." In *The Revival of Pragmatism: New Essays on Social Thought, Law, and Culture,* edited by Morris Dickstein. Durham, NC: Duke University Press.

Wible, James. 1998. *Economics of Science*. London: Routledge.

Williamson, Oliver E. 1985. *The Economic Institutions of Capitalism*. New York: Free Press.

Wilson, Edward O. 1998. *Consilience: The Unity of Knowledge*. New York: Alfred A. Knopf.

Winston, Clifford. 2006. *Market Failure vs. Government Failure*. Washington, DC: Brookings Institution Press.

Wittgenstein, Ludwig. [1953] 1999. *Philosophical Investigations*. Upper Saddle River, NJ: Prentice Hall.

Yee, Albert S. 1996. "The Causal Effects of Ideas on Policies." *International Organization* 50(1): 69–108.

Zahar, Elie. 1983. "Logic of Discovery or Psychology of Invention?" *British Journal for the Philosophy of Science* 34(3): 243–61.

Index